THE ROAD NORTH

300 YEARS OF CLASSIC
SCOTTISH TRAVEL WRITING

Edited by June Skinner Sawyers

www.theinpinn.co.uk

In fond memory of
James Porter, Margaret Skinner Porter,
Susannah Page Porter McIntyre,
James Keiller Porter and
Annie Skinner Porter Hugo

The In Pinn is an imprint of
Neil Wilson Publishing
303a The Pentagon Centre
36 Washington Street
GLASGOW
G3 8AZ
Tel: 0141-221-1117
Fax: 0141-221-5363
E-mail: info@nwp.sol.co.uk
http://www.theinpinn.co.uk/

First published September, 2000
Reprinted September 2001

A catalogue record for this book is
available from the British Library.

ISBN 1-897784-95-3

Typeset in Cochin
Designed by Mark Blackadder

Printed by WS Bookwell, Finland

CONTENTS

❊   ❊   ❊

THE HIGHLANDS

THE WESTERN ISLES

THE NORTHERN ISLES

ACKNOWLEDGEMENTS

❊ ❊ ❊

The author and publisher are most grateful to all authors, publishers and copyright owners who have allowed the reprinting of those extracts in this book which are not in the public domain. These are:

Edmund Burt: 'Letter XV' from *Burt's Letters from the North of Scotland*. Reprinted by permission of Birlinn.

James Campbell: 'Stories in Stone' from *Invisible Country*. Reprinted by permission of the Orion Publishing Group.

Derek Cooper: 'My Gaelic Went into the Sea' from *The Road to Mingulay*. Reprinted by permission of Taylor & Francis Books Ltd.

Sir Alastair Dunnett: 'The Forbidden Island' from *The Canoe Boys*. Reprinted by kind permission of Lady Dorothy Dunnett and Neil Wilson Publishing.

Seton Gordon: 'A Sea-girt Home of the Peregrine' from *Hebridean Memories*. Reprinted by kind permission of the estate of Catriona Macdonald Lockhart and Neil Wilson Publishing.

Neil Gunn: 'Out to Sea' from *Off in a Boat*. Reprinted by kind permission of Diarmid Gunn.

Emily Hiestand: 'South of the Ultima Thule' from *The Very Rich Hours*. Copyright © 1992 by Emily Hiestand. Reprinted by permission of Beacon Press, Boston.

Alison Johnson: 'Tarbert' from *A House by the Shore*. Reprinted by permission of Victor Gollancz.

David McFadden: 'An Innocent Flirtation in Tongue' from *An Innocent in Scotland: More Curious Rambles and Singular Encounters* by David McFadden © 1999. Used by written permission, McClelland & Stewart, Inc. *The Canadian Publishers*.

Bettina Selby: Part of chapter 16 on Lewis from *The Fragile Islands*. © Bettina Selby, 1989 and reprinted with her kind permission.

Margaret Fay Shaw: 'South Uist' from *From the Alleghenies to the Hebrides* by Margaret Fay Shaw. Reprinted by permission of Birlinn.

Nan Shepherd: 'The Plateau' from *The Living Mountain* by Nan Shepherd. Reprinted by permission of the late Mrs. Sheila Clouston's estate.

Paul Theroux: 'The Flyer to Cape Wrath' from *The Kingdom by the Sea*. Copyright © 1984 by Paul Theroux, reprinted by permission of The Wylie Agency.

Colm Tóibín: 'The Language of the Tribe' from *The Sign of the Cross*. Copyright © Colm Tóibín, reprinted by permission of A.P Watt Ltd on behalf of Colm Tóibín and Pantheon Books, New York.

INTRODUCTION

❊　　　❊　　　❊

For more than three centuries Scotland has been a popular travel destination. The qualities that attracted earlier generations continue to appeal to the modern traveller. A sense of grandeur. A darkly romantic past. A feeling of utter remoteness. But still there is something more.

Scotland is familiar yet different.

Some come for the solitude – to get away from it all – others for sheer adventure – to replenish and rejuvenate the spirit. The diversity of the land itself is impressive from the gently undulating hills of the Borders to the snow-capped peaks of the Highlands, big sky country where the brooding mountains seem a bit more menacing and huge boulders amid a primordial landscape cast deep shadows long into the twilight night.

Each of the travellers in this collection went to Scotland for their own individual reasons; even so, one suspects that many were searching for the same thing: escape into another world perhaps, a connection to an older and presumably wiser culture, a longing for – what? – a sense of the ineffable.

When Martin Martin toured the Western Isles in the late seventeenth century, it was considered a foolhardy if not downright dangerous venture. At that time there were no roads on the islands, while actually getting there was itself treacherous, since it often required a journey across storm-tossed waters in an open boat under typically unpredictable Hebridean skies. But Martin, a native of Skye and a Gaelic speaker, made his historic trek and in the process his writing became a classic of travel literature, referred back to time and again by later generations of travellers.

Martin set the standard that others would follow: Daniel Defoe in 1726. Naturalist James Robertson from 1767 to 1771. Thomas Pennant first in 1769 and again in 1772. William and Dorothy Wordsworth in 1803. John Keats in 1818. William

Cobbett in 1832. Most famously, Samuel Johnson and James Boswell in 1773 (who carried along with them a copy of Martin's tome). Writers and artists, too, felt compelled to come here. In 1804 James Hogg embarked on a four-week tour of the Hebrides. A decade later, in August 1814, Sir Walter Scott sailed to Skye aboard the *Pharos*. Hugh Miller travelled to the Hebrides in 1844. Later years brought Ivor Brown, Alasdair Macalpine MacGregor, Frank Fraser Darling, and many more.

Some, like Johnson, came to study the customs and habits of a particular people – the Highlanders – who, even though they shared the same island, were barely known to Lowlanders and the English, exotic creatures who may have well been from Patagonia or Siberia. Others possessed a scientific mindset, such as Joseph Banks, who is credited as being the 'discoverer' of Fingal's cave on Staffa. (In 1830 composer Felix Mendelssohn, inspired by his own visit to Staffa, would compose 'The Hebrides' overture.) Fingal's cave soon became a place of pilgrimage for Wordsworth, Keats, Scott, and other like-minded romantics.

Still others came to marvel at the wondrous scenery. Whereas earlier visitors found the Highland landscapes severe, even grim, later generations reveled in its wild unadorned beauty. For example, no matter how execrable the weather, how inhospitable the dwelling, the Wordsworths – William and Dorothy – never wavered from their romantic ideal of Scotland.

Women travel writers also ventured north, alone or in the company of trusted companions. In 1775 Mary Anne Hanway replied to Samuel Johnson in the form of *A Journey to the Highlands of Scotland, with Occasional Remarks on Dr. Johnson's Tour.* Offended by Dr. Johnson's unduly harsh criticism of Scotland, Hanway chastised the good doctor for his uncharitable behaviour. Twenty or so years later Sarah Murray's *Companion and Useful Guide to the Beauties of Scotland* celebrated the physical attributes of the country.

Above all, the Highlands provided an endless source of fascination. From Martin Martin to Paul Theroux, the Highlands have attracted the most attention, garnered the most superlatives. Artists Edwin Landseer, Horatio McCulloch, and Joseph Turner created wildly romantic vistas of mountains, seas, and lochs. Once rejected as a barbarous region populated by uncouth people who spoke an archaic and useless langauge, the Highlands would eventually come to symbolize all things Scottish to the rest of the world: tartan, kilts, bagpipes, mountainous landscapes.

The Highlands conformed to the peculiarly eighteenth-century notion of 'noble primitivism' where an ancient and proud people espoused simple yet profound virtues despite surrounded by abject poverty and who retained a depth of knowledge and genuine love of literature unsurpassed in even the most civilised of literary circles. Visitors – abetted by the Scots themselves – subscribed to this mythical Scotland that existed primarily in their very vivid imagination.

Today the consumption of heritage in Scotland is very big business indeed. 'In Scotland, heritage and tourism are inextricably linked,' writes David McCrone, Angela Morris, and Richard Kiely in *Scotland the Brand*. Indeed, according to McCrone and his colleagues, Scottish tourism in the 1990s brought in some £2 billion annually and employed more than 180,000 people, making it the country's biggest employer.

The Scottish tourist industry can be traced back to at least 1820, when the foundation of what would become a multi-million pound industry became established. Sir Walter Scott did more than anyone to popularise travel to Scotland. Although Scotland was already a well-known destination by the time of his birth in 1771, his work made a substantial impact on tourism and would for many decades to come. In particular, *The Minstrelsy of the Scottish Border* (1802-03), *The Lay of the Last Minstrel* (1805), and *The Lady of the Lake* (1810) turned the Borders and the Trossachs and Loch Katrine in particular to the attention of travellers south of the border. After 1815, more and more Americans began to visit too.

❋   ❋   ❋

The Road North is intended to be a representative rather than a comprehensive sampling of three hundred years of travel writing on Scotland. Thus, many writers who have visited Scotland and put pen to paper are not here. As any editor knows, time, money, and other mundane concerns often dictate or at least help influence content. A listing of the writers not featured in this volume is enough to fill another book. One could easily have included James Hogg, Robert

Burns, Virginia Woolf, Frank Darling, Hugh MacDiarmid, George Orwell, Hugh MacLennan, Louis MacNiece, Archibald MacLeish, George Mackay Brown, David Mamet, and Carl MacDougall, to name more than a few, if space and economic restrictions so allowed.

What remains though is a rich stew of various styles, voices, and places. Arranged geographically, *The Road North* takes readers on a virtual journey through Scotland during the last three hundred years from urban pavements to remote glens to faraway islands. It includes the impressions of such classic writers as Daniel Defoe, Edmund Burt, and Thomas Pennant. Of course, no collection of travel writing on Scotland would be complete without the trenchant commentaries of Johnson and Boswell. Nineteenth-century observers include Dorothy Wordsworth, American writers Washington Irving and Henry James, England's poet laureate Robert Southey, and native Scot Alexander Smith.

As we approach the twentieth century, the Scotland that emerges from these pages is one that most of us would recognise. The tartan bloom has rubbed off a bit, replaced by a more authentic urban grit and rustic realism.

Naturalist Seton Gordon concentrates on the bird and animal life of Tiree. Nan Shepherd celebrates the magic of the Cairngorms. The prolific H. V. Morton travels to gloomy Glencoe and, in probably the finest travel essay written on Scots and Scottish identity, Edwin Muir examines the enigmatic topic of the elusive and paradoxical Scottish psyche.

Two faces of Glasgow are presented: the renaissance city of Jan Morris and the Catholic city of Colm Toibin. In the far north, James Campbell visits bleak Kildonan, site of the one of the worst episodes of the Highland Clearances and twinkly-eyed David McFadden encounters eccentric after eccentric on his picaresque circuit while Paul Theroux discovers the near-impossible, a corner of Scotland far removed from anywhere that allows him to see the world with a fresh set of eyes, as if for the first time – truly a rare occurrence in our information-saturated age. Meanwhile, native Scots Alastair Scott and Michael W. Russell travelled the breadth of the land in search of a country and found a little bit of themselves.

The Hebrides are well represented. Both Neil Gunn and Sir Alastair Dunnett discovered their Scotland off the cold and choppy waters of the west coast – Gunn in a small boat, Dunnett in a canoe. Gavin Maxwell discovered his Scotland, surrounded by nothing more than the earth and sky, and several four-legged companions.

John McPhee, a masterly writer who makes even the most mundane subject come alive, spent many months in his ancestral homeland of Colonsay. Derek Cooper conversed with the locals to discover their take on life on the isles. Alison Johnson converted a minister's manse into a superb inn on the Isle of Harris and shares some hilarious stories of her entertaining ordeal.

It's hard to say why people react the way they do to a particular place. You may as well try to explain why people fall in love. Hence, South Uist cast its spell on Margaret Fay Shaw on first sight and never let go. Bettina Selby returned to the Outer Hebrides time after time but found that the Isle of Lewis spoke directly to her inner soul. As pilgrims do, John J. O Riordain made a tremendous effort, travelling by train, bus, and ferry, to get to Iona, often called the cradle of Scottish Christianity. He offers his own spiritual interpretation of the famed island. W. R. Mitchell journeys to faraway St. Kilda, on the edge of the known world.

Finally, Emily Hiestand, John McKinney, and Lawrence Millman travel back in time to the northern isles of Orkney, Shetland and Foula, where the light seems different and the accents recall their shared Scandinavian past.

❈   ❈   ❈

The Scotland we think we know is as much a product of our collective imagination – a *tabula rasa* of the mind – as it is an actual place. It can be whatever we want it to be: urban bustle, quiet retreat, rugged outpost. Admittedly, much has changed since the early travellers first scribbled down their initial impressions. And yet much remains the same. The mountains and lochs that Boswell and Johnson witnessed with their own eyes are still there for all to see. The inhabitants, although more sophisticated and very much a part of the modern world, are still Scots – with all that that entails. And countless people – natives and visitors alike – still travel to this ancient and complex land in search of something quite apart from the ordinary.

The road north beckons still.

THE
LOWLANDS

DANIEL DEFOE
(1660-1731)

❖   ❖   ❖

We remember Daniel Defoe today as the author of Robinson Crusoe *(1719), which many critics consider the first great English novel. Inspired by the life of Alexander Selkirk (1676-1721) who hailed from the town of Largo in Fife, Crusoe became a huge success – the blockbuster of its day.*

Born in London in 1660, the son of a merchant, Defoe enjoyed a very diverse career: poet, critic, journalist, and, eventually, novelist. The success of Robinson Crusoe *brought him a degree of financial security that he had never experienced before, although, ironically, he died alone and in poverty in 1731.*

For many years Defoe had a tremendous urge to traverse the entire breadth of the British island. And indeed Defoe spent a considerable amount of time visiting parts of England, Scotland, and Wales, performing various public and private duties.

A Tour Through the Whole Island of Great Britain was published in three volumes between 1724 and 1726. It was intended not as a typical guidebook but rather a trenchant commentary on the present state of British life and customs, with special emphasis placed on Britain's economic health. But it is also one man's journal of a particular place at a particular time. Being a patriotic Englishman, Defoe often compares the Scottish way of life with the English. The comparison, if not always pleasant, certainly makes for provocative reading.

❖   ❖   ❖

The Borders

from **A TOUR THROUGH THE WHOLE ISLAND
OF GREAT BRITAIN**

Sir,

I am now just enter'd Scotland, and that by the ordinary way from
Berwick. We tread upon Scots ground, after about three miles
riding beyond Berwick; the little district between, they say, is
neither England or Scotland, and is call'd Berwickshire, as being
formerly a dependant upon the town of Berwick; but we find no
towns in it, only straggling farm-houses; and one sees the Tweed on
one side, which fetches a reach northward, the sea on the other, and
the land between lies so high, that in stormy weather 'tis very bleak
and unpleasant; however, the land is good, and compar'd to our next
view, we ought to think very well of it.

Mordintown lying to the west, the great road does not lie
thro' it, but carries us to the brow of a very high hill, where we had
a large view into Scotland: but we were welcom'd into it with such
a Scots gale of wind, that, besides the steepness of the hill, it oblig'd
us to quit our horses, for real apprehensions of being blown off, the
wind blowing full north, and the road turning towards the north, it
blew directly into our faces: And I can truly say, I never was
sensible of so fierce a wind, so exceeding keen and cold, for it
pierc'd our very eyes, that we could scarcely bear to hold them
open.

When we came down the hill, the strength of the wind was
not felt so much, and, consequently, not the cold. The first town we
come to is as perfectly Scots, as if you were 100 miles north of
Edinburgh; nor is there the least appearance of any thing English,
either in customs, habits, usages of the people, or in their way of
living, eating, dress, or behaviour; any more than if they had never
heard of an English nation; nor was there an Englishman to be seen,
or an English family to be found among them.

On the contrary, you have in England abundance of
Scotsmen, Scots customs, words, habits, and usages, even more
than becomes them; nay, even the buildings in the towns, and in the

villages, imitate the Scots almost all over Northumberland; witness their building the houses with the stairs (to the second floor) going up on the outside of the house, so that one family may live below, and another above, without going in at the same door; which is the Scots way of living, and which we see in Alnwick and Warkworth, and several other towns; witness also their setting their corn up in great numbers of small stacks without doors, not making use of any barns, only a particular building, which they call a barn, but, which is itself no more than a threshing-floor, into which they take one of those small stacks at a time, and thresh it out, and then take in another; which we have great reason to believe was the usage of the antients, seeing we read of threshing-floors often; but very seldom, of a barn, except that of the rich glutton.

Being down this hill, we pass'd a bridge over the little river Eye, at the mouth of which there is a small harbour, with a town call'd Eyemouth, or, as some call it, Heymouth, which has of late been more spoken of than formerly, by giving the title of Baron to the late Duke of Marlborough, who was Duke of Marlborough, Marquiss of Blandford, and Baron of Eyemouth in Scotland; and, by virtue of this title, had a right of peerage in the Parliament of Scotland. But notwithstanding all this, I never heard that he did any thing for the town, which is, at present, just what it always was, a good fishing town, and some fishing vessels belong to it; for such it is a good harbour, and for little else.

From this bridge we enter upon a most desolate, and, in winter, a most frightful moor for travellers, especially strangers, call'd Coudingham, or, to speak properly, Coldhingham Moor; upon which, for about eight miles, you see hardly a hedge, or a tree, except in one part, and that at a good distance; nor do you meet with but one house in all the way, and that no house of entertainment; which, we thought, was but a poor reception for Scotland to give her neighbours, who were strangers, at their very first entrance into her bounds.

Having pass'd this desart, which indeed, makes a stranger think Scotland a terrible place, you come down a very steep hill into the Lothains, so the counties are divided, and they are spoken of in plural; because as Yorkshire is divided into East and West Riding, so here is the East, and West, and Mid Lothain, or Louthain, and therefore justly call'd Lothains in the plural.

From the top of this hill you begin to see that Scotland is not all desart; and the low lands, which then show themselves, give you a prospect of a fruitful and pleasant country: As soon as we come down the hill, there is a village call'd Cockburnspeth, vulgarly Cobberspeth, where nature forms a very steep and difficult pass, and where, indeed, a thousand men well furnish'd, and boldly doing their duty, would keep out an army, if there was occasion.

The first gentleman's house we met with in Scotland was that of Donglass, the seat of Sir James Hall; a gentleman so hospitable, so courteous to strangers, so addicted to improve and cultivate his estate, and understood it so well, that we began to see here a true representation of the gentry of Scotland; than whom, I must say, without compliment, none in Europe, understand themselves better, or better deserve the name of gentlemen. We began to see that Scotland was not so naturally barren, as some people represent it, but, with application and judgment, in the proper methods of improving lands, might be made to equal, not England only, but even the richest, most fruitful, most pleasant, and best improv'd part of England ...

WASHINGTON IRVING
(1773-1859)

❊   ❊   ❊

Washington Irving is considered the first American writer to have earned literary acclaim both at home and abroad. Born in New York City, the son of an Orcadian merchant, Irving created two of the most memorable characters in American literature, Rip Van Winkle and Ichabod Crane. He also wrote much non-fiction, including the massive five-volume Life of George Washington.

Irving made many friends in literary circles on both sides of the Atlantic – he included Sir Walter Scott among his acquaintances. Like Sir Walter, Irving is not read much today (the younger generation more than likely recognizes the name thanks to cinematic adaptations, such as, most recently, Tim Burton's The Legend of Sleepy Hollow*) and yet during his long career he influenced many people, including Charles Dickens, William Makepeace Thackeray, Herman Melville, Nathaniel Hawthorne, and Edgar Allen Poe.*

In Abbotsford *Irving pays a visit to the baronial estate of Sir Walter Scott, located in the heart of the Scottish Border country, near Melrose.*

❊   ❊   ❊

Abbotsford

Late in the evening of the 29th of August, 1816, I arrived at the ancient little border town of Selkirk, where I put up for the night. I had come down from Edinburgh, partly to visit Melrose Abbey and its vicinity, but chiefly to get a sight of the 'mighty minstrel of the North.' I had a letter of introduction to him from Thomas Campbell, the poet; and had reason to think, from the interest he had taken in some of my earlier scribblings, that a visit from me would not be deemed an intrusion.

On the following morning, after an early breakfast, I set off in a post-chaise for the abbey. On the way thither, I stopped at the gate of Abbotsford, and sent the postilion to the house with the letter of introduction, and my card, on which I had written that I was on the way to the ruins of Melrose Abbey, and wished to know whether it would be agreeable to Mr. Scott (he had not yet been made a Baronet), to receive a visit from me in the course of the morning.

While the postilion was on his errand I had time to survey the mansion. It stood some short distance below the road, on the side of a hill sweeping down to the Tweed, and was as yet but a snug gentleman's cottage, with something rural and picturesque in its appearance. The whole front was overrun with evergreens, and immediately above the portal was a great pair of elk horns, branching out from beneath the foliage, and giving the cottage the look of a hunting-lodge. The huge baronial pile, to which this modest mansion in a manner gave birth, was just emerging into existence: a part of the walls, surrounded by scaffolding, already had risen to the height of the cottage, and the court-yard in front was encumbered by masses of hewn stone.

The noise of the chaise had disturbed the quiet of the establishment. Out sallied the warder of the castle, a black greyhound; and, leaping on one of the blocks of stone, began a furious barking. His alarm brought out the whole garrison of dogs: –

'Both mongrel, puppy, whelp and hound,
And curs of low degree:'

all open-mouthed and vociferous. I should correct my quotation: not a cur was to be seen on the premises. Scott was too true a sportsman and had too high a veneration for pure blood, to tolerate a mongrel.

In a little while the 'Lord of the Castle' himself made his appearance. I knew him at once by the descriptions I had read and heard, and the likenesses that had been published of him. He was tall, and of a large and powerful frame. His dress was simple and almost rustic. An old green shooting-coat, with a dog whistle at the buttonhole, brown linen pantaloons, stout shoes that tied at the ankles, and a white hat that had evidently seen service. He came limping up the gravel-walk, aiding himself by a stout walking-staff;

but moving rapidly and with vigour. By his side jogged along a large iron-gray staghound, of most grave demeanour, who took no part in the clamour of the canine rabble, but seemed to consider himself bound, for the dignity of the house, to give me a courteous reception.

Before Scott reached the gate, he called out in a hearty tone, welcoming me to Abbotsford, and asking news of Campbell. Arrived at the door of the chaise, he grasped me warmly by the hand: 'Come, drive down, drive down to the house,' said he; 'Ye're just in time for breakfast, and afterwards ye shall see all the wonders of the Abbey.'

I would have excused myself on the plea of having already made my breakfast. 'Hut, man,' cried he, 'a ride in the morning in the keen air of the Scotch hills is warrant enough for a second breakfast.'

I was accordingly whirled to the portal of the cottage, and in a few moments found myself seated at the breakfast table. There was no one present but the family, which consisted of Mrs. Scott; her eldest daughter, Sophia, then a fine girl about seventeen; Miss Ann Scott, two or three years younger; Walter, a well-grown stripling; and Charles, a lively boy, eleven or twelve years of age.

I soon felt myself quite at home, and my heart in a glow, with the cordial welcome I experienced. I had thought to make a mere morning visit, but found I was not to be let off so lightly. 'You must not think our neighbourhood is to be read in a morning like a newspaper,' said Scott; 'it takes several days of study for an observant traveller, that has a relish for auld-world trumpery. After breakfast you shall make your visit to Melrose Abbey; I shall not be able to accompany you, as I have some household affairs to attend to; but I will put you in charge of my son Charles, who is very learned in all things touching the old ruin and the neighourhood it stands in; and he, and my friend, Johnnie Bower, will tell you the whole truth about it, with a great deal more, that you are not called upon to believe, unless you be a true and nothing-doubting antiquary. When you come back, I'll take you out on a ramble about the neighbourhood. To-morrow we will take a look at the Yarrow, and the next day we will drive over to Dryburgh Abbey, which is a fine old ruin, well worth your seeing.' – In a word, before Scott had got through with his plan, I found myself committed for a visit of several days, and it seemed as if a little realm of romance was suddenly open before me.

❋   ❋   ❋

One of my pleasantest rumbles with Scott about the neighourhood of Abbotsford was taken in company with Mr. William Laidlaw, the steward of his estate. This was a gentleman for whom Scott entertained a particular value. He had been born to a competency, had been well educated, his mind was richly stored with varied information, and he was a man of sterling moral worth. Having been reduced by misfortune, Scott had got him to take charge of his estate. He lived at a small farm, on the hill side above Abbotsford, and was treated by Scott as a cherished and confidential friend, rather than a dependent.

As the day was showery, Scott was attended by one of his retainers, who carried his plaid. This man, whose name, I think, was George, deserves especial mention. Sophia Scott used to call him her father's grand vizier; and she gave a playful account one evening, as she was hanging on her father's arm, of the consultations which he and George used to have about matters relating to farming. George was tenacious of his opinions, and he and Scott would have strong disputes, in front of the house, as to something that had to be done on the estate, until the latter, fairly tired out, would abandon the ground and the argument, exclaiming, 'Well, well, George, have it your own way.'

After a time, however, George would present himself at the door of the parlour, and observe, 'I hae been thinking over the matter, and upon the whole, I think I'll take your honour's advice.'

Scott laughed heartily when this anecdote was told to him. 'It was with him and George,' he said, 'as it was with an old laird and a pet servant, whom he had indulged, until he was positive beyond all endurance. "This won't do!" cried the old laird, in a passion. "We can't live together any longer, – we must part." "An' where the deil does your honour mean to go?" replied the other.'

I would, moreover, observe of George, that he was a firm believer in ghosts, and warlocks, and all kinds of old wives' fables.

He was a religious man too, mingling a little degree of Scottish pride in his devotion; for, though his salary was but twenty pounds a year, he had managed to afford seven pounds for a family bible. It is true he had one hundred pounds clear of the world, and was looked up to by his comrades as a man of property.

In the course of our morning's walk, we stopped at a small house belonging to one of the labourers on the estate. The object of Scott's visit was to inspect a relic which had been digged up in the Roman camp; and which, if I recollect right, he pronounced to have been a tongs. It was produced by the cottager's wife, a ruddy healthy-looking dame, whom Scott addressed by the name of Ailie. As he stood regarding the relic, turning it round and round, and making comments upon it, half grave, half comic, with the cottage group around him, all joining occasionally in the colloquy, the indomitable character of Monkbarns was again brought to mind, and I seemed to see before me that prince of antiquarians and humorists, holding forth to his unlearned and unbelieving neighbours.

Whenever Scott touched, in this way, upon local antiquities, and in all his familiar conversations about local traditions and superstitions, there was always a sly and quiet humour running at the bottom of his discourse, and playing about his countenance, as if he sported with the subject. It seemed to me as if he distrusted his own enthusiasm, and was disposed to dwell upon his own humours and peculiarities; yet, at the same time, a poetic gleam in his eye would show that he really took a strong relish and interest in the theme.

'It was a pity,' he said, 'that antiquarians were generally so dry; for the subjects they handled were rich in historical and poetic recollections, in picturesque details, in quaint and heroic characteristics, and in all kinds of curious and obsolete courtesies and ceremonials. They are always groping among the rarest materials for poetry, but they have no idea of turning them to poetic use. Now, every fragment from old times has, in some degree, its story with it; or gives an inkling of something characteristic of the circumstances and manners of its day, and so sets the imagination at work.'

For my own part, I never met with an antiquarian so delightful, either in his writings or his conversation; and the quiet subdued humour that was prone to mingle in his disquisitions, gave them, to me, a peculiar and an exquisite flavour. But he seemed, in fact, to undervalue every thing that concerned himself. The play of his genius was so easy, that he was unconscious of its mighty power; and made light of those sports of intellect that shamed the efforts and labours of other minds.

Our ramble this morning took us again up the Rhymer's Glen, and by Huntley Bank, and Huntley Wood, and the silver waterfall overhung with weeping birches, and mountain ash, those delicate and beautiful trees which grace the green shaws and burn sides of Scotland. The heather, too, that closely woven robe of Scottish landscape, which covers the nakedness of its hills and mountains, tinted the neighbourhood with soft and rich colours. As we ascended the glen, the prospect opened upon us: Melrose, with its towers and pinnacles, lay below; beyond was the Eildon Hills, the Cowdenknowes, the Tweed, Gala Water, and all that storied vicinity; the whole landscape varied by gleams of sunshine and driving showers.

Scott, as usual, took the lead, limping along with great activity; and in joyous mood; giving scraps of border rhymes and border stories. Two or three times, in the course of our walk, there were drizzling showers, that I supposed would put an end to our ramble; but my companion trudged on as unconcernedly as if it had been fine weather. At length I asked whether we had not better seek some shelter. 'True,' said Scott, 'I did not recollect that you were not accustomed to our Scottish mists. This is a lachrymose climate, "evermore showering". We, however, are "children of the mist", and must not mind a little whimpering of the clouds, any more than a man must the weeping of an hysterical wife. As you are not accustomed to be wet through, as a matter of course, in a morning's walk, we will bide a bit under the lee of this wall, until the shower is over.'

Taking his seat under shelter of a thicket, he called to his man George, for his tartan; the, turning to me, 'Come,' said he, 'come under my plaidy, as the old song goes:' so, making me nestle down beside him, he wrapped part of the plaid round me, and took me, as he said, under his wing.

While we were nestled together, he pointed to a hole in the opposite bank of the glen. 'That,' he said, 'was the hole of an old grey badger, who was, doubtless, snugly housed in this bad weather.' Sometimes he saw him at the entrance, like a hermit at the door of his cell, telling his beads, or reading a homily. He had a great respect for the venerable anchorite, and would not suffer him to be disturbed. He was a kind of successor to Thomas the Rhymer, and, perhaps, might be Thomas himself, returned from Fairyland, but still under fairy spell.

Some accident turned the conversation upon [James] Hogg, the poet, in which Laidlaw, who was seated beside us, took a part. Hogg had once been a shepherd in the service of his father, and Laidlaw gave many interesting anecdotes of him, of which I now retain no recollection: they used to tend the sheep together when Laidlaw was a boy, and Hogg would recite the first struggling conceptions of his muse. At night, when Laidlaw was quartered comfortably in bed in the farm-house, poor Hogg would take to the shepherd's hut, in the fold on the hill side, and there lie awake for hours together, and look at the stars and make poetry, which he would repeat the next day to his companion.

Scott spoke in warm terms of Hogg, and repeated passages from his beautiful poem of Kilmeny, to which he gave great and well-merited praise. He gave, also, some amusing anecdotes of Hogg and his publisher, Blackwood, who was at that time just rising into the bibliographical importance which he has since enjoyed.

Hogg, in one of his poems, I believe 'The Pilgrims of the Sun', had dabbled a little in metaphysics, and, like his heroes, had got into the clouds. Blackwood, who began to affect criticism, argued stoutly with him as to the necessity of omitting or elucidating some obscure passage. Hogg was immovable.

'But, man,' said Blackwood, 'I dinna ken what ye mean in the passage.' 'Hout hout, man,' replied Hogg impatiently, 'I dinna ken always what I mean mysel'.' There is many a metaphysical poet in the same predicament with honest Hogg.

Scott promised to invite the Shepherd to Abbotsford during my visit; and I anticipated much gratification in meeting with him, from the account I had received of his character and manners, and the great pleasure I had derived from his works. Circumstances, however, prevented Scott from performing his promise; and, to my great regret, I left Scotland without seeing one of its most original and national characters.

ROBERT SOUTHEY
(1774-1843)

❉   ❉   ❉

Poet, essayist, and biographer, Robert Southey was poet laureate of England in 1813. Although not well read today, he was an important and well-regarded figure of his time. A graduate of Oxford University, in 1803 he settled in Keswick in the Lake District where he befriended the Romantic poets Samuel Taylor Coleridge (who became his brother-in-law) and William Wordsworth.

In 1819 Southey travelled to Scotland and undertook a six-week-long journey with the famed Scots engineer Thomas Telford as his constant companion and wrote down his observations. He was interested in the social conditions of the country, which led him to New Lanark, a planned community south of Glasgow recognised for its humane working conditions and enlightened labour policies. Southey, however, formed his own opinions.

❉   ❉   ❉

New Lanark

from JOURNAL OF A TOUR IN SCOTLAND

Tuesday, September 28. – Hamilton is a dirty old town, with a good many thatched houses in the street – implying either poverty, or great disregard of danger from fire. 15 miles to Lanark, thro' a beautiful country, the Clyde being generally in sight. No part of England, the Lake-Land alone excepted, is more lovely than this. And, the number of *quintas* show that the Scotch are fully sensible of its beauty: the Portugueze word occurs naturally to me, and we want a word of home-growth – *villa* is not English – *seat* has another meaning – and *gentlemens-houses* of too Dutch-like a form of composition. Among these are two modern Gothic buildings which must have been very expensive: both look well, and one of them, as far as

I could distinguish its parts, appeared to have been built in the old fashion of Scotland and the Low Countries adapted to modern comfort with good taste and effect – in that fashion it had round towers at the corners, and pointed roofs. The ground about the lower falls of the Clyde belongs to Robert Owen of Lanark; he has made a circuitous walk to them, with good intention, but somewhat unluckily for us, to whom a long walk was thus made necessary thro' a heavy shower. It is a good scene, tho' we saw it to disadvantage, the water being very low.

After breakfast we walked to New Lanark, which is about a mile from the town. The approach to this establishment reminded me of the descent upon the baths of Monchique, more than any other scene which I could call to mind. The hills are far inferior in height, neither is there so much wood about them; but the buildings lie in such a dingle, and in like manner surprize you by their position, and their uncommon character. There is too a regular appearance, such as belongs to a conventual or eleemosynary establishment. The descent is very steep: such as is implied by saying you might throw a stone down the chimnies.

A large convent is more like a cotton-mill than it is like a college – that is to say, such convents as have been built since the glorious age of ecclesiastical architecture, and these are by far the greater number. They are like great infirmaries, or manufactories; and these mills which are three in number, at a distance might be mistaken for convents, if in a Catholic country. There are also several streets, or rather rows of houses for the persons employed there; and other buildings connected with the establishment. These rows are cleaner than the common streets of a Scotch town, and yet not quite so clean as they ought to be. Their general appearance is what might be looked for in a Moravian settlement.

I had written to Owen from Inverary; and he expected us, he said, to stay with him a week, or at the very least three days; it was not without difficulty that we persevered in our purpose of proceeding the same evening to Douglas Mill.

He led us thro' the works with great courtesy, and made as full an exhibition as the time allowed. It is needless to say anything more of the Mills than that they are perfect in their kind, according to the present state of mechanical science, and that they appeared to be under admirable management; they are thoroughly clean, and so carefully ventilated, that there was no unpleasant smell in any of the apartments. Everything required for the machinery is made upon the spot, and the expence of wear and tear is estimated at 8000£ annually. There are stores also from which the people are supplied with all the necessaries of life. They have a credit there to the amount of sixteen shillings a week each, but may deal elsewhere if they chuse. The expences of what he calls the moral part of the establishment, he stated at 700£ a year. But a large building is just compleated, with ball and concert and lecture rooms, all for 'the formation of character'; and this must have required a considerable sum, which I should think must surely be set down to Owen's private account, rather than to the cost of the concern.

In the course of going thro' these buildings, he took us into an apartment where one of his plans, upon a scale larger than any of the Swiss models, was spread upon the floor. And with a long wand in his hand he explained the plan, while Willy and Francis stood by, with wondering and longing eyes, regarding it as a plaything, and hoping they might be allowed to amuse themselves with it. Meantime the word had been given: we were conducted into one of the dancing rooms; half a dozen fine boys, about nine or ten years old, led the way, playing on fifes, and some 200 children, from four years of age till ten, entered the room and arranged themselves on three sides of it. A man whose official situation I did not comprehend gave the word, which either because of the tone or the dialect I did not understand; and they turned to the right or left, faced about, fell forwards and backwards, and stamped at command, performing manoeuvres the object of which was not very clear, with perfect regularity. I remembered what T. Vardon had told me of the cows in Holland. When the cattle are housed, the Dutch in their spirit of cleanliness, prevent them from dirtying their tails by tying them up (to the no small discomfort of the cows) at a certain elevation, to a cross string which extends the whole length of the stalls: and the consequence is that when any one cow wags her tail, all the others must wag theirs also. So I could not but think that these puppet-like motions might, with a little ingenuity, have been produced by the great water-wheel, which is the *primum mobile* of the whole Cotton-Mills. A certain number of the children were then drawn out, and sung to the pipe of a music master. They afterwards danced to the piping of the six little pipers. There was too much of all this, but the children seemed to like it. When the exhibition was over, they filed off into the adjoining school room.

I was far better pleased with a large room in which all the children of the establishment who are old enough not to require the constant care of their mothers, and too young for instruction of any kind, were brought together while their parents were at work, and left to amuse themselves, with no more superintendence than is necessary for preventing them from hurting themselves. They made a glorious noise, worth all the concerts of New Lanark, and of London to boot. It was really delightful to see how the little creatures crowded about Owen to make their bows and their curtesies, looking up and smiling in his face; and the genuine benignity and pleasure with which he noticed them, laying his hand on the head of one, shaking hands with another, and bestowing kind looks and kind words upon all.

Owen in reality deceives himself. He is part-owner and sole Director of a large establishment, differing more in accidents than in essence from a plantation: the persons under him happen to be white, and are at liberty by law to quit his service, but while they remain in it they are as much under his absolute management as so many negro-slaves. His humour, his vanity, his kindliness of nature (all these have their share) lead him to make these *human machines* as he calls them (and too literally believes them to be) as happy as he can, and to make a display of their happiness. And he jumps at once to the monstrous conclusion that because he can do this with 2210 persons, who are totally dependent upon them – all mankind might be governed with the same facility. *Et in Utopia ego*. But I never regarded man as a machine; I never believed him to be merely a material being; I never for a moment could listen to the nonsense of Helvetius, nor suppose, as Owen does, that men may be cast in a mould (like the other parts of his mill) and take the impression with perfect certainty. Nor did I ever disguise from myself the difficulties of a system which took for its foundation the principle of a community of goods. On the contrary I met them fairly, acknowledged them, and rested satisfied with the belief (whether erroneous or not) that the evils incident in such a system would be infinitely less than those which stare us in the face under the existing order. But Owen reasons from his Cotton Mills to the whole empire. He keeps out of sight from others, and perhaps from himself, that his system, instead of aiming at perfect freedom, can only be kept in play by absolute power. Indeed, he never looks beyond one of his own ideal square villages, to the rules and proportions of which he would square the whole human race. The *formation of character!* Why the end of his institutions would be, as far as possible, the destruction of all character. They tend directly to destroy individuality of character and domesticity – in the one of which the strength of man consists, and in the other his happiness. The power of human society, and the grace, would both be annihilated.

Yet I admire the man, and like him too. And the Yahoos who are bred in our manufacturing towns, and under the administration of our Poor Laws are so much worse than the Chinese breed which he proposes to raise, that I should be glad to see his regulations adopted, as the Leeds people have proposed, for a colony of paupers. Such a variety in society would be curious; and might as well be encouraged as Quakerism and Moravianism.

Owen walked with us to the Inn: and we set off just in time to accomplish a stage of 8 miles to Douglas Mill, before night fell. The Inn was formerly the Miller's house; a new one must be built, because it is out of repair, and because the new road will be at some little distance from it. Our accommodations there were good.

JAN MORRIS

✻   ✻   ✻

*Jan Morris is the travel writer's travel writer – her essays are considered
classics of the genre. She has crisscrossed the globe countless times in search
of a story. Wherever she goes, she leaves her own indelible mark. She views the
world through a pair of very perceptive eyes and, fortunately for us, is able and
more than willing to share her vision. Whatever she writes about, her modus
operandi remains the same: to offer an individual response to a particular
place, 'a wanderer's response.'*

     Her best-known books include the Pax Britannica *trilogy (*Heaven's
Command, Pax Britannica, *and* Farewell to the Trumpets*),* Spain,
Among the Cities, Journeys, Venice, Oxford, The Matter of Wales,
Destinations, Manhattan '45, *the autobiographical* Conundrum, *and,
most recently,* Lincoln: A Foreigner's Quest. *She has also edited* The
Oxford Book of Oxford *and two Welsh travel anthologies. Her first novel,*
Last Letters from Hav, *was nominated for the 1985 Booker Prize.*

     This delightful piece on the 'new' Glasgow is from Locations.

✻   ✻   ✻

Glasgow: A Reincarnation

from LOCATIONS

Ay, well, they talk a lot, she said in her almost impenetrable Glasgow
accent, *but they havna changed much really.* She was one of God's
Glaswegians, pawky, tough, stocky, fun, with a face pallid from too
much smoking but enlivened by a scatter of freckles around her
nose, which gave her a gingery youthful look. I assumed that she
was simply expressing a half-serious native scepticism. Everyone
knows of course that once-grimy, once-slummy, once-violent old

Glasgow has changed a lot – Glasgow's Miles Better, as the celebrated civic slogan has it, Glasgow is Where the Action Is, There's A Lot Glasgowing On. With Barcelona, perhaps, Glasgow is the trendiest city in Europe, gawked at night and day by tourists and travel writers.

Presently I realized, however, that the woman with the freckles was expressing something more profound. We were sitting in adjacent red plastic seats in the concourse of Glasgow Central Station, which is itself a famous example of Glasgow's self-improvement. Everything in that nineteenth-century prodigy is painted and shiny again, with Muzak playing brightly, flower-boxes blooming, a floor of pale terrazzo tiling and a jolly kind of trumpet call to introduce the train announcements. But the longer I looked around me the more it dawned upon me that my companion was right. They hadn't changed much really. They had merely restored a splendid Victorian artefact to its original self, not just in fabric, but in spirit too.

This must have been, I now saw, just how Glasgow Central seemed to its customers a century ago – all this spanking brightness and cockiness. Its heroic glass roof looks brand new. Its intricate forest of iron-girdering seems futuristic still. Not only the fresh-painted woodwork of its restaurants, or the plushy comfort of its Central Hotel, but the sleek gleaming trains, too, lined up yellow and blue at their platforms, the elegant new station delicatessen, even the Muzak and the electronic fanfare – all represented the very essence of Victorian panache. I was experiencing exactly the excitement that my great-grandparents would have experienced, if they had chuffed into Glasgow Central around the time of Queen Victoria's Golden Jubilee. It was not just a face-lift, more a rebirth.

They havna changed much really. What we see in Central Station we see in Glasgow as a whole: a glitzy reincarnation, a city returning to kind, and behaving as it was brought up to behave.

It was old long before Victoria's Golden Jubilee. It was a medieval market, cathedral, and university town, and its port prospered in the tobacco and cotton trades. But it grew into greatness with the British Empire, Victoria's empire of steam, iron, and ships, and in the heyday of the imperial system it was immensely successful. Second City of the British Empire was the catchphrase then. Glasgow's heavy industries exported their products all over the world, its River Clyde was lined with famous shipyards, and its city centre burgeoned into a grand exhibition of Victorian style.

If you think this style was sombre or pompous, come to Glasgow now, where you can see much of it just as it was meant to be, before the smoke of the generations blackened it, and economic decline blunted its assurance. Wherever you look in central Glasgow, festive, buoyant, romantic Victorian architecture greets you. In Glasgow especially it was an architecture of lightness, expressed in a virtuoso use of vistas and cheerful elaborations of every kind. Glass abounds – Glasgow is full of big windows and conservatories – and the skyline is punctuated by fretted and whimsical shapes, with towers like telescopes, and cupolas, and weathervanes, and entertaining bobbles, turrets, and bumps.

It is not all great architecture, heaven knows, but two undeniably great architects did work in Glasgow during the Victorian century – Alexander Thomson in High Victorian times, Charles Rennie Mackintosh at *fin de siècle*. They gave such particular twists to Victorianism that between them they created a unique civic manner, recognizable everywhere in striking fenestration, Art deco ornamentation, curious interpretations of classical modes, touches of the Egyptian and bits of Scottish medievalism. And interacting always with these elements of genius are countless examples of the truest Glasgow building form, the tenement – a low-rise apartment block really, of an especially communal kind, represented in a myriad ashlar and sandstone terraces, crescents, esplanades and winding city streets, and built in reds and creams which, now that the detritus of the industrial age have been removed, turn out to be the real Glasgow colours.

All this has been spectacularly revitalized. Forty years ago the Glasgow presence seemed almost obliterated by decay and dogma. The Empire was lost, the shipyards were closing, the port was moribund, nobody wanted the marvellous steam engines of the North British Locomotive Company. Glasgow's occupation was gone. The city was neglected and impoverished, and when in the 1950s they first tried to revivify the old place, the fashionable socio-logical theories of the day only made things worse. Acres of traditional tenements were destroyed then, ill-built ugly tower blocks went up around the city perimeter, and the unity of the city was whittled away in loveless housing estate and ill-advised ring road.

Just in time the tide was turned. Refurbishment replaced demolition as social policy. The last of the horrible tower blocks was built (and the first are now being pulled down). Millions of pounds of public and private money was poured into the cleaning up of the city, the cherishing of its arts and the restoration of its old ebullience. If you sail up the Clyde to Glasgow now you still pass mile after mile of dead docks and abandoned shipyards, quays forlorn and derelict, disused cranes, ruined works, broken piles, and overgrown watersteps. Only a couple of shipyards are still at work. Only a lonely Cypriot freighter, perhaps, loads a melancholy cargo of scrap metal, scrunched up there and then from a pile of old cars upon the quay.

But when your boat approaches the city centre, at the famous old landing-stage called Broomielaw, then a palpable sense of vigour and high hope greets you after all. Old buildings look spruce and confident, new ones sprout up all around. In the city of the shippers and the ironmasters, slinky boutiques, smooth art galleries, discos, clubs and urbane restaurants proliferate. To canned Vivaldi expensively dressed infants throw teddy-bears at one another across the mosaic floor of the elegant Princes Square shopping centre. One evening I went direct from a reception for one of America's most celebrated photographers to a reading by one of Britain's most controversial novelists, and at my favourite Glasgow restaurant (a foliage-filled glass-roofed courtyard in the university quarter) my fellow-diners these days seem to look less like Glaswegians on a night out than delegates to a permanent convention of Milanese fashion designers.

Mind you, the pride had never faltered. Glasgow has always been intensely fond of itself, even in hard times, and more than anywhere else in Britain, has aspired to the condition of a city-State. The freckled woman freely admitted that there was nowhere quite like Glasgow. You know the auld song, don't you? – and she broke into a somewhat tobacco-thickened and screechy soprano – *I'm only a common old working chap, As anyone here can see, But when I've had a couple of drinks on a Saturday, GLASGOW BELONGS TO ME!* There are few cities that have celebrated themselves with such profligate consistency down the years – the bookshops are full of books about Glasgow, the museums are stacked with Glasgow material, there are innumerable songs about Glasgow, countless poems about Glasgow, acres of Glasgow paintings, and more than one bestselling dictionary of the Glasgow dialect.

This is a Victorian phenomenon too. Glasgow shared the powerful nineteenth-century impetus towards municipal government and self-sufficiency. Everywhere City Halls were the prime architectural expressions of this movement, and there is no mistaking the self-esteem of Glasgow's own City Chambers, in George Square, which are rich in all the symbolisms of civic complacency. When the Chambers were completed in 1888 Glasgow's focus moved there from the ancient power-centre of the cathedral and the High Street markets, and to this day the life of the city revolves largely around George Square, which is no Piazza San Marco or Place de la Concorde, but is certainly full of character.

It too has been enthusiastically rejuvenated. At one end stands the towering mass of the Chambers themselves, encrusted with emblematic figures and topped by one of those telescopic towers. The Merchant House at the other end is an ornate palace of monetarism, surmounted on its domed turret by a gilded three-masted ship. The hotel on the north side has lately had a bright new glassy terrace added to it, and on the south a mighty royal crest adds authority to the Italianate General Post Office. There are lawns and trees and ornamental flower-beds, and two supercilious-looking lions, frequently ridden by impertinent children, guard the granite Cenotaph which is Glasgow's memorial to its war dead. All around the square are statues. Some commemorate universal heroes – Walter Scott on a tall central colum, Burns and Gladstone and Queen Victoria herself, nonchalantly carrying a sceptre and wearing a crown while riding side-saddle on a horse. Some are of worthies perhaps less exactly remembered – General Sir John Moore, Field-Marshal Lord Clyde, or Thomas Graham the chemist.

And one at least, and that the most telling of the lot, is of somebody most of us have never heard of – James Oswald, MP, whose effigy was erected, its inscription tells us, 'by a few friends'. One feels that the friends are all around there still, for even now

George Square has a tight-knit family feel to it, as though all the people sitting on its benches, admiring its flowers, clambering over its Cenotaph lions, are really kith and kin. This is the power of Glasgow, which has sustained it through all hazards. People talk to each other easily on those benches. People share gambles, compare extortionate prices, take their shoes off to give their poor feet a rest. The 5-year-old boy riding his motorized buggy around the benches smiles indiscriminately at us all as he blasts past yet again. His father proudly tells us how much he paid for the machine. Several women raise canny eyebrows at one another, as if to say well, some people ha' more money than sense.

Sitting there among the citizens, looking at those statues, thinking about Mr Oswald and his friends, cursing the buggy-boy, while the big buses slide around the square and the City Chambers look paternalistically down – sitting in this place, at once so old-fashioned and yet so contemporary, so proud of itself but so neighbourly, once again I feel time reunited. In my mind I easily reclothe the people in crinolines and stove-pipe hats, and metamorphose the buses into horse-drawn trams, the taxis into polished black hansoms, the chequered caps of the policemen into tall bobbies' helmets, and the motor-buggy into a mercifully silent hobby-horse.

Ay, well, that's all very well (the freckled woman says), *but life's not all statues in George Square – and what's a wee bairn doing with a contraption like that anyway, he'll damage himself in the end.* She is right again, of course. Life wasn't all statues in Glasgow's Victorian prime, either, when social contrasts were fearful and many of those picturesque tenements were among the worst slums in Europe.

I often saw her, as I wandered the city. She was one of those eyebrow-raisers in the square, of course. She was scrabbling among the second-hand clothes in the dingy shambles of Paddy's Market. She was dubiously examining the contents of her purse outside cutprice stores, and she was for ever hastening, huddled against the wind in her shabby anorak, along the pot-holed desolate streets of the Gorbals.

The Gorbals is her home, figuratively if not actually. Forty years ago the Gorbals was the most famously squalid and dangerous part of Glasgow, a place where the old tenements had been allowed to decay into an appalling nadir of misery and sickness, and where the tower blocks that replaced them had become legends of rubbish-strewn, graffiti-smeared, crime-ridden disillusionment. In the Gorbals the woman with the freckles is always visible, hanging out the washing from loveless balconies, yelling at recalcitrant children, or labouring home from the supermarket with her shopping-bag (containing frozen fish-fingers, a can of peas, a tabloid newspaper, two bottles of stout and a packet of filter-tips ...)

Much of outer Glasgow, away from the newly glistening city centre and the lavish western suburbs, remains dismal – nothing like so luridly poverty-stricken as it once was, but still depressed and depressing. Unemployment is high. Crime is all too common. Drugs are easy to get. The vast housing estates of the fifties and sixties, however imaginatively refurbished, can still seem cruelly inhuman. They have tried putting post-modernist roofs on the worst of the flat-topped tower blocks, partly for cosmetic purposes, partly to keep the damp out, but they still seem grim artificial places, lacking all spontaneity, lacking sociable shops and good boozy pubs and corners to gossip in.

Yet here is really the pith of Glasgow. 'I'm only a common working chap', says that song, and nobody will deny that the strength of Glasgow's character, the source of its humour and its comradeship, has always lain in its inimitable and gregarious prole-tariat – all those freckled women, many of them Irish, with their husbands, and their children, their aunts and their cousins (including dear Hamish in Philadelphia and the one they prefer not to talk about in Australia), multiplied ten thousand times and inten-sified with each generation for a couple of hundred years. Whether they are punks or municipal officers, wives of layabouts or mothers of scholarship boys, Glasgow's working people are always ready to talk, and always quick with a riposte, a confidence, or an enquiry. I asked a man in a street the way to the police courts, and in no time at all he was giving me a lecture on sea-power in World War II. I paused to tie up my shoe-lace, and two passing women asked how much I had paid for my shoes – far too much, they instantly pronounced. A youth who shared my café table merrily told me about his time in gaol – attempted murder was the charge – and at Paddy's Market several ancient drunks took me aside to assure me, more or less, that Glasgow belonged to them.

Glasgow has traditionally been a staunchly socialist city, a city of the working man, with fierce sectarian rivalries, militant unions, formidable football teams, gang wars, rumbustious saloon and paddle-steamer pleasures. Its poverty has been, in a sense, its strength, binding its people together in the fortitude of hardship, and there is an angry school of thought that says this old tradition is now being betrayed. What is happening to the city, says this line of argument, is a treachery to Glasgow's truest values, and an affront to its heritage. The city is being perverted into a different kind of place altogether, dominated by a different kind of society – yuppified, gentrified, emasculated. That common old working chap is being sold down the drain. The brawny workmen of the old days, who actually made things, are betrayed to the purveyors of advertising slogans, package tours, and imaginary money.

But then can you wonder, in a city with such a history, such a people, that a kind of inverted Luddism pines for the pistons, the turbines, the camaraderie, the mighty ships, the steam, grime, and virility of the past?

❀   ❀   ❀

But it is not so different, after all. Self Help! Free Trade! Full Steam Ahead! These were the slogans of the Victorians, who maintained that prosperity for the great industrialists meant prosperity for the proletariat too. It never did, of course, but the reasoning is the same now, and although Glasgow is still governed by a Labour administration, today as in the old days it breathes the ethos of capitalist opportunism.

The difficulty is that there is no longer any obvious reason why a great city should thrive in the west of Scotland, far from the power centres of the new Europe. On the other hand there is no obvious reason why it shouldn't, either, so the main instrument of revival has been propaganda. A tireless publicity machine has, during the past decade, blazoned Glasgow's merits to the world, and made this not just the Cultural City of Europe, but the Hype City too. Glasgow is a metropolis of brochures, a capital of self-justificatory statistics, and an object lesson in that eminently Victorian virtue, chutzpah.

For the Victorians of course were terrific bluffers and braggarts. There was never an instrument of propaganda like the British Empire in its prime, inculcating not only among its rivals and subjects, but no less among its own people, the conviction that British was inevitably Best. The Glaswegian Victorians presented their city as a very exhibition of brag, glorifying all the achievements that had made Glasgow a true power in the world. 'Let Glasgow Flourish' was the city's abbreviated official motto, but its fuller version was more apposite really – 'Lord, let Glasgow Flourish by the Spreading of the Word'.

Glasgow's publicists today have less to boast about, but they are approaching their task in just the same way. As I see it, they are trying to restore the fortunes of their city by sheer will-power. Glasgow's Miles Better because it says it's better. There's a Lot Glasgowing On because Glasgow has willed it so. The theory is that the brazen publicity of it all, if arid in itself, will prove futile in the end: the livelier, more attractive, more fun the city seems in the eyes of the world, the more prosperity will return to it.

Not that it is all chutzpah. The new Glasgow really does have a lot to offer, and much of it would perfectly satisfy the old Victorians. The vast St Enoch's Centre is the largest glass-covered shopping centre in Europe. The new Burrell Collection, housed in a lovely pavilion in a park, is my favourite museum in the world. The Glasgow manner, that beguiling mixture of power and delicacy, now fecundly permeates everything, in interiors and exteriors, in logos and packagings and the décor of hamburger bars. Many of the tenements have been superbly modernized. The proliferation of art – opera, theatre, symphonic music, ballet, rock, film, literature, painting – reminds me of the days of nineteenth-century patronage, when noble institutions of culture sprang out of the wealth of Europe.

Even the woman with the freckles admits that Glasgow is miles better. She is as fervent a civic patriot as anyone else, and she is as pleased as anyone by the new gusto of the place. It may be half-spurious, it may not have wiped the graffiti off her ghastly tower block or taken her husband from under her feet by finding him a job, but at least it means that when she crosses the river to spend her social security money she is going to a city centre full of life and light and colour. She has been notorious always for her extravagant love of glitter-clothes and ornament, and Glasgow today is just the place for rhinestones.

So the city has succeeded in recapturing the exuberance of its Victorian past. Can it also recapture the success? The publicists claim, of course, that it is already happening, and that new businesses and service industries are already flocking in, but for myself I prefer to reserve judgement for a decade or two. They talk a lot ...

In any case one can only admire the bounce of it all, the general readiness to accept change and start afresh. That is very Glasgow too. It was in this city, after all, that the Industrial Age was born, changing all way all great cities lived for ever: down by the Clyde on a spring Sunday in 1765 James Watt first realized the principle of the steam engine. There are a few signs in Glasgow still of the city that this revelation made redundant – a craggy archaic house or two, the stern cathedral, the tough old tower that once marked the city's centre. Most of it, though, Glasgow got rid of without many qualms, eagerly grasping the new order; and most of Glasgow now, I sense, shares in the excitement of today's Post-industrial Revolution.

For that is what we are seeing in Glasgow – a great, famous, and most lovable city in revolution. It is like an experiment with time. If it works, Glasgow may be as thriving a business centre of the new Europe as it was once a booming industrial centre of the British Empire. It it fails – well they havna changed much anyway. They certainly havna changed the popular character, which remains as vivid as ever, or the deeper personality of a city that has remained always, through bad luck and good, through all historical vagaries, so irrepressible and incorrigibly itself.

Would you mind saying that again now? (says the freckled lady caustically, lighting another cigarette). *'Irrepressibly and incorrigibly itself.' Well that's a grand wee thing to say about a place, whatever it means.*

COLM TÓIBÍN

❋   ❋   ❋

Winner in 1995 of the American Academy of Arts and Letters' E. M. Forster Award, Colm Tóibín is one of Ireland's finest and most accomplished young writers. He is the author of two highly acclaimed novels, The South *and* The Heather Blazing. *His non-fiction books include* Dubliners *(with photographs by Tony O'Shea),* Homage to Barcelona *and* Bad Blood.

    A lapsed Catholic, Tóibín views Glasgow in 'The Language of the Tribe' from an Irish Catholic perspective and arrives at some surprisingly provocative conclusions. Tóibín has a good eye for dialogue and knows when and how to cut to the chase. A marvellous piece of reporting.

❋   ❋   ❋

The Language of the Tribe

from THE SIGN OF THE CROSS:
TRAVELS IN CATHOLIC EUROPE

I went to Scotland in February 1993 expecting a shadowy version of Northern Ireland. I arrived armed with certain information: it was a deeply sectarian and divided society; there was discrimination against Catholics; the Scottish Labour Party was mainly Catholic while the Scottish National Party was mainly Protestant; the football matches between Rangers and Celtic were examples of pure, naked hatred between Protestants and Catholics.

    There were things I needed to know. Why, for example, had the violent conflict between Catholics and Protestants in Northern Ireland not flared up in Scotland? Could it do so in the future? How exactly were Catholics discriminated against? What exactly was the atmosphere like in these famous Rangers-Celtic encounters?

In 1986 I had gone to Belfast to report for a Dublin radio programme on the difference between a night's drinking on the Protestant Shankill and on the Catholic Falls. I had no trouble making contact with the Catholics, and I had no fears for my safety. It took some time, however, to get in touch with people from the Shankill who could take me drinking and guarantee my safety. It was the summer after the Anglo-Irish Agreement, and sectarian assassinations had resumed in Belfast; there was considerable ill-feeling against the Republic and its citizens among Protestants in the Shankill.

Friday night was to be the Protestant night; I met my minders in the Crown Bar in the neutral territory of the centre of Belfast. I did not expect my Catholic minders to be there as well; I was surprised to see them. But it is a popular bar. I could not introduce my two sets of minders to each other. My Catholic friends did not think I should go up to the Shankill; they would never do so. They viewed my Protestant minders suspiciously and suggested that I stay in the Crown Bar. I told them I'd see them the following night. I knew that they were worried.

My Protestant friends took me in a taxi to a place called the Malvern Bar. They asked if the name meant anything to me. I replied that it was where a Catholic barman had been murdered in the 1960s. They thought this was a huge black joke, taking me to this bar, the site of such a famous sectarian murder. There was very little malice in their laughter; it was more a sort of banter which is common in Belfast. They were amused at my being an outsider.

I survived the Malvern, several other bars, a great deal of drink and a lot of grim laughter. I was not introduced to many people. (My name is clearly Catholic.) After the bars shut we went to a drinking club which looked more like a sports hall full of tables and loud talk. After a few drinks, I noticed that my minders were missing. One of them, after a while, walked over casually, sat down opposite me and said, 'Our instructions are: "Get your Fenian friend out of here now." So turn around this second and walk out, don't look at anyone, and get on to the main road as quickly as you can.'

I did what he said.

The next night, I went to a Republican drinking club with my Catholic minders. There was a sign on the wall saying that any band who played too loudly would not be allowed to play again. One of my companions, making sure he had the attention of the entire company, asked me if I knew what this meant. I replied that I did not. 'It means they'll be shot,' he said. 'Any band who plays too loud will be shot.' They all laughed. Their Fenian friend had no trouble getting into other Catholic drinking clubs in the city, and felt much more relaxed that evening with his own tribe than he did with the Shankill Protestants.

A month after this, I set off walking along the Irish border, and I wrote a book, called *Bad Blood*, about my experiences. Every step of the way I was aware of the Protestant/Catholic divide. Sometimes it took the form of hatred or deep hurt, but often it was simply there: it lay under everything, and it explained most things. When I went to Glasgow in 1993 I carried with me all this baggage about conflict between Catholic and Protestants; my view of the place was profoundly affected by my experiences in Northern Ireland. It is possible that I asked all the wrong questions.

It was easy at first. I arrived in the city a few days before a Rangers and Celtic match, and I moved among journalists and academics asking about the background to the famous rivalry between the two football teams. Here are some of the things I heard:

'Protestants are richer. The poorer classes, the Catholics, who came here first from Ireland after the potato famine, vote Labour. But it is not discussed: people here are too afraid to bring religion into it.'

'There are a lot of Masons in the police, but also some Catholics. Rather than religion, it would be social standing, but that would favour Protestants.'

'Eighty-five per cent of the prison population is Catholic.'

[When I contacted The Scottish Office to check this, I received the following information:

Below are the percentage figures for 1993 of receptions within Scottish prisons broken down by religion.

Church of Scotland	57.7
Roman Catholic	33.7
Church of England	1.1
Other Religion	0.6
No Religion	6.8
	100*

*Components may not add to total due to rounding.

These figures should be treated with some degree of caution as the information is collected by asking the prisoner when he is first received into the establishment. Please also note that we do not know whether the prisoner is a practising or non-practising churchgoer.]

'Sixty-five per cent of the population is Protestant; thirty per cent is Catholic.'

[According to The Scottish Office, this is not a question asked on the census form.]

'Protestant kids still have better schools, but there was a bigger gap in the 1950s than there is today.'

'There is tremendous sympathy among Catholics here towards Catholics in Northern Ireland. There was bitterness during the hunger strikes. When Bobby Sands died open conflict would have been easy if a leader had emerged. It would have just taken one man.'

'People here are afraid to talk too much about the Protestant/Catholic/Irish subject. It's taboo. People here will say a Dundee bastard, but not a Protestant bastard or a Catholic bastard. People don't want a Northern Ireland situation.'

'On *The Scotsman* [newspaper] in Edinburgh I could have told you who was Protestant and who was Catholic the minute I went there.'

'In Glasgow the Rangers and Celtic matches channel away energies and bigotry. If they didn't have great intensity, things might spill over into violence.'

'Celtic [the Catholic team] dominated Scottish football in the mid-1960s. In 1967 it was the first British team to win the European Cup. It won the Scottish League nine years in a row. Now it has gone right into reverse. Poor old Celtic! It is run by two old families who are suspicious of change. The club is going backwards, while Rangers is buying up all the best players.'

'I always said that I wouldn't attend the game. The atmosphere is evil. For ninety minutes normal rational, good-living people ... [pauses] ... you can feel the hatred in the air. Don't go.'

'Rangers were incensed when Celtic won nine in a row. They went around Scotland and bought everyone's best players.'

'Evil? You could go tomorrow and it could be a quiet game.

The popular theory is that it is a cathartic exercise for both sides.'

'Until 1912 you could still find Catholic players playing for Rangers. Round about 1910/1912 Harland & Woolf [the Belfast shipbuilding company] came over to Clyde and brought a large section of Protestant foremen from Belfast. Rangers was going through a bad patch and somebody saw that you could ally a club to a side. Things stayed like that from 1912; Rangers never knowingly fielded a Catholic. Celtic maintained an open recruiting policy.'

'There are reasons why you didn't have Northern Ireland here. Municipal housing was never allocated on the basis of religion. There was no discrimination and Catholics had allied themselves with the Labour Party in Scotland. The discrimination against Catholics was in banking and insurance. Politically, Catholics had power at local level and at party level.'

'More than half the population of Glasgow has Irish connections.'

'Most of the police are Protestants. Most people in jail are Catholics.'

'The match is a tribal ritual. Celtic has had two very bad seasons, but the fans turn out. It has nothing to do with Scotland. It is an Irish situation imported into Scotland. The Catholic population in Glasgow is Irish.'

'The fans are turning against the management of Celtic.'

'There were no Catholic broadcasters on BBC radio in the 1950s. Things changed when commercial TV came in.'

'The two sides have a different way of looking at the world. The Church of Scotland has great virtues – thrift, an ability to work hard. Calvinist theology is a better training for accountants than Catholic theology. Catholicism is romantic and fanciful. I'm not sure that you want romantic and fanciful accountants.'

'The signing up of Maurice Johnson [a Catholic, to Rangers, in 1987] was a stroke of pure genius. At a stroke it removed an area in which Rangers were vulnerable. He was extremely courageous and a good player.'

'The Rangers/Celtic divide is the focus for a sectarianism in Glasgow which doesn't exist. Ninety per cent of the Irish came from Donegal, they were labourers and second class citizens. Celtic became their focus, a way of celebrating their identity. You couldn't work in a bank; you couldn't be a lawyer, or a journalist – in those years *The Glasgow Herald* wouldn't employ a Catholic – you could be a publican or a bookie – dear God the property they own in Glasgow now!'

'In 1890 Glasgow was the richest city in the world per capita.'

'The Celtic style of playing is full of panache; the Rangers style is dull and boring.'

'The virtues here are wit, intelligence, enthusiasm and irony.'

'Scottish people are more concerned about the nature of the union with England than with the Protestant/Catholic divide.'

'The Pope's visit was important. There was great pride that he had come. It was beautiful sunny weather. It was felt to be a Scottish occasion. It was a distinct watershed in the history of the nation. The Catholic community changed because of it.'

In one of my early encounters in Glasgow I asked an innocent question. There is a new movement in Scottish writing, full of social engagement and formal energy. I could list ten or twelve Scottish writers, most of them uncompromising figures, distant from southern English gentility. I casually asked a journalist in Glasgow who among the writers was Catholic and who was not. I presumed that maybe half the writers were Catholics. He stopped and thought for a while. He shook his head. He said it was funny that he had never been asked the question before, or thought about it. There must be one, he replied, but he couldn't think of a name.

Unless I wanted to include Muriel Spark. She was a convert, I said, that was different. Do you mean, I asked him, that all of the writers, with their street credibility and their working-class heroes, are Protestants? Yes, he said. And do you mean, I went on, that no one has ever raised this matter? Correct, he said. And do you mean that most people do not think it is a significant fact? Correct, once more.

Irish nationalism was constructed by writers as much as by politicians or revolutionaries; some of these – Yeats, for example, or Lady Gregory, or Synge – were Protestants but they had offered their power and support to a Catholic nation. In Northern Ireland writers like Brian Friel or Seamus Heaney, both Catholics, were essential aspects of the nationalist community's sense of itself, even when they did not write about politics. In the Republic, writers like Patrick Kavanagh and John McGahern had named our world for us. Maybe it was my problem: but I could not imagine coming from a nation, or a community or a place which did not have writers.

And surely, I thought, there were stories to be told: the arrival of unskilled and unlettered men and women from Donegal in Ireland into this strange world of factory-work and mines and labour politics; the slow melting into Glasgow of these outsiders; the adherence to Celtic football club; the pub life of the city; the idea for the generation which benefited from free education that they belonged in the city and were outsiders at the same time. I could not understand why there were no Catholic writers in Scotland.

Late one night during the Edinburgh Festival in 1993, I raised the matter with a distinguished Scottish poet. He couldn't think of a Catholic writer either, and, as the night wore on, I mentioned the discrimination against Catholics in banking and insurance in Scotland, the Masonic influence in the police. And the no writers. I happened to state that this sounded to me, an outsider, like Alabama in, say, 1954. Scotland was now the only place in the world where to be a Catholic was to be at a distinct disadvantage. Northern Ireland was just as bad, but there was a general recognition of the problem and numerous committees and bodies to deal with it. No one in Scotland even admitted it was happening.

My friend, the poet, told me I was completely wrong. It just wasn't like that. I came from Ireland where Catholics and Protestants openly opposed each other. I wasn't like that in Scotland, he repeated. I was asking the wrong questions, he said. I asked him how he would reply if there were no women writers in Scotland, or, in another society where blacks represented 30 per cent of the population (as Catholics do in Scotland), no black writers?

On the Thursday before the Celtic versus Rangers match I telephoned a journalist in London, whom I knew to be a Glasgow Catholic, and asked him if he knew of any Catholic writers in Scotland. I was in luck. He did not hestitate. He gave me a name – Thomas Healy – and a telephone number. I went to a bookshop and bought the two books by Healy that were on sale. They were both published by Polygon, the first, *It Might Have Been Jerusalem* in 1991, the second, *Rolling*, in 1992. I began to read *Rolling*.

It was a novel about manic drinking and pure loneliness and the desperate search for redemption. There was a knotted, tortured edge to the prose, and there was no effort to make things easy for the reader. I presumed – maybe I had no right to presume this – that the novel came directly from personal experience. There was a sense that nothing in it had been made up, and that it had taken real honesty and effort to write down and shape what had happened. It had that same sharpness as a great deal of the best modern Scottish writing.

I telephoned Thomas Healy and we arranged to meet that evening. He nominated a modern, well-lit pub in the suburbs. I ordered a pint and sat there waiting for him. He was a tall, thin man in his forties, nervous and polite. He explained that he was not drinking himself, but made clear that he did not mind if I had another pint. He had gone up to the priest, he said, and taken the pledge. I knew about the pledge. It was something that people in Ireland and done up to the 1950s, and maybe later. If you were a heavy drinker and you wanted to stop, you went to see a priest and made a pledge never to drink again, or not to drink for a certain period. But it was, at least in my experience in Ireland, a thing of the past. But not here.

Things were bad at home, he said. His mother had been in hospital but he did not think she was happy there and he had taken her home. He had to look after her: it was important that she was well looked after.

He'd had a difficult time, he told me, with London agents and publishers. At one point, he said, he was in such a rage that he threw the only copy of a typescript into the fire, as did the protagonist of *Rolling*. He had made very little money from his two books. We talked then about money and publishing.

I mentioned that there seemed to be a great camaraderie among Scottish writers. I mentioned James Kelman, Alisdair Gray and Jeff Torrington. He nodded, but said that he did not know any of them. I asked him if he was the only Catholic writer in Scotland, or if he could think of any others. He thought for a while and then laughed. No one, he said, had ever raised the subject before. He had never thought about it; but it was true. Maybe there were one or two others, but he couldn't think of them. He shook his head and looked into his drink. It was odd, he said, that no one had ever raised the matter before.

He was quiet-spoken and, of course, sober. His eyes grew bright when he talked about books and writing. Sometimes he mentioned a detail about his own life that tallied with the narrative in *Rolling*: stories about cycling or boxing or time spent in Germany. I hadn't finished the book yet, but that night after I left Thomas Healy I read it to the end, to the raw, brutal honesty of the last pages, so full of ambiguity and unresolved pain that it did not matter whether he was Protestant, Catholic or Hindu. Nevertheless, it remained true that he was the only Catholic writer in Scotland that anyone could think of.

On my first day in Glasgow I met Dr Andrew Noble from the English Department of Strathclyde University and asked him if there was anyone I should see over the next few days. He suggested an ex-student, one of the most brilliant he had come across, who now taught English. He gave me his name, Jim McCormack and his number. We arranged to meet at my hotel.

I was surprised to find a man in his fifties, more or less the same age as Andrew Noble. Once more, this was something which would not happen in Ireland. People go to university after school, in general, or not at all. There is no state grant system in the Republic of Ireland for adults. Jim McCormack's name is Irish, and there was a sort of soft, immediate friendliness about him which reminded me of home. I asked him about his Irish forebears.

His father came from Ireland in 1934 to work in the pits, joining his uncle and cousins; his mother was born in Scotland, but her parents were from Newry in Ireland. Her father had been in the British Army; he had served in Ireland. The owner of the mine where his father worked also owned the village, but he invested no money in the mines, which became death traps. Jim McCormack remembered talk about priests having to go down and minister to those who were dying or dead in the pits, phrases like 'they brought him up in a bag' being used in stories told about accidents, women in black shawls living in dread of rock falls or explosions.

His father was deeply Catholic, not pious, but devoted, he barely drank at all and was fiercely respectable. You were never far from Ireland. If you listened to Mass on the radio and the priest had an English accent, someone would say 'put that off, it's not our kind of Mass.' During the war, his father had a plot of land. He would hold up a piece of clay and say: 'That could be your grandfather's place in Lisnaskea [in Northern Ireland], clay is the same all over the world.'

St Patrick's Day was the big day for Catholics in Scotland; Lent was suspended for the celebration. They knew all the hymns as their hymns: 'Hail glorious St Patrick, dear saint of our isle.' When the King and Queen came to Scotland after the war, his mother and father would not go to see them.

A real battle was fought in Scotland, he said, between the Church and the political left. The priests were demented about it. It was a sin to read the *Daily Worker*. He met men on the plots who had fought in Spain against Franco, lay scholars, men who had educated themselves on Voltaire, Shaw, O'Casey, Hugh MacDiarmid and Dominic Behan. It was common in Catholic families for the father to be a communist and the mother a devout Catholic who never missed Mass.

There were Protestants down the mines too, but they could also get jobs in the steelworks. There was a joke about people with Catholic names: 'He needn't apply for a job in the Bank of Scotland.' In Glasgow, Catholics who did law tended to become criminal lawyers because they couldn't get jobs as business lawyers.

His father told him that he would break his back before he would allow him to become a miner. He won a place in a secondary school and began to read. The cult of Fatima was huge at the time and the discussion over how long you could kiss a girl before committing a sin was current. He read Jacques Maritain, Bloy and Peguy and Waugh. But he loved and respected the older men who had tried to run a revolution in Scotland, men who had spoken to Lenin. There was a spirit in Scotland which could have done well, he said.

That radical spirit in Glasgow survived, he believed, and emerged again in the arts, in the theatre with groups such as 7:84 and the Citizens' Theatre. The place was alive with singers, poets, writers, drama groups, and that to him was the flowering of the old socialist/communist world.

He himself came to work in the city as a clerk in a shipping office. He discovered jazz and began to write poetry. Over the years he published a good deal of poetry in magazines and periodicals. He continued to read. In 1959 he got married and started to work as a bus conductor. In 1964 he went to university to study English and got a good first. He became head of the English Department in a Catholic school. Nowadays, he said, things were becoming more strictly Catholic in such schools; for certain promotions you needed to get a certificate from the local parish priest, which you never needed before. They would not bother the older teachers but they were tightening up. The state schools in Glasgow were essentially Protestant schools; he taught in a Catholic school by choice. He understood the jokes, he said drily.

The Thatcher thing had had a dreadful effect on Glasgow, he said; the kids all wanted to be accountants and lawyers whereas before they wanted to be writers. In the late 1960s the students would read you their poems over the phone. Now you didn't have poets coming out of schools any more. At the same time there was huge unemployment and the place was jumping with drugs.

He mentioned reading James Baldwin and realising that the Irish working class in Scotland tended to despise themselves. For him, then, the idea of communism gave you a sort of dignity as an Irish Catholic in Glasgow. I asked him about Catholic writers, told him how no one seemed to have thought of this before I had come along with my Irish sectarian attitudes. He hadn't thought of it before either. He supposed Protestants had a sense of belonging that Catholics did not have. As a writer, he had been invited by Philip Hobsbawm, who had helped writers both in Northern Ireland and Scotland, to come to his workshop, but he had never gone along.

'I'm not sure,' he said, 'that it's easy to be creative in a culture in which you're not at home. The Protestants feel at home in their province, shout how they may about independence.'

To be a Catholic in Scotland, he said, is to be fundamentally different. The same Unionist mind-set exists in Scotland as in Northern Ireland; the feeling that this country belongs to them rather than to Catholics. Catholics are not really trusted. And it should be remembered, he added, that when people came over from Ireland they took any job, and they undercut local workers, and this caused bitterness.

The writers, he said, came from foremen's homes and felt a terrible anger at petit-bourgeois values. They belonged, he said. I could see he was thinking about this as he spoke; he was unsure if he could put his finger on what it was that caused him never to strike out as a writer, never to feel confident enough to make it his life. It still seemed to be astonishing that no one of his class or generation had become a writer, and only Thomas Healy represented the next generation.

I asked him why there had never been a civil rights movement in Scotland or a spill-over of the violence from Northern Ireland? Catholics in Scotland simply did not know enough about Northern Ireland, he said; their enemy was not Britain, but the Rangers' symbol. The conflict was about wages and conditions, and there was no discrimination in the allocation of state housing. The Catholics accepted that it was not their country. They gloried in that fact. And there was a romantic element in the Irish connection rather than anything real.

The Catholic zeal of his youth was something that still amazed him, the amount of energy the Church invested in keeping Scottish Catholics safe from communism. They had staged plays about Our Lady of Fatima, the apparitions at Knock, the history of St Dominic; bishops came to see the performances. We had been drinking and talking for some time now and I could sense that what he had told me had stirred things in him, old ideas and memories. I don't remember if I said that there were at least two or three novels in what he had told me, and more, perhaps, in what he had left out, and that his country, despite itself, needs Catholic novelists, especially lapsed ones.

The following night, the eve of the match, I went to Hereghty's pub, one of the famous bastions for Celtic supporters in the city, and joined in the festivities. They were drinking with speed and ferocity. The group of young men to my right ordered treble whiskys and gulped back in one go, shaking their heads and gasping when they had finished. One of them looked as if he was going to be sick. I was introduced as a journalist from Ireland, and people bought me pint after pint until I had three of them lined up in front of me. I was with my tribe.

There was only one woman in the bar; she was sitting near the door. When I remarked on this, I was informed that she might feel isolated, but what about the Rangers supporter? I didn't believe that there was a Rangers supporter in the bar, but they pointed to him and one of the company took me over and introduced me. Was he sure he was in the right bar? I asked him. He laughed. This wasn't Belfast, he said. He was a regular here, and he was always made welcome. Once, he said, when Celtic had lost really badly he had come into the bar as usual, and the fans had thanked him for coming that night, as though his presence cheered them up.

It would not be as easy, he said, for a Celtic fan to drink in a Rangers pub on the night before a match, although no harm would probably come to him. He didn't know why, he said, but the atmosphere would be more tense.

The atmosphere grew tense in Hereghty's during the last ten minutes of drinking time. People swallowed pints in two gulps and reached for another one or a double whisky. When they talked about Celtic, they moaned about the management. Rangers had a better ground, they had more money and could buy in top-class players. Celtic was now a poor relation and the fans hated the idea because Celtic had once been their main source of pride.

The next day, half an hour before the match, a group of Celtic fans stood close to where the Rangers supporters entered the stands and shouted, 'Oou, aah, up the 'RA! Ouu, aah, up the 'RA!' The 'RA was the IRA. They waved an Irish tricolour. Some police came by on horseback and others in a car. The fans continued to shout, 'Oou, aah, up the 'RA!' until one of them was snatched and put in the back of a police car. 'Scum,' one of his friends shouted at the police on horseback. And then there was more trouble as the police tried to detain this fan as well.

All this was noteworthy because it was isolated. The two groups of supporters were not involved in any scuffles or fights with each other. They took different routes to the ground. There was no real sense of aggression or violence. Everything was carefully monitored by the police. It could have been an ordinary match between two competing sides in any English city.

In my search for a ticket I had mentioned that I didn't care whether I sat with the Rangers fans or the Celtic supporters. Everyone thought that I was mad. As a Southern Irish Catholic I had no place on the Rangers side, I was assured. I was, by definition, a Celtic supporter.

When the match started I did not feel like a Celtic supporter. Celtic waved the Irish tricolour; Rangers waved Union Jacks. Celtic sang the Irish national anthem, 'The Soldiers' Song'; Rangers sang 'Rule Britannia'. There was a peculiar unreality about it, since this was Glasgow, and it was unlikely that either side had spent much time in England or in Ireland, places to which they now swore such fierce loyalty. All this emotion seemed wasted on these clapped-out images and clapped-out songs. This was parody without any humour, without the slightest hint of irony. It was intense, misplaced fanaticism. The Rangers crowd now sang 'The Sash', a Unionist anthem from Northern Ireland. A big group of Celtic supporters massed together in what is known as The Jungle chanted, 'Oou, aah, up the 'RA!'

At the beginning the Celtic fans excelled at exuding a feeling of grievance. If there was the least foul which escaped the referee's notice, they all booed and whistled and pointed their fingers. And then at dull moments in the game they chanted their sectarian slogans. But the rest of the time they forgot themselves, they simply wanted their team to win, and they went crazy if there was the remotest possibility of Celtic scoring a goal. They went wild when there was a near miss; they howled with despair and disappointment at bad play. And in the thirty-seventh minute when Celtic scored a goal, they danced with joy and screamed with delight. The Jungle, thick with green and white scarves and Irish flags, was transformed into a soup of smiling, yelping fans. I suddenly discovered that I was a Celtic fan too, that I was shouting and jumping as well. I wanted Celtic to win.

Then the Celtic fans had some great fun taunting the Rangers supporters. 'Can you hear Rangers sing? No, no, no', and 'What's It Like To Follow Shite?' and 'It's So Fucking Easy'. The goal had made all the difference. The match was now exciting. I watched every move, wanting our side to score again, wanting another goal to come and transform us all.

In the second half Rangers sang 'We are the Billy Boys', a reference to King William of Orange and the Battle of the Boyne, in which the Protestant side defeated the Catholics in 1690, and our side came back with 'Roddy McCorley', a rousing if melancholy ballad about an Irish Catholic hero on his way to be hanged. In the eighth minute we scored a goal. The Rangers fans did not move. There was not a sound from them, and thus it was easy to point over and shout 'Can you hear Rangers sing? No, no, no' once more.

It was not long before Rangers scored. It shouldn't have happened and our goalie, Packie Bonner from Donegal, hit the ground with his fist in rage and frustration. But we were still winning, even though Rangers were ahead in the League, still in line for the European Cup and were now singing about being a Euro-army.

After the game most of the supporters stayed behind for a while to roar and cheer and wave their flags and shout abuse. As they left there were police everywhere to make sure that each group stuck to its own patch and went back to its watering hole in an orderly fashion. I stood in the car park and watched the Rangers fans leaving the stadium. A few Celtic fans stood on the other side of the wire and jeered them, making very rude signs. And a few of the Rangers fans made rude signs in return, but soon they grew bored and went off.

They were only half in earnest, just as the sectarian confrontation at the match seemed only half serious, a game full of empty slogans which meant nothing to the participants, left-over parts of what had been imported from Ireland. These slogans meant nothing much in Scotland, where there was no IRA and where the followers of William of Orange did not control political parties.

Back in the hotel later, Irish supporters of Celtic, who had come all the way from Dublin, and others who had come from England, were too drunk to talk. They moved unsteadily around the bar, muttering things I could only half understand. One of them had fallen asleep on a bench and his friends were trying to wake him up so they could go out on the town and celebrate some more. They were having a great time: their team had won, they were with their tribe, and there was hope still.

HENRY JAMES
(1843-1916)

❊   ❊   ❊

One of the most versatile American men of letters, Henry James was a novelist, short story writer, playwright, critic and essayist. From 1866 to 1869 and from 1871 to 1872 he was a contributor to the Nation *and the* Atlantic Monthly. *Over the years he also wrote his fair share of travel writing.*

Born in New York, James spent his youth shuttling back and forth between Europe and America. At age nineteen he briefly attended Harvard Law School. When, two years later, he published his first short story, a literary career was launched. A prolific writer, among his best-known works include The Europeans *(1878),* Daisy Miller *(1879),* Washington Square *(1880),* The Portrait of a Lady *(1881),* The Bostonians *(1886),* The Turn of the Screw *(1898), and* The Wings of a Dove *(1902).*

In 1878 this most European of American writers spent some time in Scotland, and wrote down his observations.

❊   ❊   ❊

In Scotland

from COLLECTED TRAVEL WRITINGS:
GREAT BRITAIN AND AMERICA

Edinburgh, September 25, 1878.

NOW THAT the metropolis is so inanimate I hardly need apologize to you for writing from a livelier place than London. It is not making an exorbitant claim for Edinburgh to say that at present it deserves this description, for it has simply gained by the departed life of its sister capital. This afternoon, with a military band playing in the

long green garden below Princes Street, in the shadow of the
magnificent mass of the Castle Rock, with a host of well-dressed
people collected to listen to the music; with the brilliant terrace
above adorned with prosperous hotels and besprinkled with tourists
divided between the attractions of shop-fronts and the striking
picture formed by the Old Town and its high-perched citadel – this
admirable Edinburgh looked like a very merry place. Scotland is a
highly convenient play-ground for English idlers, and Edinburgh,
during the early autumn, comes in for a great deal of the bustle
produced by the ebb of the southern tide. For the last six weeks this
annual concert has been irrigating (not to say irritating) the Scottish
moors and mountains; and it is hardly too much to say that at this
period you must come to Scotland to see what England is about.

When I came hither myself, a little more than a fortnight ago,
there were still plenty of members of the large class which has
autumnal leisure to spare, hurrying northward. The railway-
carriages were occupied, and the platforms of the stations
ornamented, by ladies and gentlemen in shooting-jackets of every
pattern and hue. I say 'ladies' advisedly, for the fairer members of
these groups had every appearance of being sporting characters. I
do not know what may be the feminine costume of this particular
period in America, but here it consists of a billycock hat with a very
small brim, a standing collar of a striped or figured linen, like that
belonging to a 'fancy' shirt, a scarf in a sailor's knot, a coachman's
overcoat, made of some cross-barred material like the nether integu-
ments of a 'nigger-minstrel,' and a petticoat clinging as closely as a
pair of tight trousers and effectually completing the illusion. The
proper accessories of such a figure are a gentleman draped rather
than redundantly, and an aggregation of luggage consisting of a
good many baskets and bath tubs, of several *fasces* of fishing-rods,
and divers gun-cases that look like carpet-bags flattened and
elongated by steam-pressure; the whole set off by a couple of
delightful setters or retrievers fastened to the handle of a trunk, and,
amid the bustle of the railway-platform, turning themselves about
and sniffing at this and that in touching bewilderment. A friend of
mine, an American, was once asked to mention the two features of
English life which had made most impression on him. He hesitated
a moment, and then he said, 'The dogs and the children.' The

children apart, it is worth coming to Scotland simply to encounter the very flower of the canine race – the beautiful silken-eared animals that follow in the train of the happy Englishmen who have hired a moor at a thousand pounds for six weeks' grouse-shooting. England is certainly the paradise of dogs; nowhere are they better appreciated and understood. But Scotland is their seventh heaven. Of course all the Englishmen who cross the Tweed have not paid a thousand pounds down as the basis of their entertainment, though the number of gentlemen who have permitted themselves this fancy appears to be astonishing. Tourists of the more vulgar pattern, who have simply come to enjoy the beauties of nature and to read the quotations, in the guidebooks, from Sir Walter Scott, are extremely numerous, and Scotland, as regards some of the provisions that she makes for them, takes on the air of a humbler Switzerland. One must admit, however, that though the Scotch inns are much better than the English, they do not push their easy triumph very far; they bear the same relation to the Swiss hotels that the scenery of the Highlands does to that of the Alps. But if their merits are not unalloyed, it is not for want of resolution – as, for instance, in the matter of the table d'hôte. The table d'hôte in the British Islands is essentially an importation, an exotic, a drooping and insalubrious flame. But like all new converts the Scotch innkeepers are immoderate; they are of the opinion that of a good thing there can never be too much ...

'This admirable Edinburgh,' I said just now; and I must venture to emphasize the fresh approbation of a susceptible stranger. The night of my arrival here was a superb one; the full moon had possession of a cloudless sky. I saw, on my way from the station, that it was working wonders on some very remunerative material; so that after a very brief delay I came forth into the street, and presently wandered all over the place. There is no street in Europe more spectacular than Princes Street, where all the hotels stand in a row, looking off, across the long green gulf that divides the New Town from the Old, at the dark, rugged mass of the latter section. But on the evening of which I speak Princes Street was absolutely operatic. The radiant moon hung right above the Castle and the ancient houses that keep it company on its rocky pedestal, and painted them over with a thousand silvery, ghostly touches.

They looked fantastic and ethereal, like the battlements of a magician's palace. I had not gone many steps from my hotel before I encountered the big gothic monument to Scott, which rises on the edge of the terrace into which Princes Street practically resolves itself. Viewing it in the broad daylight of good taste, I am not sure that I greatly care for this architectural effort, which, as all the world knows, consists of a colossal canopy erected above a small seated image of the great romancer. It looks a little too much like a steeple without a church, or like a great deal too big for the head it covers. But the other night, in the flattering moonlight, it presented itself in all respects so favorably that I found myself distinctly what the French call *ému*, and said to myself that it was a grand thing to have deserved so well of one's native town that she should build a towering temple in one's honor. Sir Walter's great canopy is certainly an object which a member of the scribbling fraternity may contemplate with a sort of reflex complacency. I carried my reflex complacency – a rather awkward load – up the Calton Hill, whose queer jumble of monuments and colonnades looked really sublime in the luminous night, and then I descended into the valley and watched the low, black mass of Holyrood Palace sleeping in its lonely outlying corner, where Salisbury Crags and Arthur's Seat seemed rather to lose than to define themselves in the clarified dusk. The sight of all this really splendid picturesqueness suggested something that has occurred to me more than once since I have been in Scotland – the idea, namely, that if that fine quality of Scotch conceit which, if I mistake not, all the world recognizes, is, as I take it to be, the most robust thing of its kind in the world, the wonder after all is not great. I have said to myself during the last fortnight that if I were a Scotchman I too should be conceited, and that I should especially avail myself of this privilege if I were a native of Edinburgh. I should be proud of a great many things. I should be proud of belonging to a country whose capital is one of the most romantic and picturesque in Europe. I should be proud of Scott and Burns, of Wallace and Bruce, of Mary Stuart and John Knox, of the tremendously long list of Scotch battles and heroic deeds. I should brag about the purple of the heather and the colors of the moors, and I should borrow a confidence (which indeed I should be far from needing) from the bold, masculine beauty of my native mountains. Above all, I should take comfort in belonging to a country in which natural beauty and historical association are blended only less perfectly than they are blended in Italy and Greece; whose physiognomy is so intensely individual and homogenous, and, as the artists say, has so much style.

ALASTAIR SCOTT

*   *   *

Born in Edinburgh in 1954, Alastair Scott lives on Skye with his wife Sheena. A photographer, writer and broadcaster, he is the author of numerous books, including Scot Free, A Scot Goes South, A Scot Returns, *and* Tracks Across Alaska.

Like many of his countrymen, Scott suffers from a hopeless wanderlust. An incorrigible traveller, he has explored nearly seventy countries around the world. In Native Stranger, *he returns home, seeking to sample modern Scotland in all its rich diversity from Unst in the Shetlands to Hawick in the Borders. Along the way he offers portraits of prominent and not-so-famous Scots, from the late novelist George Mackay Brown and poet Sorley Maclean to historian James Hunter and politician Alex Salmond.*

Scott is a very personable writer – warm, witty, and entertaining. Gordon, the Caddy is one of the many 'characters' that Scott met on his travels.

*   *   *

Caddy, St Andrews

from NATIVE STRANGER:
A JOURNEY IN FAMILIAR AND
FOREIGN SCOTLAND

Since Alloa, which sounds like a Hawaiian greeting until you get there, neat brown signs had informed me that I was on the Mill Trail. In heritage centres heavy with wistful nostalgia I learned about the area's golden age of tartan and serge, and how, a century later in times of no work, even the sweat shops and slave labour of former tyrannical institutions assume that coating of Good-Old-

Days reverence.

The Mill Trail turned, unofficially, to the Beer Trail (Alloa Breweries) and then the Farm Trail. Fife was arable and had been ploughed into dark brown squares, or put under plastic to boost the growth of what I took to be infant strawberries. The land coasted by with self-satisfied ease, showing the practised hand of repaying handsome dividends, and saved its hills for real hills, abrupt conical laws: Largo Law, Kellie Law, Norman's Law, Blacklaw, Lucklaw. The map of Fife read like a new act of privitisation.

Ever since leaving the Highlands and Islands I had failed to recognise a collective identity that could truly be described as a separate culture. In landscape and dialects, Lanimers and Common Ridings, distinctive elements were present but they didn't hold together as a strong entity in the way that language, religion, common grazings, peat and isolation bonded the entity of 'Highland'. As a counterpoint to the north, 'Lowland' relied on strength of numbers for its corporate image rather than on the sum of its living differences. Through the Borders and up the east coast, thus far, longer histories of accessibility and industrialisation had moulded lifestyles into a general sameness.

Here and there that sameness inhabits pockets of character. Around Fife's coast are some of Scotland's most worshipped fishing villages – Dysart, Elie, Anstruther, Crail – which boast more artists on their piers than lobster pots. Like great auks, they are pretty, beautiful even, but past their best, museum pieces. Pittenweem was my favourite, less likely to appear on canvas than any of the others, but in September it died less than the others too. It had fishermen. They sat around in huddles, gossiping; old storm-beaten faces, whiskery, ruffled by wrinkles, their mouths down-turned and loose like a cod's. In their dotage and infirmity old fishermen have always the salty smells of their youth, the constancy of the sea and the credible lie of its long friendship. I envy them that solace.

St Andrews seemed to have everything for the retiree. It had the sea for old fishermen, and for landlubbers it had those rare qualities which are only found in small university towns; the frequent sounds of laughter in the streets and a high percentage of young people who, if not gainfully employed, are at least not disrup- tively unemployed. Its population lent the place a warm, carefree sense of abandon while its wide streets and aged buildings lent it dignity. Apart from its perishingly chill wind, St Andrews struck as being a grand place in which to grow old. And of course it had golf.

'Some folk think ye kin buy golf, know what ah mean? – best gear an' a' that, but ye cannae. Ye got tae ler-run it,' Gordon the Caddy said. 'D'ye play much yersel?'

'No, hardly at all. Just a wee bit for fun.'

For fun. That wasn't really true. I found golf intensely frustrating. It was the devastation of losing your rattle over the side of the pram, the joy of having it returned to you, only to lose the bloody thing again. Golf balls were one pound's worth of devious bloodymindedness.

I withheld a piece of information from Gordon the Caddy. Amongst my illustrious sporting ancestors (Mary, Queen of Scots, was not one of them) I had an aunt who hit a mean golf ball. She represented Great Britain in the Curtis Cup on three occasions, was a regular in internationals and then turned professional when Slazenger put her name, Jean Donald, on their clubs. But my standard of play forced me to keep Jean a secret on a golf course. People always had unreasonable expectations that talent was unfailingly hereditary. To be a bad golfer was acceptable, but to be a bad golfer when there were birdies and eagles in the genes, was either freakish or negligent.

And besides, I suffered a pathological dislike of losing golf balls. If a round of the game didn't allow for the odd half-hour here and there to root around in the rough for my errant ball, I wasn't interested. A choice of four clubs tended to suffice for my needs, but a tour of the Golf Museum in St Andrews showed me that one more might well have lifted my game. It was described as 'ane scraper'.

What distinguished Scottish golf from the *kolf* of Holland, the museum also enlightened me, was that Scottish golf always aimed for holes. The more adventurous Dutch aimed for trees or people's front doors. The earliest reference to golf in Scotland appears in a statute in 1457, and by 1618 it was sufficiently popular for James VI to award a trade monopoly (which went unrecognised) in golf balls. Leith's five-hole course was the oldest in Scotland but somehow St Andrews stole the show and by 1650, its twenty-two holes had become recognised as the game's 'home'. Today the town has five and a half courses. In May the Old Course was already fully booked until October.

It was a Sunday, the only day the Old Course is given a rest. For six days a week, a round cost £50 per player, foursomes only, teeing off every twelve minutes from 7 am to 6 pm ... this was serious money. Quite aside from the other four-and-a-bit courses, the Old Course alone netted £1,000 an hour.

Caddies cost £20 on top of the fee for the round. I hired one ('Pay afterwards') and was allocated Gordon. He was one of my more extravagant travel expenses.

'Wha's yer clubs then?'

'I haven't got any.'

'Ye whit ... nae clubs ... ?'

I explained that all I wanted to do was to walk around the Old Course with a guide and learn something about what went on. Gordon looked insulted. I fished out two ten-pound notes.

Gordon the Caddy brightened. 'Nae bother, pal.'

We set off. He began with a summary of his life's injuries and ailments. Apparently his first eighteen years had been trouble-free but his 'guarantee must hiv ren oot'. He lost half a thumb on a Normandy beach. He held up the stump. 'Shortly after, broke ma leg, bad, aye, fib *an'* tib it wis. Then ... '

'Excuse me, but is that the Royal and Ancient Clubhouse?'

'Aye, that's it.' He became my guide again. 'Yon flagpole there's the mast frae the *Cutty Sark*. Now, the club house dates back to . . .' and he told me all about it.

'Can we go inside?'

'Not a hope in hell. Ah've been here thirteen year an ah've niver yet been inside. Last year I caddied fer Clint Eastwood – ' he guddled in a pocket and pulled out a photograph. Proof. Credentials. Clint Eastwood and a grinning Gordon. '– an Clint says, "Ah fancy goin in there." "No way," ah says, but he goes in and a moment later he gets thrown oot.'

'How do you become a member?'

'It helps if you hiv a title, and loads a money ... an the last thing ye do is show any interest in becoming a member. Oh aye, that's yer chances jist deid. There's about 1,600 o' them. There's one. There's the Major.'

He pointed to a hirpling set of plus-fours and tweed jacket approaching the main door. The Major opened it with his own key. He disappeared through another door beyond a bowl of water laid out for members' dogs. Gordon led me round to a side window where we pressed our noses against the pane. We could almost smell the antiquity of oak panelling, plush, leather and vellum. Past club captains looked strangely out of place, hijacked from a fox pack. The Major joined another tweed-wrapped ancient reading a newspaper and sank into an adjacent chasm of padded chair. Around the room were rows of lockers. 'Some o' they lockers hivnae been opened in a hunner an' fifty years,' Gordon whispered.

We set off up the first fairway.

' ... ah got appendicitis. Well, they took that oot and then whit happened? ... TB ... tub burrk yule ohsis. Ah wis nine months ina sanatorium wi that ... '

'What club would you advise me to use here?'

Gordon stopped to consider this unnecessary question. He turned his stout and apparently indestructible frame this way and that until he spotted a landmark. The breeze played with his white hair which stuck out in punkish quiffs. 'Ah hivnae seen ye hit anything yet so ah couldnae say whit club, but frae that stank there, it's a hunner an twenty three yards tae the hole. An see they flags, it's the right one. Ye've got tae remember here that the fairways share greens. Double greens they are. Now, ye can always tell where y'are by adding up the holes. Greens add up tae eighteen, fairways tae nineteen. So if yer on the fourteenth green that's shared wi the fourth. If yer on the fourteenth fairway, the one alongside is the fifth.'

I nodded politely at this piece of mind-boggling logic and realised that if you didn't have a caddy on the Old Course you certainly needed to pack a calculator along with your irons and scrapers.

By the time we reached the tenth, Gordon had exhausted his catalogue of calamities. My grasp on the timescale of his heart attack and quadruple heart bypass (he pulled up his jersey and shirt to reveal the scar, 'That's ma zipper') was shaky but his recent hernia and gallstones brought me bang up to date: Gordon, caddy, retired baker, van driver, steel worker, telephonist, film extra (crowd scene, *Chariots of Fire*) and civil servant, aged 69.

It wasn't my type of course at all. Rangers patrolled constantly to ensure the flow of players remained unhindered. The greens were cut twice a day and were ridiculously fast. I preferred challenging greens with rogue tufts of grass and dips and sheep droppings. On these billiard tables my putts would have ended up in the fields. And to cap it all, five minutes was the maximum allowance for a lost ball.

We reached the famous seventeenth where, Gordon said, more great reputations had been ruined than on any other hole in the world. Tommy Nakajima's was one. In the 1978 Open he was lying in joint second place when he teed off on the seventeenth. He got within putting distance of the hole in two. His putt was long and went into a bunker. He took another seven shots to get out and end the hole, but by then he was twentieth and had lost £100,000 in prize money. 'We call this bunker the Sands of Nakajima now ... unofficial like.'

We passed the Old Course Hotel which had netting on its roof to protect its slates, a pock-marked wall, two cracked windows and a figure (paying £170 per night without breakfast) daringly having coffee in a glass conservatory. Golf at St Andrews was funded essentially by Americans (85 per cent) and Japanese (5 per cent).

'Oh aye! Gone! It's aye goin'. Somebody's stolen the eighteenth flag again.' A bare pole marked the final green. The disappointing flag was simply high jinks or souvenir hunters but St Andrews was developing a fearsome reputation for the theft of golf clubs. Warning notices were liberally posted. I felt disappointed. Crime, and my caddy's susceptibility to rupture, fracture, inflammation and arrest had badly tainted my round. Until Gordon remarked:

'Ye know, ah must hiv walked doon the eighteenth hunners of times, but when ah walk doon wi' a playin' guest, ah still feel a thrull. Fer maist folk who come here this is a once-in-a-lifetime experience. A great privilege. Some get really emotional, an it aye affects me tae.'

This was a startling revelation from a man who had just admitted to keeping a log of air crashes. His records went back to the 1920s. He listed the date, aircraft, cause of accident, number of dead and, where possible, their names. He thought he might get it published some day.

'An see that beach there?' St Andrew's sands were half a mile wide and ran to infinity. 'That's where ah wis shot in *Chariots o' Fire.*'

I nodded appreciatively and thanked him for the tour. He looked disappointed. I thought, *he's surely not expecting a tip, is he?*

'Are ye nae wantin' a photie o' me ... ?'

MICHAEL W. RUSSELL

❊   ❊   ❊

Michael W. Russell is a television producer and director as well as a Member of the Scottish Parliamant. He is also the former chief executive of the Scottish National Party. Educated in Ayrshire and Edinburgh, he has lived in various parts of Scotland. Author of A Poem of Remote Lives: The Enigma of Werner Kissling, 1895-1988, *a biography of German photographer and filmmaker Werner Kissling, he now makes his home in Argyll.*

During the early months of 1998 Russell retraced portions of Edwin Muir's famous journey from the Lowlands to the Highlands in Depression-era Scotland to discover how much the country and the people have changed over the decades. Russell's long trek took him to Edinburgh, the Borders, Dumfries and Galloway, Ayrshire, Lanarkshire, Glasgow, Stirling, Perth, Dundee, Aberdeen, Inverness, and the Western Isles, before finally returning home to Argyll.

Unlike Muir, the Scotland that Russell finds is a quite different land, one that still has problems certainly and yet for the first time in recent memory a place that is also full of possibilities. The people who populate this 'new' Scotland dare to dream, dare once again to hope.

❊   ❊   ❊

Stirling and Perth

from IN WAITING:
TRAVELS IN THE SHADOW OF EDWIN MUIR

For most of the people outside the central belt and the other major Scottish cities such as Aberdeen and Dundee, a car is not a luxury, but a necessity. In fact, if you don't live within a city or a large town, public transport is either not available, or not reliable and convenient. Muir's Scotland was different. Trains went from every hole in the hedge and buses joined every village to their neighbouring town. The car partly killed that type of infrastructure, but it was also killed by a lack of foresight from local government allied to a lack of involvement in basic public transport services for which we are still paying the price.

A sensible public transport system would create holding areas for cars outside each major city, with first-class, frequent public transport from these places into every part of each city. And it would make such public transport either free or extremely cheap and accessible every hour of the day and night. The only solution which we are offered at the moment seems to be to make the use of the motor car (irrespective of where the driver lives) an increasing financial burden while failing to offer any improvement for the public element. Lots of sticks, but precious few carrots.

In any case for all of rural Scotland there is likely to be no transport alternative to the car. If I, living in Argyll, want to travel by bus or train to Edinburgh, I might as well don my Marco Polo gear, wave my wife and son good-bye, and set out on the great journey. I would first of all have to walk down a 500-yard track (my choice, I admit, and I'm prepared to fully accept my responsibility for stage one), then I'd take a bus (one every two hours) to Dunoon, which would take almost an hour. The boat trip across would be another half-hour, and then a train to Glasgow would take 40 minutes. I would change stations (15 minutes) and take an hour-long train journey to Edinburgh, with a further 15-minute walk to my office. Total time: almost four hours – or more if I am staggering under the weight of my laptop and my overnight bag. But more pertinently, the cost is also prohibitive – about £25 all in compared to the ferry fare of about £5.00 if you buy the tickets in bulk, and the £10 worth of diesel I would need (all right, all right, I know that I alo have to cost in car depreciation, the running costs, etc, etc ... but it is not only cheaper, it *seems* cheaper).

Some of my neighbours would have an even more difficult time. Sandy MacQueen, who lives across the loch would be best to take his boat over to the Island of Bute (an hour and a half to Rothesay) and catch a ferry to the mainland from there. If not he would have to walk a three-mile track and get one of the increasingly rare buses – the best would be the subsidised Post Bus – to start his trip to Dunoon.

Somehow we're going to have to live with the car in rural Scotland (and perhaps be a bit more fair on petrol and ferry prices), whilst making it easy in the towns and cities to use what is laid on for us. Best to lay it on first, and make it attractive, than try and force a change. Motorway tolls and punitive car tax increases are not the first steps, even with some vague commitment to hypothecation of the proceeds. Governments have a tendency to forget such promises once the money starts rolling in.

There is virtually no public transport to the field of Bannockburn, which I pass on my way to Stirling. But the sight of it always gives me sore feet, as I have marched to it from the centre of Stirling year in and year out on the third Saturday in June. The SNP's Bannockburn Rally has been a fixed point in the nationalist calendar for many years. In the 60s and 70s there were usually two or three thousand marchers, complete with pipe bands and regalia.

Today the numbers are down to two or three hundred at each event – not a sign of lessening of interest in nationalism, but more a sign that such interest need not be expressed by an annual airing of the Saltire. Younger party members are keener to campaign than to march (it used to be the other way round at university) and the time is right for a different type of event to mark the anniversary of the battle – a festival or a fair perhaps?

Muir 'remembered' about Bannockburn when leaving Stirling by way of the Wallace Monument on the other side of the town. At that time there was a dispute about the real site of the battle, and who should preserve the field. The National Trust won, and it is now a typical NT property – superficially attractive, but with a host of regulations about its use and a seemingly paranoic fear pervades the place preventing anyone from actually being passionate about it.

Unlike Culloden, Bannockburn has little atmosphere left. There is nothing brooding about the site – it is wide and open, and crossed by the M90 – and only at the modern-day statue of Bruce does one get any impression of the magnitude of what was won here: nothing less than Scotland's freedom and an independent state that lasted for almost four hundred years thereafter.

I park the Land-Rover and walk out onto the field. At the borestone I meet an elderly American couple, trying to make sense of the place. Al and Jean are from New York, and she claims Scottish ancestry. We talk about Scotland and its past and I describe the events leading up to 1314. They, however, are more interested in how I know about this – we get on to politics and they tell me they have come to Scotland this year, for their first visit, because they had read about the referendum and about how we are going to be independent.

I try to explain to them that we aren't quite independent yet but the concept is difficult for them. 'You mean', says Al, 'that you are still going to be giving your oil away? And that you can't raise taxes? Are you nuts, or something?'

They have the idea, and I agree that we may be nuts, but we are working on a cure. Unusually it is Jean that is the redneck of the pair – in looking at the panorama around us I mention Dunblane and the gun ban, and she reacts almost violently. 'Guns ain't the problem,' she spits, 'it's the people with the guns.' She warms to the subject, much to Al's embarrassment. 'If those teachers had had guns, they would have blown that guy away,' she asserts, beginning to poke me in the chest. 'If those policemen had had guns, they would have sorted the guy out before he did what he did ... [poke, poke] ... if the parents of the kids he had tried it on with before ... [she is well informed – there must be a National Rifle Association briefing sheet on this in America] ... had had guns, they would have dealt with him.'

For once in my life I am beginning to wish I had a gun. But I can't stop her, or change her mind. Of all the gulfs that separate us from our cousins across the pond, gun laws are the most intractable. I once had to appear on NBC talking about the SNP proposals for a ban on all handguns, and it was as if I had told the French that total abstinence (and a prohibition on cheese and Gauloise) was the only way forward. Incredulity was the kindest part of it.

The fusillade subsides, and I give them a lift into Stirling, as they have taken a taxi out. They are going on to Inverness, and then back to Glasgow. They too are using the trains, but they seem enchanted by them. Enchanted, that is, by everything but the lack of seats and the speed. 'Why don't you guys go a bit faster, and have enough places for everyone?' asks Al. I say I don't know as I have probably done enough to confuse them for one day. A dissertation on the troubles brought on by privatisation would have been an explanation too far.

Muir found Stirling 'bright, solid and stylish' but as usual, when standing looking at the 'impressive prospect' that can be seen from the castle he could not help remarking on the old tenements in the town which had, like those 'in almost all Scottish historical cities...largely degenerated into slums'. Now the slums have become fashionable homes and restaurants – even fashionable hotels – and the one-way traffic system, with its chicanes and bumps for 'calming' traffic makes the whole area quieter though I suspect much less authentic.

I can never visit Stirling Castle without recalling the final moments of *Tunes of Glory*, the film of the Kennaway novel, and the snow drifting into the ramparts as the pipes die away. Even at one of the final Runrig concerts held here on a summer evening in 1997 I felt cold, but also moved. Or rather I did once I had persuaded a large German fan to take down his huge banner (*The Black Forest says Hullo to Runrig – You are the Greatest*) which was blocking the view of the stage for about 20 percent of the audience.

Stirling lies at the heart of Scotland – but just as the heart, whilst vital, is not the most attractive of organs, Stirling itself always seems one of the less desirable of Scottish towns. Rather than concentrating on the town's assets, one is always mindful of what one can see from it and where it lies – to the east the flat land of the Forth, and the refinery stacks of Grangemouth, as well as a smudge on the landscape of the Hillfoots villages; to the west beyond the carse the start of the conglomeration that has Glasgow in its midst; to the south a nondescript landscape edging into industrialisation. Only to the north do the hills of the Highlands offer the prospect of real, fresh, rural Scotland.

I am going north, and set out again past Stirling Bridge and the university, which is really in Bridge of Allan, the neighbouring town. Soon I am skirting Dunblane, driving on the bypass that sweeps in a lazy half-circle round that unhappy little town. For years Dunblane was simply a name on the road – the old A9 passed through it, and in the summer it was not uncommon to be stuck for 20 minutes in the traffic queue that built up on either side of the roundabout above the old town centre. Then the new road was built, and only rarely did I find myself driving down to the Cathedral and the attractive main street, usually because I needed a paper, or a bottle of wine to take home. Dunblane was, and is, a commuter town with a good rail service, to Glasgow in particular. A number of acquaintances at the BBC lived there, travelling in each day. It was one of many such towns, no more remarkable than any other.

Now its name is unforgettable. I suspect for many Scots the day of the tragedy will become like the day of Kennedy's assassination for Americans. One will remember where one was when the news came through, and how one hovered around the television trying to make sense of the unfolding story. I was showing the SNP's bank manager round the office for the first time, when I glanced at the Teletext that is always on in the press office. 'Ten Children Dead'. I went over and checked the story – by the time I had refreshed the screen it was up to 'Eleven Children'. And it went on rising.

For the rest of the day there was a constant stream of phone calls – enquiries about what we were saying, which seemed irrelevant, and friends who just wanted to talk. Margaret Ewing went to Dunblane (she used to live there) and was shattered by the experience – seeing at first hand not only the grief but also meeting those who were trying to cope with it, and seeing the enormity of what they had witnessed. Hardened journalists rang to debate in private the ethics of dealing with the story, and how they didn't want to intrude but had to report it. My wife and I talked about how it could happen anywhere, even in her little school of 20 pupils, which – like all schools – had no security and an open door.

The day after I had the worst migraine of my life: physically sick perhaps with the difficulty of comprehending the sheer evil of the event. 'Evil' is a word I eschew, preferring to account for wrong by the damage that individuals suffer in their lives, and hoping for reformation rather than bringing into play arbitrary judgement. But evil is the only word for it. A blackness within an individual so great – perhaps a pain so great – that it turned into a rain of death upon those who had no blame, and who turned their faces to their intruder at first in enquiry and welcome and only then in innocent, wounded, uncomprehending terror.

I drive on past the town; now frozen in the echo of the pistol shots that have changed this place forever. It deserves to be left in peace, to bind itself up and to heal itself, supported by our anguished love, but not burdened with our continued, prurient, enquiries.

Between Stirling and Perth the countryside starts to rise up, erecting little hills as homages to the Highlands to come. Off to the right is Sheriffmuir – another Scottish battle scene, though the drive to it does not repay any curiosity: there is nothing there but a few houses, and the pub that used to house Hercules the Bear, whose escape in the Western Isles some years ago caused me not a little worry, as he swam off to freedom from an island that I could see clearly from my bedroom in Benbecula.

I pass Blackford, home to both the sleeping Tullibardine Distillery and the constantly operational Highland Spring water plant, the former now under the ownership of Jim Beam Brands and the latter owned by Arabs and aggressively marketed throughout the world. Muir would have been amazed that the same Scottish water upon which the whisky industry depends has become an important asset in its own right, and will be more important still in the next century, when water becomes a scarce resource. In fact Muir would probably be amazed by many of the ways in which Scots now earn their living – bottling water, assembling with infinite care small slivers of silicon that could contain all his books hundreds of times over; erecting windmills to generate power; selling hamburgers to car drivers at small glass side windows – even running the day to day affairs of political parties.

All these can certainly be fitted into the endless interplay of 'exploiters and exploited' that Muir observed with disgust (and which, in its 1934 form he believed had led to the decline of Scotland and its identity), but somehow that definition does not quite fit our country today. The market economy can still be savage and unrestrained – the legions of the unemployed that still exist will testify to that – but equally it can be inventive, creative and positive: it can re-invent itself in a million ways, and bring a million new benefits to society.

'The market has no morality' was a Michael Heseltine boast,

intended to signify the need for governments to keep out of freebooting capitalism. But the market is operated by human beings, who do have moral choices. They do not have to bow to every market trend or force, or make profit the only criteria by which they will be judged. They can make moral choices about the level of profit, about the need to invest in human beings as well as plant and machinery, and then can seek to ameliorate any negative effects of the market on employees and communities.

They can, in short, bring morality into the market place as a factor – and bring in human decency and human responsibility too, the responsibility of one person to another; the duty of care. The ludicrous construct of [British prime minister Tony] Blair's 'third way' would make a little (though not much) sense if this is what it meant – if it meant listening to people and their concerns, and accepting the legitimate fears and concerns of trade unions and their members. But this is not a 'third way' at all – it is a modern version of European Social Democracy, in which individuals have rights and exercise those in tandem with their duties as members of society: and in which society too can exercise care and responsibility.

A true socialism – Muir's socialism – is possibly the ideal way to regulate human life. But it is also impossible to achieve, at least at this moment in time. The best we can do is to accept and embrace the benefits of capitalism and find ways of regulating and reforming its worst aspects. Ways that can provide a shield for the failures of the market, but still enjoy its successes, and use them to invest in our future.

I am thinking about social theory when I find myself speeding past the Gleneagles Hotel, a temple of capitalist success which has wisely invested in a splendid new golf course that edges the road. I am glad that such excesses exist – which probably condemns me to the purists as the worst sort of romantic hedonist. But inventing a new golf course is a noble activity: a blending of ingenuity and culture to create something that will test and reward in unequal measure. From there I skirt the long village of Auchterarder and start the hill climb to Perth. Off to my left is the wonderfully named Findo Gask, the sign to which used to beckon me from the old road every time I came this way. Eventually I went, and drove for miles without finding anything. Does it exist? Is it my Nirvana, I wonder, which I am fated forever to seek? Or is it just yet another superb Scottish placename, the romance of which is far greater than its actuality.

I am very fond of Perth and was even before I spent five weeks here in the run up to the constituency by-election in 1995. It is a pity that Muir devotes only one line to it – 'I stopped in Perth to buy a basket of strawberries and pushed on to a remote part of Angus where I wished to see a married couple, old friends of mine, who were running a farm there' – as to me it is one of the most Scottish of towns, and yet also one of the most modern. Like all Scottish towns it has simply grown – so driving in is a patchwork experience, moving past modern estates to Edwardian villas and on to car showrooms, tyre depots and then into the town centre itself.

Perth sits comfortably on the River Tay, and the best of the centre also abuts onto the river itself, with traffic guided over two bridges, which are (unusually) the boundaries of the city. Perth is a city, and calls itself such – with some justification as it is the fastest-growing conurbation in Scotland, and will, in size, overtake Dundee early in the next century. It has already overtaken Dundee in attraction.

There is little in the centre that is really old – or at least looks that way, apart from St John's Kirk, which is the cradle of the Scottish Reformation. The impressive City Chambers look late-18th century, tarted up a bit in the next century, but they sit cheek by jowl with shops and offices, and with a wealth of pubs and restaurants that make the city a good place to spend an evening. Such an integration of civic activity and service is just the right note to strike.

Perth is also rich in hotels, my favourite being the Salutation – though its claim to be the oldest hotel in Scotland is probably bogus. None the less, and despite the ravages of the all-purpose modern hotel interior designer, it has a comfortable and antique feel, with a splendid window in the first floor dining room that gives a view of a single city street that speaks volumes about the place. And it certainly did play host to Charles Edward Stewart during his triumphal sweep down Scotland in 1745 – a sweep that was exceeded in speed only by his retreat the following year!

Modernism has made the main shopping thoroughfare as

bland as anywhere else in Scotland – there is even an indoor mall – yet the streets constantly surprise, producing small faded cafés, and strange shops dedicated to odd fashions or pursuits in every nook and cranny. Even the straight and ordered Victorian part of the centre – slightly grim with its severe tenements – has a variety that is hard to find elsewhere.

Perth is also prosperous – an Aga dealership gives testimony to the wealth of the surrounding countryside, as does a Laura Ashley outlet. But its community spirit means that the Perth Theatre lies almost next to that imported centre of home counties good taste, and round the corner one can hire a kilt from an old-fashioned tailor that looks (and is) planted in the last century. Perth City Halls lie at the heart of the city and although they are too small now for the type of political conference that is the norm, there has been an attempt to make them more attractive by sprinkling pavement cafés around. Inside the wood-panelled splendour has been restored and the gold leaf re-gilded: only the massive organ sits mute, waiting for someone knowledgeable enough to make its sound fill the building.

Pehaps I like Perth because I associate it with success: it was here that Alex Salmond became SNP leader in 1990, and at the same time, as his campaign manager, I avoided being defeated for the party office I held. I spent the only real sleepless night of my life before that vote, working out in my head again and again whether we had really done things the right way, and if so was there any possibility of defeat. My head said no, but my usual caution said, 'Of course ... anything can happen.' And in 1995 I ran the campaign that won the by-election – again saying to myself for days before that we must win because no one else could, yet constantly questioning whether the right things were taking place, and whether the right campaign was being run. But I also associate Perth with long evenings and pleasant dinners, good company and dry weather and a sense of wellbeing enhanced by the surroundings and the people.

There is no doubt that this eastern part of Scotland (we are only 20 miles or so from the sea, and the river Tay that runs through here will soon be broad enough to require a massive road bridge at Dundee) is drier and the ambient weather better than the west where I live and where I was brought up. That fact seems to be reflected in the bustle and style of the city – less hiding from the rain and the wind, and more openness and casual conversation. Perhaps I am imagining it, but the strong voices of the farmers and their wives greeting each other in the open streets is a sound I don't associate with Oban or Fort William: there the conversation is more intimate, the gatherings more huddled.

Tonight I am having dinner with work colleagues, preparing for a special party conference. Out of the richness of choice we select a Thai restaurant (I have been there before with the BBC) and we have an excellent meal, though the table keeps expanding as more people turn up, and the nervous waiter is beginning to have a breakdown as his work expands also. The talk revolves in small groups, occasionally widening to embrace the whole table, the falling apart again into twos and threes. Inevitably it is about what we share – the minutiae of the moment, of polls and problems, and possibilities ahead. Allison Hunter – with whom I have run six by-elections and innumerable other campaigns – mentions an incident from the last campaign here: within moments we are reminiscing about events and personalities and drawing in an audience of younger party members, now staff, who are sharing the culture and, in the semiotic parlance, 'owning' the incidents.

This is not a unique event: any group of people who work together know the syndrome, and know that it is a fragile covering of common experiences that lies over the vast deep of personal lives, ambitions, histories and futures. We are, in William MacIlvanney's phrase, 'swapping names like conversation', but it is the conversation that unites us, and it is therefore comforting, reassuring and re-enforcing. Eventually we pay, and walk out into an early summer street that is still bright with the reflected light of northern hemisphere evenings. There are shafts of sunlight lying along the road, spilling into the town from the surrounding hills. A couple of us walk to the river, which is rolling and surging towards the sea, but controlled and quiet in this season, glassy on its top in the calm air.

Much later I am ensconced in MP Roseanna Cunningham's office, reacting to a new poll and coming to terms with the fact that to the younger members of our staff the confidence and self-assertion of Scottish voters is not a surprise, but an inevitability.

Even if it declines from here on in, even if Scotland draws back for a moment from embracing its future and stepping onto the world stage as itself, it will still only be a temporary setback for them.

They are confident – with the confidence of youth – that the future does belong to them, and that such a future will be better, more open and more generous than the age in which they grew up. For me, that hope is summed up in a place like Perth. An ancient city, it has taken part in many of the major events of our history, yet has gone on growing and developing and being renewed. It took the Union in its stride, and it can take a new future just as well. To the outside it may seem quiet and conservative. But it has a will and a spirit of its own. It wants to be part of the world, and it will make it on its own terms.

The river keeps on running to the sea. The town keeps on growing. And the people keep on living here, welcoming new blood and enlisting them in the quiet, determined, civilised, cause of the city.

DOROTHY WORDSWORTH
(1771-1855)

✻   ✻   ✻

Although her famous brother William casts a giant shadow on her own work and accomplishments, Dorothy Wordsworth exerted considerable influence over the Romantic writers. It wasn't until many years after her death that her letters, poetry, and, above all, her journals come to the public's attention.

In the summer and autumn of 1803, Dorothy Wordsworth, accompanied by William, and, briefly, poet Samuel Taylor Coleridge went on a tour of Scotland, a remarkable journey of nearly 700 miles. Sir Walter Scott suggested that the party make their way to Loch Lomond, the Trossachs, and, finally, the Western Isles. They travelled in an Irish jaunting car, that is, an open-air horse-drawn vehicle. This journey was fruitful on many levels. It inspired, for example, her brother to compose a series of evocative Highland poems, including 'Stepping Westward,' 'To a Highland Girl', and, especially, the haunting 'A Solitary Reaper'.

This journey marked Dorothy's fist visit to Scotland, and she made the most of it. Her enthusiasm and open-mindedness to new experiences are apparent on almost every page. Candid and refreshingly blunt – she was not afraid to criticise her hosts when warranted – she also found great pleasure in the country's rustic simplicity and in the genuine warmth of its people.

✻   ✻   ✻

Loch Lomond and The Trossachs

from JOURNALS OF DOROTHY WORDSWORTH

Thursday, August 25th. – We were glad when we awoke to see that it was a fine morning – the sky was bright blue, with quick-moving clouds, the hills cheerful, lights and shadows vivid and distinct. The village looked exceedingly beautiful this morning from the garret windows – the stream glittering near it, while it flowed under trees through the level fields to the lake. After breakfast, William and I went down to the waterside. The roads were as dry as if no drop of rain had fallen, which added to the pure cheerfulness of the appearance of the village, and even of the distant prospect, an effect which I always seem to perceive from clearly bright roads, for they are always brightned by rain, after a storm; but when we came among the houses I regretted even more than last night, because the contrast was greater, the slovenliness and dirt near the doors; and could not but remember, with pain from the contrast, the cottages of Somersetshire, covered with roses and myrtle, and their small gardens of herbs and flowers. While lingering by the shore we began to talk with a man who offered to row us to Inch-ta-vannach; but the sky began to darken; and the wind being high, we doubted whether we should venture, therefore made no engagement; he offered to sell me some thread, pointing to his cottage, and added that many English ladies carried the thread away from Luss.

Presently after Coleridge joined us, and we determined to go to the island. I was sorry that the man who had been talking with us was not our boatman; William by some chance had engaged another. We had two rowers and a strong boat; so I felt myself bold, though there was a great chance of a high wind. The nearest point of Inch-ta-vannach is not perhaps more than a mile and a quarter from Luss; we did not land there, but rowed round the end, and landed on that side which looks towards our favourite cottages, and their own island, which, wherever seen, is still their own. It rained a little when we landed, and I took my cloak, which afterwards served us to sit down upon in our road up the hill, when the day grew much finer, with gleams of sunshine. This island belongs to Sir James Colquhoun, who has made a convenient road, that winds gently to the top of it.

We had not climbed far before we were stopped by a sudden burst of prospect, so singular and beautiful that it was like a flash of images from another world. We stood with our backs to the hill of the island, which we were ascending, and which shut out Ben Lomond entirely, and all the upper part of the lake, and we looked towards the foot of the lake, scattered over with islands without beginning and without end. The sun shone, and the distant hills were visible, some through sunny mists, others in gloom with patches of sunshine; the lake was lost under the low and distant hills, and the islands lost in the lake, which was all in motion with travelling fields of light, or dark shadows under rainy clouds. There are many hills, but no commanding eminence at a distance to confine the prospect, so that the land seemed endless as the water.

What I had heard of Loch Lomond, or any other place in Great Britain, had given me no idea of anything like what we beheld: it was an outlandish scene – we might have believed ourselves in North America. The islands were of every possible variety of shape and surface – hilly and level, large and small, bare, rocky, pastoral, or covered with wood. Immediately under my eyes lay one large flat island, bare and green, so flat and low that it scarcely appeared to rise above the water, with straggling peat-stacks and a single hut upon one of its out-shooting promontories – for it was of a very irregular shape, though perfectly flat. Another, its next neighbour, and still nearer to us, was covered over with heath and coppice-wood, the surface undulating, with flat or sloping banks towards the water, and hollow places, cradle-like valleys, behind. These two islands, with Inch-ta-vannach, where we were standing, were intermingled with the water, I might say interbedded and intervened with it, in a manner that was exquisitely pleasing. There were bays innumerable, straits or passages like calm rivers, landlocked lakes, and, to the main water, stormy promontories. The solitary hut on the flat green island seemed unsheltered and desolate, and yet not wholly so, for it was but a broad river's breadth from the covert of the wood of the other island. Near to these is a miniature, an islet covered with trees, on which stands a small ruin that looks like the remains of a religious house; it is overgrown with ivy, and were it not that the arch of a window or gateway may be distinctly seen, it would be difficult to believe that it was not a tuft of trees growing in the shape of a ruin, rather than a ruin overshadowed by trees. When we had walked a little further we saw below us, on the nearest large island, where some of the wood had been cut down, a hut, which we conjectured to be a bark hut. It appeared to be on the shore of a little forest lake, enclosed by Inch-ta-vannach, where we were, and the woody island on which the hut stands ...

＊   ＊   ＊

I have said so much of this lake that I am tired myself, and I fear I must have tired my friends. We had a pleasant journey to Tarbet; more than half of it on foot, for the road was hilly, and after we had climbed one small hill we were not desirous to get into the car again, seeing another before us, and our path was always delightful, near the lake, and frequently through the woods. When we were within about half a mile of Tarbet, at a sudden turning looking to the left, we saw a very craggy-topped mountain amongst other smooth ones; the rocks on the summit distinct in shape as if they were some buildings raised up by man, or uncouth images of some strange creature. We called out with one voice, 'That's what we wanted!' alluding to the frame-like uniformity of the side-screens of the lake for the last five or six miles. As we conjectured, this singular mountain was the famous Cobbler, near Arrochar. Tarbet was before us in the recess of a deep, large bay, under the shelter of a hill. When we came up to the village we had to inquire for the inn, there being no signboard. It was a well-sized white house, the best in the place. We were conducted up-stairs into a sitting-room that might make any good-humoured travellers happy – a square room, with windows on each side, looking, one way, towards the mountains, and across the lake to Ben Lomond, the other.

There was a pretty stone house before (*i.e.* towards the lake) with some huts, scattered trees, two or three green fields with hedgerows, and a little brook making its way towards the lake; the fields are almost flat, and screened on that side nearest the head of the lake by a hill, which, pushing itself out, forms the bay of Tarbet, and, towards the foot, by a gentle slope and trees. The lake is narrow, and Ben Lomond shuts up the prospect, rising directly from the water. We could have believed ourselves to be by the side of Ulswater, at Glenridden, or in some other of the inhabited retirements of the lake. We were in a sheltered place among mountains; it was not an open joyous bay, with a cheerful populous village, like Luss; but a pastoral and retired spot, with a few single dwellings. The people of the inn stared at us when we spoke, without giving us an answer immediately, which we were at first disposed to attribute to coarseness of manners, but found afterwards that they did not understand us at once, Erse being the language spoken in the family. Nothing but salt meat and eggs for dinner – no potatoes; the house smelt strongly of herrings, which were hung to dry over the kitchen fire.

Walked in the evening towards the head of the lake; the road was steep over the hill, and when we had reached the top of it we had long views up and down the water. Passed a troop of women who were resting themselves by the roadside, as if returning from their day's labour. Amongst them was a man, who had walked with us a considerable way in the morning, and told us he was just come from America, where he had been for some years, – was going to his own home, and should return to America. He spoke of emigration as a glorious thing for them who had money. Poor fellow! I do not think that he had brought much back with him, for he had worked his passage over: I much suspected that a bundle, which he carried upon a stick, tied in a pocket-handkerchief, contained his all. He was almost blind, he said, as were many of the crew. He intended crossing the lake at the ferry; but it was stormy, and he thought he should not be able to get over that day. I could not help smiling when I saw him lying by the roadside with such a company about him, not like a wayfaring man, but seeming as much at home and at his ease as if he had just stepped out of his hut among them, and they had been neighbours all their lives. Passed one pretty house, a large thatched dwelling with outhouses, but the prospect above and below was solitary.

The sun had long been set before we returned to the inn. As travellers, we were glad to see the moon over the top of one of the hills, but it was a cloudy night, without any peculiar beauty or solemnity. After tea we made inquiries respecting the best way to go to Loch Ketterine; the landlord could give but little information, and nobody seemed to know anything distinctly of the place, though it was but ten miles off. We applied to the maid-servant who waited on us: she was a fine-looking young woman, dressed in a white bed-gown, her hair fastened up by a comb, and without shoes and stockings. When we asked her about the Trossachs she could give us no information, but on our saying, 'Do you know Loch

Ketterine?' she answered with a smile, 'I *should* know the loch, for I was bred and born there.' After much difficulty we learned from her that the Trossachs were at the foot of the lake, and that by the way we were to go we should come upon them at the head, should have to travel ten miles to the foot of the water, and that there was no inn by the way. The girl spoke English very distinctly; but she had few words, and found it difficult to understand us. She did not much encourage us to go, because the roads were bad, and it was a long way, 'and there was no putting-up for the like of us'. We determined, however, to venture, and throw ourselves upon the hospitality of some cottager or gentleman. We desired the landlady to roast us a couple of fowls to carry with us. There are always plenty of fowls at the doors of a Scotch inn, and eggs are as regularly brought to table at breakfast as bread and butter.

THE
HIGHLANDS

QUEEN VICTORIA
(1819-1901)

✣   ✣   ✣

Queen Victoria participated in a love affair with Scotland that lasted most of her adult life. In 1842 she made her first visit there and came away pleased. A scant 20 years earlier George IV visited Edinburgh, donning a kilt and thus essentially offered a royal endorsement of Scottish, and in particular, Highland culture. Now the young queen followed suit. She made three successful tours of Scotland in 1842, 1844, and 1847.

Like many people of her day, Victoria had been introduced to Scotland through the writing of Sir Walter Scott. The images that formed in her mind were of the most romantic kind: gallant Highlanders living a noble life amid both poverty and splendour. And when she actually set foot in Scotland, she was not disappointed. She received a warm welcome wherever she went. Finally, in 1848 she acquired Balmoral Castle, turning it into a holiday home for the royal family. It was a place to get away from the pressures of her and husband Prince Albert's busy life and to bask in the glory of the countryside.

In 1868 she published Leaves from the Journal of Our Life in the Highlands, *which proved to be a durable crowd-pleaser.*

✣   ✣   ✣

Grampian
Ascent of Ben Muich Dhui

from LEAVES FROM THE JOURNAL OF OUR LIFE
IN THE HIGHLANDS FROM 1848 TO 1861

Friday, October 7, 1859.

Breakfast at half-past eight. At ten minutes to nine we started, in the sociable, with Bertie and Alice and our usual attendants. Drove along the opposite side of the river. The day very mild and promising to be fine, though a little heavy over the hills, which we anxiously watched. At *Castleton* we took four post-horses, and drove to the *Shiel of the Derry*, that beautiful spot where we were last year – which Albert had never seen – and arrived there just before eleven. Our ponies were there with Kennedy, Robertson, and Jemmie Smith. One pony carried the luncheon-baskets. After all the cloaks, &c. had been placed on the ponies, or carried by the men, we mounted and began our 'journey'. I was on 'Victoria', Alice on 'Dobbins'. George McHardy, an elderly man who knew the country (and acts as a guide, carrying luggage for people across the hills, 'on beasts' which he keeps for that purpose), led the way. We rode (my pony being led by Brown most of the time going up and down) at least four miles up *Glen Derry*, which is very fine, with the remnants of a splendid forest, *Cairn Derry* being to the right, and the *Derry Water* running below. The track was very bad and stony, and broken up by cattle coming down for the 'Tryst'. At the end of the glen we crossed a ford, passed some softish ground, and turned up to the left by a very rough, steep, but yet gradual ascent to *Corrie Etchan*, which is in a very wild rugged spot, with magnificent precipices, a high mountain to the right called *Ben Main*, while to the left was *Cairngorm of Derry*. When we reached the top of this very steep ascent (we had been rising, though almost imperceptibly, from the *Derry Shiel*), we came upon a loch of the same name, which reminded us of *Loch-na-Gar* and of *Loch-na-Nian*. You look from here on to other wild hills and corries – on *Ben A'an*, &c. We ascended very gradually, but became so enveloped in mist that we could see nothing – hardly those just before us! Albert had walked a good deal; and it was very cold. The mist got worse; and as we rode along the stony, but almost flat ridge of *Ben Muich Dhui*, we hardly knew whether we were on level ground or the top of the mountain. However, I and Alice rode to the very top, which we reached a few minutes past two; and here, at a cairn of stones, we lunched in a piercing cold wind.

Just as we sat down, a gust of wind came and dispersed the mist, which had a most wonderful effect, like a dissolving view – and exhibited the grandest, wildest scenery imaginable! We sat on a ridge of the cairn to take our luncheon, – our good people being grouped with the ponies near us. Luncheon over, Albert ran off with Alice to the ridge to look at the splendid view, and sent for me to follow. I did so; but not without Grant's help, for there were quantities of large loose stones heaped up together to walk upon. The wind was fearfully high, but the view was worth seeing. I cannot describe all, but we saw where the *Dee* rises between the mountains called the *Well of Dee – Ben-y-Ghlo* – and the adjacent mountains, *Ben Vrackie* – then *Ben-na-Bhourd* – *Ben A'an*, &c. – and such magnificent wild rocks, precipices, and corries. It had a sublime and solemn effect; so wild, so solitary – no one but ourselves and our little party there.

Albert went on further with the children, but I returned with Grant to my seat on the cairn, as I could not scramble about well. Soon after, we all began walking and looking for 'cairngorms', and found some small ones. The mist had entirely cleared away below, so that we saw all the beautiful views. *Ben Muich Dhui* is 4,297 feet high, one of the highest mountains in *Scotland*. I and Alice rode part of the way, walking wherever it was very steep. Albert and Bertie walked the whole time. I had a little whisky and water, as the people declared pure water would be too chilling. We then rode on without getting off again, Albert talking so gaily with Grant. Upon which Brown observed to me in simple Highland phrase, 'It's very pleasant to walk with a person who is always "content".' Yesterday, in speaking of dearest Albert's sport, when I observed he never was cross after bad luck, Brown said, 'Every one on the estate says "there never was so kind a master"; I am sure our wish is to give satisfaction.' I said, they certainly did.*

By a quarter-past six o'clock we got down to the *Shiel of the Derry*, where we found some tea, which we took in the 'shiel',† and started again by moonlight at about half-past six. We reached *Castleton* at half-past seven – and after this it became cloudy. At a quarter-past eight precisely we were at *Balmoral,* much delighted and not at all tired; everything had been so well arranged and so quietly, without any fuss. *Never* shall I forget this day, or the impression this very grand scene made upon me; truly sublime and impressive; such solitude!

---

* We were always in the habit of conversing with the Highlanders – with whom one comes so much in contact in the Highlands. The Prince highly appreciated the good-breeding, simplicity, and intelligence, which makes it so pleasant, and even instructive to talk to them.
† 'Shiel' means a small shooting-lodge.

NAN SHEPHERD
(1893-1981)

❋　　　❋　　　❋

Novelist and critic, Nan Shepherd was raised in Aberdeen and graduated from university there in 1915. Until 1956 she worked as a lecturer at Aberdeen College of Education. She has written three novels, The Quarry Wood *(1928),* The Weatherhouse *(1930), and* A Pass in the Grampians *(1933), the latter about a young woman's coming of age in North-east Scotland.*

Shepherd is also a fine nature writer. In The Living Mountain, *she writes passionately about the mountains that she loves so dearly.*

❋　　　❋　　　❋

The Plateau

from THE LIVING MOUNTAIN:
A CELEBRATION OF THE CAIRNGORM
MOUNTAINS OF SCOTLAND

Summer on the high plateau can be delectable as honey; it can also be a roaring scourge. To those who love the place, both are good, since both are part of its essential nature. And it is to know its essential nature that I am seeking here. To know, that is, with the knowledge that is a process of living. This is not done easily nor in an hour. It is a tale too slow for the impatience of our age, not of immediate enough import for its desperate problems. Yet it has its own rare value. It is, for one thing, a corrective of glib assessment: one never quite knows the mountain, nor oneself in relation to it. However often I walk on them, these hills hold astonishment for me. There is no getting accustomed to them.

The Cairngorm Mountains are a mass of granite thrust up

through the schists and gneiss that form the lower surrounding hills, planed down by the ice cap, and split, shattered and scooped by frost, glaciers and the strength of running water. Their physiognomy is in the geography books – so many square miles of area, so many lochs, so many summits of over 4000 feet – but this is a pallid simulacrum of their reality, which, like every reality that matters ultimately to human beings, is a reality of the mind.

The plateau is the true summit of these mountains; they must be seen as a single mountain, and the individual tops, Ben MacDhui, Braeriach and the rest, though sundered from one another by fissures and deep descents, are no more than eddies on the plateau surface. One does not look upward to spectacular peaks but downward from the peaks to spectacular chasms. The plateau itself is not spectacular. It is bare and very stony, and since there is nothing higher than itself (except for the tip of Ben Nevis) nearer than Norway, it is savaged by the wind. Snow covers it for half the year and sometimes, for as long as a month at a time, it is in cloud. Its growth is moss and lichen and sedge, and in June the clumps of Silene – moss campion – flower in brilliant pink. Dotterel and ptarmigan nest upon it, and springs ooze from its rock. By continental measurement its height is nothing much – around 4000 feet – but for an island it is well enough, and if the winds have unhindered range, so has the eye. It is island weather too, with no continent to steady it, and the place has as many aspects as there are gradations in the light.

Light in Scotland has a quality I have not met elsewhere. It is luminous without being fierce, penetrating to immense distances with an effortless intensity. So on a clear day one looks without any sense of strain from Morven in Caithness to the Lammermuirs, and out past Ben Nevis to Morar. At midsummer, I have had to be persuaded I was not seeing further even than that. I could have sworn I saw a shape, distinct and blue, very clear and small, further off than any hill the chart recorded. The chart was against me, my companions were against me, I never saw it again. On a day like that, height goes to one's head. Perhaps it was the lost Atlantis focused for a moment out of time.

The streams that fall over the edges of the plateau are clear – Avon indeed has become a by-word for clarity: gazing into its depths, one loses all sense of time, like the monk in the old story who listened to the blackbird.

> *Water of A'n, ye rin ʃae clear,*
> *'Twaʃ beguile a man of a hundreʃ year.*

Its waters are white, of a clearness so absolute that there is no image for them. Naked birches in April, lighted after heavy rain by the sun, might suggest their brilliance. Yet this is too sensational. The whiteness of these waters is simple. They are elemental transparency. Like roundness, or silence, their quality is natural, but is found so seldom in its absolute state that when we do so find it we are astonished.

The young Dee, as it flows out of the Garbh Choire and joins the water from the Lairig Pools, has the same astounding transparency. Water so clear cannot be imagined, but must be seen. One must go back, and back again, to look at it, for in the interval memory refuses to recreate its brightness. This is one of the reasons why the high plateau where these streams begin, the streams themselves, their cataracts and rocky beds, the corries, the whole wild enchantment, like a work of art is perpetually new when one returns to it. The mind cannot carry away all that it has to give, nor does it always believe possible what it has carried away.

So back one climbs, to the sources. Here the life of the rivers begins – Dee and Avon, the Derry, the Beinnie and the Allt Druie. In these pure and terrible streams the rain, cloud and snow of the high Cairngorms are drained away. They rise from the granite, sun themselves a little on the unsheltered plateau and drop through air to their valleys. Or they cut their way out under wreaths of snow, escaping in a tumult. Or hang in tangles of ice on the rock faces. One cannot know the rivers till one has seen them at their sources; but this journey to the sources is not to be undertaken lightly. One walks among elementals, and elementals are not governable. There are awakened also in oneself by the contact elementals that are as unpredictable as wind or snow.

This may suggest that to reach the high plateau of the Cairngorms is difficult. But no, no such thing. Given clear air, and the unending daylight of a Northern summer, there is not one of the summits but can be reached by a moderately strong walker without distress. A strong walker will take a couple of summits. Circus walkers will plant flags on all six summits in a matter of fourteen hours. This may be fun, but is sterile. To pit oneself against the mountain is necessary for every climber: to pit oneself merely against other players, and make a race of it, is to reduce to the level of a game what is essentially an experience. Yet what a race-course for these boys to choose! To know the hills, and their own bodies, will enough to dare the exploit is their real achievement.

Mastering new routes up the rock itself is another matter. Granite, of which the Cairngorms are built, weathers too smoothly and squarely to make the best conditions for rock-climbing. Yet there is such challenge in the grandeur of the corries that those who climb cannot leave them untasted. The Guide Book and the *Cairngorm Club Journal* give the attested climbs, with their dates, from the end of last century onwards. Yet I wonder if young blood didn't attempt it sooner. There is a record of a shepherd, a century and a half ago, found frozen along with his sheep dog, on a ledge of one of the Braeriach cliffs. He, to be sure, wandered there, in a blizzard, but the men who brought down the body must have done a pretty job of work; and I can believe there were young hot-heads among that hardy breed to whom the scaling of a precipice was nothing new. Dr George Skene Keith, in his *General View of Aberdeenshire*, records having scrambled up the bed of the Dee cataract in 1810, and Professor McGillivray, in his *Natural History of Braemar*, tells how as a student, in 1819, he walked from Aberdeen University to his western home, straight through the Cairngorm group; and lying down to sleep, just as he was, at the foot of the Braeriach precipices, continued next morning on his way straight up out of the corrie in which he had slept. On a later visit, searching out the flora of these mountains, he seems to have run up and down the crags with something of the deer's lightness. There are, however, ways up and down some of these corries that may be scrambled by any fleet-footed and level-headed climber, and it is doubtless these that the earlier adventurers had used. The fascination of the later work lies in finding ways impossible without the rope; and there are still many faces among these precipices that have not been attempted. One of my young friends lately pioneered a route out of the Garbh Choire of Braeriach, over rock not hitherto climbed. To him, one of the keenest young hillmen I know (he has been described, and recognised at a railway terminus, as 'a little black fellow, load the size of himself, with a far-away look in his eyes'), the mere setting up of a record is of very minor importance. What he values is a task that, demanding of him all he has and is, absorbs and so releases him entirely.

It is, of course, merely stupid to suppose that the record-breakers do not love the hills. Those who do not love them don't go up, and those who do can never have enough of it. It is an appetite that grows in feeding. Like drink and passion, it intensifies life to the point of glory. In the Scots term, used for the man who is *abune himsel'* with drink, one is *raised*; *fey*; a little mad, in the eyes of the folk who do not climb.

Fey may be too strong a term for that joyous release of body that is engendered by climbing; yet to the sober looker-on a man may seem to walk securely over dangerous places with the gay abandon that is said to be the mark of those who are doomed to death. How much of this gay security is the result of perfectly trained and co-ordinated body and mind, only climbers themselves realize; nor is there any need to ascribe to the agency of a god either the gay security, or the death which may occasionally, but rarely, follow. The latter, if it does occur, is likely to be the result of carelessness – of failing in one's exaltation to observe a coating of ice on the stone, of trusting to one's amazing luck rather than to one's compass, perhaps merely, in the glow of complete bodily well-being, of over-estimating one's powers of endurance.

But there is a phenomenon associated with this *feyness* of which I must confess a knowledge. Often, in my bed at home, I have remembered the places I have run lightly over with no sense of fear, and have gone cold to think of them. It seems to me then that I could never go back; my fear unmans me, horror is in my mouth. Yet when I go back, the same leap of the spirit carries me up. God or no god, I am *fey* again.

The *feyness* itself seems to me to have a physiological origin. Those who undergo it have the particular bodily make-up that functions at its most free and most live upon heights (although this, it is obvious, refers only to heights manageable to man and not at all to those for which a slow and painful acclimatisation is needful). As they ascend, the air grows rarer and more stimulating, the body feels lighter and they climb with less effort, till Dante's law of ascent on the Mount of Purgation seems to become a physical truth:

> *This mountain is such, that ever at the beginnin below 'tis toilsome, and the more a man ascends the less it wearies.*

At first I had thought that this lightness of body was a universal reaction to rarer air. It surprised me to discover that some people suffered malaise at altitudes that released me, but were happy in low valleys where I felt extinguished. Then I began to see that our devotions have more to do with our physiological peculiarities than we admit. I am a mountain lover because my body is at its best in the rarer air of the heights and communicates its elation to the mind. The obverse of this would seem to be exemplified in the extreme of fatigue I suffered while walking some two miles underground in the Ardennes caverns. This was plainly no case of a weary mind communicating its fatigue to the body, since I was enthralled by the strangeness and beauty of these underground cavities. Add to this eyes the normal focus of which is for distance, and my delight in the expanse of space opened up from the mountain tops becomes also a perfect physiological adjustment. The short-sighted cannot love mountains as the long-sighted do. The sustained rhythm of movement in a long climb has also its part in inducing the sense of physical well-being, and this cannot be captured by any mechanical mode of ascent.

This bodily lightness, then, in the rarefied air, combines with the liberation of space to give mountain *feyness* to those who are susceptible to such a malady. For it is a malady, subverting the will and superceding the judgment: but a malady of which the afflicted will never ask to be cured. For this nonsense of physiology does not really explain it at all. What! am I such a slave that unless my flesh feels bouyant I cannot be free? No, there is more in the lust for a mountain top than a perfect physiological adjustment. What more there is lies within the mountain. Something moves between me and it. Place and a mind may interpenetrate till the nature of both is altered. I cannot tell what this movement is except by recounting it.

H. V. MORTON
(1892-1979)

❈   ❈   ❈

Far too few people read H. V. Morton anymore – many of his books are out of print – but for several decades the Englishman was one of the most popular (and prolific) travel writers around. In the 1920s and 1930s his In Search of *series had captured the imagination of readers throughout the world. Whether travelling to England, Scotland, Ireland, or other sites beyond the British Isles, Morton exhibited a discerning intelligence and superb craftsmanship.*

Morton wrote about Scotland often, most famously in In Search of Scotland *(1929) and its sequel* In Scotland Again *(1933).* In Search of Scotland *is representative of Morton at his finest. Opinionated and very much a product of his time, Morton nevertheless is still a pleasure to read.*

❈   ❈   ❈

Glencoe

from IN SEARCH OF SCOTLAND

Along the road from Ballachulish where the river Coe pours into Loch Leven is a comfortable little village which boasts the most grotesque signpost in the British Isles:

THE VILLAGE OF GLENCOE
SCENE OF THE FAMOUS MASSACRE
TEAS AND REFRESHMENTS, TOBACCO AND CIGARETTES

This statement relieves the feeling of gloom with which a traveller approaches the scene of the clan massacre. The only writer who found Glencoe cheerful was Andrew Lang. Macaulay's description is well known, so is that by Dorothy Wordsworth; perhaps the best, however, is the not so familiar letter by Dickens in Forster's *Life*.

'All the way,' wrote Dickens, 'the road had been among moors and mountains with huge masses of rock which fell down God knows where, sprinkling the ground in every direction, and giving it the aspect of the burial place of a race of giants. Now and then we passed a hut or two, with neither window nor chimney, and the smoke of the peat fire rolling out at the door. But there were not six of these dwellings in a dozen miles; and anything so bleak and wild and mighty in its loneliness, as the whole country, it is impossible to conceive. Glencoe itself is perfectly *terrible*. The pass is an awful place. It is shut in on each side by enormous rocks from which great torrents come rushing down in all directions. In amongst these rocks on one side of the pass (the left as we came) there are scores of glens, high up, which form such haunts as you might imagine yourself wandering in, in the very height and madness of a fever. They will live in my dreams for years – I was going to say as long as I live, and I seriously think so. The very recollection of them makes me shudder ... '

I went on into this mountain pass ready, even anxious, to shudder at it. But, alas, the sun was shining! Glencoe in this mood – the mood that Lang must have known – is not frightful: it is awesome, it is stark, it is, like all the wild mountains of Scotland, a lesson in humility. Man has never existed for it; it is, at least in sunlight, not unfriendly so much as utterly oblivious of humanity. A man suddenly shot up into the moon might gaze at the cold, remote mountains with much the same chilly awe that he looks at the Pass of Glencoe. Here is a landscape without mercy. So far as Glencoe is concerned the first germ of life has never struggled from the warm slime. It is still dreaming of geological convulsions. Glencoe in sunlight does not make a man shudder because it is beautiful. It rather encourages him to sit down and look at it for a long time as you sit down in the sand and look at the Sphinx, wondering what he – for the sphinx is masculine – can see in the sky. Perhaps it is God. Glencoe has the same expression.

The worst road in Scotland winds its way through the solitude. The iron-grey mountains fret the sky on either hand. Half the pass is in sunlight; half in cold shadow. Tough grass and soggy bogland fill the narrow valley. There is no sound but the running of icy water, brown with peat; no movement but the wind in the long grass and the slow wheeling of some sinister bird high over the hills.

The volcanic heights are gashed by sharp gullies, broadening as they descend, in which water has in the course of centuries found its way to the valley. In some of these gashes trees try to hide from the wind like men sheltering. Mostly they are great slashes in the rock, as if giants had sharpened their swords on the hills ...

The sun is covered by a cloud. The light dies in Glencoe as suddenly as a light is switched off in a room. The pass has changed colour. It is grey and hopeless. Now you see why Macaulay called it the 'Valley of the Shadow'. As you look up at the mountains, at the queer gullies and the dark glens they seem a fit abode for naked devils. It was surely in such a place as Glencoe that the Gadarene swine met their end.

I came across a young shepherd walking behind sheep which moved softly like a grey wave over the grass on invisible feet. His collie would sleuth ahead and turning in the direction of the flock, crouch in the grass with his long nose showing, watching his charges with bright, critical eyes. If any sheep strayed or nibbled too long at the grass he would spring out like a brown and white dart, and in a second the offender would be pressing his way into the grey wave and the flock would have resumed its right formation.

The shepherd gave a low whistle. The dog, which appeared to be obsessed by the sheep, heard and instantly responded, bounding in long, graceful leaps towards his man, to stand, head on one side – blue tongue out, eyes on his eyes, one of the most beautiful pictures of intelligence I have ever seen.

The shepherd said something which I did not understand. The dog immediately wheeled round and turned back the flock. The shepherd, proud to show-off his dog to me, whistled and said something else, and the dog headed the sheep back again! Another whistle and the dog raced ahead and lay obediently in the grass.

'He's a goot dog, but not so goot as his mother wass! said the shepherd carelessly, not wishing to praise his own property.

A gunshot echoed round the hills. We looked up. They were shooting to-day, explained the shepherd, and the roads over the mountains were closed. His journey to market, which on an ordinary day would have taken him a few hours, would by the main road get him in at nightfall. But sport in the Highlands takes no count of ordinary people.

GAVIN MAXWELL
(1914-1969)

❋   ❋   ❋

Born in 1914, Gavin Maxwell bought the small Hebridean island of Soay in 1945, where he tried to establish a basking shark fishery. The result was his first book, Harpoon at a Venture. *In 1956 he wrote* God Protect Me from My Friends, *a biography of the infamous Sicilian bandit, Salvatore Giuliano. Two years later in 1958 came* A Reed Shaken by the Wind, *an account of his travels with Wilfred Thesiger among the Marsh Arabs of Southern Iraq and then, in 1959,* The Ten Pains of Death, *a study of his return to Sicily and a deeply insightful work on the impoverished Sicilian peasant communities.*

But it wasn't until the publication of Ring of Bright Water *in 1960 that his literary stock began to rise. To date this beloved classic has sold more than a million copies. Readers fell in love with the story of the author's life in a remote corner of the Western Highlands, surrounded by a wild landscape of mountain and sea and of the animals that became his constant companions over the years. A children's version was published in 1962 and a sequel,* The Rocks Remain, *in 1963. Maxwell returned to his childhood in 1965 with the* The House of Elrig, *a memoir of his youth in Galloway. The Camusfearna trilogy was completed with* Raven Seek Thy Brother *in 1968. Gavin Maxwell died of cancer in 1969.*

❋   ❋   ❋

Western Highlands

from RING OF BRIGHT WATER

I sit in a pitch-pine panelled kitchen-living-room, with an otter asleep upon its back among the cushions on the sofa, forepaws in the air, and with the expression of tightly shut concentration that very small babies wear in sleep. On the stone slab beneath the chimney-piece are inscribed the words *'Non fatuum huc persecutus ignem'* – 'It is no will-o'-the-wisp that I have followed here'. Beyond the door is the sea, whose waves break on the beach no more than a stone's throw distant, and encircling, mist-hung mountains. A little group of Greylag geese sweep past the window and alight upon the small carpet of green turf; but for the soft, contented murmur of their voices and the sounds of the sea and the waterfall there is utter silence. This place has been my home now for ten years and more, and wherever the changes of my life may lead me in the future it will remain my spiritual home until I die, a house to which one returns not with the certainty of welcoming fellow human beings, nor with the expectation of comfort and ease, but to a long familiarity in which every lichen-covered rock and rowan tree show known and reassuring faces.

I had not thought that I should ever come back to live in the West Highlands; when my earlier sojourn in the Hebrides had come to an end it had in retrospect seemed episodic, and its finish uncompromisingly final. The thought of return had savoured of a jilted lover pleading with an indifferent mistress upon whom he had no further claim; it seemed to me then that it was indeed a will-o'-the-wisp that I had followed, for I had yet to learn that happiness can neither be achieved nor held by endeavour.

Looking back with distaste to the brashness of my late adolescence I perceive that I was an earnest member of the Celtic fringe, avid for tartan and twilight. This was no by-product of a Nationalistic outlook, nor could my yearnings have found outlet in that direction, for I was at that time also an arrant snob, and the movement seemed to be essentially plebeian; supported, moreover, by youths whose title to a foothold in the West Highlands was as controversial as my own. It was not to the company of such as these that I aspired; the healthier and more robust enthusiasm of tartaned hikers from the industrial cities inspired in me a nausea akin to that of Compton Mackenzie's *Macdonald of Ben Nevis*. It was not with the awe due to surviving dinosaurs that I viewed certain backwoods Highland chieftains with moustaches as long as their lineage, but with the enthusiastic reverence that the vintage-car accords to Bentleys of the 1920s. Nothing in my early life had led me to question the prescriptive rightness of the established order as it had been in the days of my grandparents; to me the West Highlands were composed of deer forests and hereditary chieftains, and the sheep, the hikers and the Forestry Commission were regrettable interlopers upon the romantic life of the indigenous aristocracy.

I was no whit abashed by the fact that I came of a lowland family who had been established in one spot for more than five hundred years, and that it was there and as a Galloway Scot that I had been born and brought up. It was a handicap, certainly, as was also my inability to perform Highland dances or to speak Gaelic; to learn would have been to acknowledge that I had not known before, and so would have been unthinkable. I did learn, however, to play a few tunes, very badly, on the bagpipes; I had had a Gaelic-speaking nurse; I had been brought up to wear a kilt – though of shepherd's plaid; and, strongest card of all and probably what started the rot, my maternal grandmother had been a daughter of the Duke of Argyll, of MacCallum Mor himself. At Inveraray Castle and at Strachur on the opposite side of Loch Fyne I passed most of my long vacs from Oxford. Inveraray under the reign of the late Duke was a temple of twilight both Celtic and other, and its atmosphere was hardly calculated to cure my disease. The melancholy beauty of Strachur and Inveraray was for me still further complicated by the agonies of first love; I was well and truly pixillated, and I soaked myself in the works of Neil Munro and Maurice Walsh when I should have been laying the foundations of a literary education. All this was basically the outcome of an inherently romantic nature tinged with melancholy, for which a special home and uniform had clearly been prepared among the precipitous hills and sea lochs of the West Highlands.

There existed during my time at Oxford a curious clique of landed gentry so assertively un-urban that we affected a way of dressing quite unsuited to University life; at all times, for example, we wore tweed shooting suits and heavy shooting shoes studded with nails and dull with dubbin, and at our heels trotted spaniels or Labrador retrievers. Some of us were Englishmen, but the majority were Scots or those whose parents were in the habit of renting Highland shootings, and I have no doubt that the cult was akin to my own, for I remember that in the autumn term the rooms of its members were hung with the heads of stags killed during the vac, and there was endless talk of the Highlands. Most of us were, in fact, a species of privileged hiker, and we were also a striking example of the fact that aristocracy and education were no longer synonymous.

My own yearning for the Highlands was in those days as tormenting as an unconsummated love affair, for no matter how many stags I might kill or feudal castles inhabit I lacked an essential involvement; I was further from them than any immigrated Englishmen who planted one potato or raised one stone upon another. It is often those who dream of a *grande passion* who find it and suffer and are the sadder for it, and so it was with me, for when at last I came to the West Highlands by right of ownership and of effort they brought me to my knees and sent me away defeated and almost bankrupt. But during that five years' struggle the false image for which I had yearned had faded, and a truer one, less bedizened with tartan but no whit less beautiful, had taken place.

Immediately after the war's end I bought the island of Soay, some four thousand acres of relatively low-lying 'black' land cowering below the bare pinnacles and glacial corries of the Cuillins of Skye. There, seventeen miles by sea from the railway, I tried to found a new industry for the tiny and discontented population of the island, by catching and processing for oil the great basking sharks that appear in Hebridean waters during the summer months. I built a factory, bought boats and equipped them with harpoon guns, and became a harpoon gunner myself. For five years I worked in that landscape that before had been, for me, of a nebulous and cobwebby romance, and by the time it was all over and I was beaten I had in some way come to terms with the Highlands – or with myself, for perhaps in my own eyes I had earned the right to live among them, and the patient unauthenticity of the Maxwell tartan no longer disturbed me.

When the Soay venture was finished, the island and the boats sold, the factory demolished, and the population evacuated, I went to London and tried to earn my living as a portrait painter. One autumn I was staying with an Oxford contemporary who had bought an estate in the West Highlands, and in an idle moment after breakfast on a Sunday morning he said to me:

'Do you want a foothold on the west coast, now that you've

lost Soay? If you're not too proud to live in a cottage, we've got an empty one, miles from anywhere. It's right on the sea and there's no road to it – Camusfearna, it's called. There's some islands, and an automatic lighthouse. There's been no one there for a long time, and I'd never get any of the estate people to live in it now. If you'll keep it up you're welcome to it.'

It was thus casually, ten years ago, that I was handed the keys to my home, and nowhere in all the West Highlands and islands have I seen any place of so intense or varied a beauty in so small a compass.

The road, single-tracked for the past forty miles, and reaching in the high passes a gradient of one in three, runs southwards a mile or so inland of Camusfearna and some four hundred feet above it. At the point on the road which is directly above the house there is a single cottage at the roadside, Druimfiaclach, the home of my friends and nearest neighbours, the MacKinnons. Inland from Druimfiaclach the hills rise steeply but in rolling masses to a dominating peak of more than three thousand feet, snow-covered or snow-dusted for the greater part of the year. On the other side, to the westward, the Isle of Skye towers across a three-mile-wide sound, and farther to the south the stark bastions of Rhum and the couchant lion of Eigg block the sea horizon. The descent to Camusfearna is so steep that neither the house nor its islands and lighthouse are visible from the road above, and that paradise within a paradise remains, to the casual road-user, unguessed. Beyond Druimfiaclach the road seems, as it were, to become dispirited, as though already conscious of its dead end at sea-level six miles farther on, caught between the terrifying massif of mountain scree overhanging it and the dark gulf of sea loch below.

Druimfiaclach is a tiny oasis in a wilderness of mountain and peat-bog, and it is a full four miles from the nearest roadside dwelling. An oasis, an eyrie; the windows of the house look westward over the Hebrides and over the tyrian sunsets that flare and fade behind their peaks, and when the sun has gone and the stars are bright the many lighthouses of the reefs and islands gleam and wink above the surf. In the westerly gales of winter the walls of Druimfiaclach rock and shudder, and heavy stones are roped to the corrugated iron roof to prevent it blowing away as other roofs here have gone before. The winds rage in from the Atlantic and the hail roars and batters on the windows and the iron roof, all hell let loose, but the house stands and the MacKinnons remain here, as, nearby, the forefathers of them both remained for many generations.

It seems strange to me now that there was a time when I did not know the MacKinnons, strange that the first time I came to live at Camusfearna I should have passed their house by a hundred yards and left my car by the roadside without greeting or acknowledgement of a dependence now long established. I remember seeing some small children staring from the house door; I cannot now recall my first meeting with their parents.

I left my car at a fank, a dry-stone enclosure for dipping sheep, close to the burn side, and because I was unfamiliar with the ill-defined footpath that is the more usual route from the road to Camusfearna, I began to follow the course of the burn downward. The burn has its source far back in the hills, near to the very summit of the dominant peak; it has worn a fissure in the scarcely sloping mountain wall, and for the first thousand feet of its course it part flows, part falls, chill as snow-water even in summer, between tumbled boulders and small mult-coloured lichens. Up there, where it seems the only moving thing besides the eagles, the deer and the ptarmigan, it is called the Blue Burn, but at the foot of the outcrop, where it passes through a reedy lochan and enters a wide glacial glen it takes the name of its destination – Allt na Fearna, the Alder Burn. Here in the glen the clear topaz-coloured water rushes and twitters between low oaks, birches and alders, at whose feet the deep-cushioned green moss is stippled with bright toadstools of scarlet and purple and yellow, and in summer swarms of electric-blue dragonflies flicker and hover in the glades.

After some four miles the burn passes under the road at Druimfiaclach, a stone's throw from the fank where I had left my car. It was early spring when I came to live at Camusfearna for the first time, and the grass at the burn side was gay with thick-clustering primroses and violets, though the snow was still heavy on the high peaks and lay like lace over the lower hills of Skye across the Sound. The air was fresh and sharp, and from east to west and north to south there was not a single cloud upon the cold clear blue; against it, the still-bare birch branches were purple in the sun and the dark-banded stems were as white as the distant snows. On the sunny slopes grazing Highland cattle made a foreground to a landscape whose vivid colours had found no place on Landseer's palette. The rucksack bounced and jingled on my shoulders; I was coming to my new home like one of the hikers whom long ago I had so much despised.

I was not quite alone, for in front of me trotted my dog Jonnie, a huge black-and-white springer spaniel whose father and grandfather before him had been my constant companions during an adolescence devoted largely to sport. We were brought up to shoot, and by the curious paradox that those who are fondest of animals become, in such an environment, most bloodthirsty at a certain stage of their development, shooting occupied much of my time and thoughts during my school and university years. Many people find an especial attachment for a dog whose companionship has bridged widely different phases in their lives, and so it was with Jonnie; he and his forebears had spanned my boyhood, maturity, and the war years, and though since then I had found little leisure nor much inclination for shooting, Jonnie adapted himself placidly to a new role, and I remember how during the shark fishery years he would, unprotesting, arrange himself to form a pillow for my head in the well of an open boat as it tossed and pitched in the waves.

Now Jonnie's plump white rump bounced and perked through the heather and bracken in front of me, as times without number at night I was in the future to follow its pale just-discernible beacon through the darkness from Druimfiaclach to Camusfearna.

Presently the burn became narrower, and afforded no foothold at its steep banks, then it tilted sharply seaward between rock walls, and below me I could hear the roar of a high waterfall. I climbed out from the ravine and found myself on a bluff of heather and red bracken, looking down upon the sea and upon Camusfearna.

The landscape and seascape that lay spread below me was of such beauty that I had no room for it all at once; my eye flickered from the house to the islands, from the white sands to the flat green pasture round the croft, from the wheeling gulls to the pale satin sea and on to the snow-topped Cuillins of Skye in the distance.

Immediately below me the steep hill-side of heather and ochre mountain grasses fell to a broad green field, almost an island, for the burn flanked it at the right and then curved round seaward in a glittering horseshoe. The sea took up where the burn left off, and its foreshore formed the whole frontage of the field, running up nearest to me into a bay of rocks and sand. At the edge of this bay, a stone's throw from the sea on one side and the burn on the other, the house of Camusfearna stood unfenced in green grass among grazing black-faced sheep. The field, except immediately opposite to the house, sloped gently upwards from the sea, and was divided from it by a ridge of sand dunes grown over with pale marram grass and tussocky sea-bents. There were rabbits scampering on the short turf round the house, and out over the dunes the bullet heads of two seals were black in the tide.

Beyond the green field and the white shingly outflow of the burn were the islands, the nearer ones no more than a couple of acres each, rough and rocky, with here and there a few stunted rowan trees and the sun red on patches of dead bracken. The islands formed a chain of perhaps half a mile in length, and ended in one as big as the rest put together, on whose seaward shore showed the turret of a lighthouse. Splashed among the chain of islands were small beaches of sand so white as to dazzle the eye. Beyond the islands was the shining enamelled sea, and beyond it again the rearing bulk of Skye, plum-coloured distances embroidered with threads and scrolls of snow.

Even at a distance Camusfearna house wore that strange look that comes to dwellings after long disuse. It is indefinable, and it is not produced by obvious signs of neglect; Camusfearna had few slates missing from the roof and the windows were all intact, but the house wore that secretive expression that is in some way akin to a young girl's face during her first pregnancy.

As I went down the steep slope two other buildings came into view tucked close under the skirt of the hill, a byre facing Camusfearna across the green turf, and an older, windowless, croft at the very sea's edge, so close to the waves that I wondered how the house had survived. Later, I learned that the last occupants had been driven from it by a great storm which had brought the sea right into the house, so that they had been forced to make their escape by a window at the back.

At the foot of the hill the burn flowed calmly between an avenue of single alders, though the sound of unseen waterfalls was loud in the rock ravine behind me. I crossed a single wooden bridge with stone piers, and a moment later I turned the key in Camusfearna door for the first time.

EDMUND BURT
(d.1755)

❖   ❖   ❖

In 1730 Edmund Burt was ordered to Scotland to work as a contractor for the government. He spent most of his time in Inverness. From there he wrote letters to an acquaintance in London on his observations. Burt was nothing if not detail-minded. He offered opinions on everything from cooking and personal hygiene to weddings and funerals. No aspect of Highland life and society was left untouched.

Burt was an engineer contracted to work on the Highland roads and bridges that were then being built under the direction of General Wade. At the time Burt wrote down his astute observations, the Highland myth had not yet been invented, Jacobitism was still a four-letter word, and the northern lands were still considered a remote and dangerous part of Britain.

Burt's Letters from the North of Scotland is considered one of the earliest and most detailed sources of information on life in the Highlands during the 18th century. Although Burt often cast a critical eye, he was no ordinary government worker, content to observe from afar. On the contrary, he had face-to-face encounters with ordinary men and women with whom he expressed outright sympathy for the poverty and hardship they had to endure. Most importantly, Burt's Letters captures the Highlands before the 'Improvers' gained control at a time when the Highland chiefs had not yet been replaced by ubiquitous landlords.

❖   ❖   ❖

Northern Highlands

Letter XVII
from BURT'S LETTERS FROM
THE NORTH OF SCOTLAND

Second Day. At mounting I received many compliments from my host; but the most earnest was, that common one of wishing me good weather. For, like the seafaring man, my safety depended upon it; especially at that season of the year.

As the plain lay before me, I thought it all fit for culture; but in riding along, I observed a good deal of it was bog, and here and there rock even with the surface: however, my road was smooth; and if I had had company with me, I might have said jestingly, as was usual among us after a rough way, 'Come, let us ride this over again'.

At the end of about a mile, there was a steep ascent, which they call a 'carne' – that is, an exceedingly stony hill, which at some distance seems to have no space at all between stone and stone. I thought I could compare it with no ruggedness so aptly as to suppose it like all the different stones in a mason's yard thrown promiscuously upon one another. This I passed on foot, at the rate of about half a mile in the hour. I do not reckon the time that was lost in backing my horses out of a narrow place withoutside of a rock, where the way ended with a precipice of about twenty feet deep. Into this gap they were led by the mistake or carelessness of my guide. The descent from the top of this carne was short, and thence I ascended another hill not so stony; and at last, by several others (which, though very rough, are not reckoned extraordinary in the Highlands), I came to a precipice of about a hundred yards in length.

The side of the mountain below me was almost perpendicular; and the rest above, which seemed to reach the clouds, was exceedingly steep. The path which the Highlanders and their little horses had worn was scarcely two feet wide, but pretty smooth; and below was a lake whereinto vast pieces of rock had fallen, which I suppose had made, in some measure, the steepness of the precipice; and the water that appeared between some of them seemed to be under my stirrup. I really believe the path where I was is twice as high from the lake as the Cross of St Paul's is from Ludgate Hill; and I thought I had good reason to think so, because a few huts beneath, on the further side of the water, which is not very wide, appeared to me each of them like a black spot not much bigger than the standish before me.

A certain officer of the army going this way was so terrified with the sight of the abyss that he crept a little higher, fondly imagining he should be safer above, as being further off from the danger, and so to take hold of the heath in his passage. There a panic terror seized him, and he began to lose his forces, finding it impracticable to proceed, and being fearful to quit his hold and slide down, lest in so doing he should overshoot the narrow path; and had not two soldiers come to his assistance, viz. one who was at some little distance before him, and the other behind, in all probability he had gone to the bottom. But I have observed that particular minds are wrought upon by particular dangers, according to their different sets of ideas. I have sometimes travelled in the mountains with officers of the army, and have known one in the middle of a deep and rapid ford cry out he was undone; another was terrified with the fear of his horse's falling in an exceeding rocky way; and perhaps neither of them would be so much shocked at the danger that so greatly affected the other; or, it may be, either of them at standing the fire of a battery of cannon. But for my own part I had passed over two such precipices before, which rendered it something less terrifying; yet, as I have hinted, I chose to ride it, as I did the last of the other two, knowing by the first I was liable to fear, and that my horse was not subject either to that disarming passion or to giddiness, which in that case I take to be the effect of apprehension.

It is a common thing for the natives to ride their horses over such little precipices; but for myself I never was upon the back of one of them; and, by the account some Highlanders have given me of them, I think I should never choose it in such places as I have been describing.

There is in some of those paths, at the very edge or extremity, a little mossy grass, and those shelties, being never shod, if they are ever so little footsore, they will, to favour their feet, creep to the very brink, which must certainly be very terrible to a stranger.

It will hardly ever be out of my memory, how I was haunted by a kind of poetical sentence, after I was over this precipice, which did not cease till it was supplanted by the new fear of my horse's falling among the rocks in my way from it. It was this:

There hov'ring eagles wait the fatal trip.

By the way, this bird is frequently seen among the mountains, and, I may say, severely felt sometimes, by the inhabitants, in the loss of their lambs, kids, and even calves and colts.

I had not gone about six miles, and had not above two, as I understood afterwards, to the place of baiting. In my way, which I shall only say was very rough and hilly, I met a Highland chieftain with fourteen attendants, whose offices about his person I shall hereafter describe, at least the greatest part of them. When we came, as the sailor says, almost broadside and broadside, he eyed me as if he would look my hat off; but, as he was at home, and I a stranger in the country, I thought he might have made the first overture of civility, and therefore I took little notice of him and his ragged followers. On his part he seemed to show a kind of disdain at my being so slenderly attended, with a mixture of anger that I showed him no respect before his vassals; but this might only be my surmise – yet it looked very like it. I supposed he was going to the glen from whence I came, for there was no other hut in all my way, and there he might be satisfied by the landlord who I was, etc.

I shall not trouble you with any more at present, than that I safely arrived at my baiting place; for, as I hinted before, there is such a sameness in the parts of the hills that the description of one rugged way, bog, ford, etc. will serve pretty well to give you a notion of the rest.

Here I desired to know what I could have for dinner, and was told there was some undressed mutton. This I esteemed as a rarity, but, as I did not approve the fingers of either maid or mistress, I ordered my man (who is an excellent cook, so far as a beefsteak or a mutton chop) to broil me a chop or two, while I took a little turn to easy my legs, weary with sitting so long on horseback.

This proved an intolerable affront to my landlady, who raved and stormed, and said, 'What's your master? I have dressed for the Laird of this and the Laird of that, such and such chiefs; and this very day,' says she, 'for the Laird of – ,' who, I doubted not, was the person

I met on the hill. To be short, she absolutely refused to admit of any such innovation; and so the chops served for my man and the guide, and I had recourse to my former fare hard eggs.

Eggs are seldom wanting at the public huts, though, by the poverty of the poultry, one might wonder how they should have any inclination to produce them.

Here was no wine to be had; but as I carried with me a few lemons in a net, I drank some small punch for refreshment. When my servant was preparing the liquor, my landlord came to me, and asked me seriously if those were apples he was squeezing. And indeed there are as many lemon trees as apple trees in that country, nor have they any kind of fruit in their glens that I know of.

Their huts are mostly built on some rising rocky spot at the foot of a hill, secure from any burn or springs that might descend upon them from the mountains; and, thus situated, they are pretty safe from inundations from above or below, and other ground they cannot spare from their corn. And even upon the skirts of the Highlands, where the laird has indulged two or three trees from his house, I have heard the tenant lament the damage done by the droppings and shade of them, as well as the space taken up by the trunks and roots.

The only fruit the natives have, that I have seen, is the bilberry, which is mostly found near springs, in hollows of the heaths. The taste of them to me is not very agreeable, but they are much esteemed by the inhabitants, who eat them with their milk: yet in the mountain woods, which for the most part, are distant and difficult of access, there are nuts, raspberries, and strawberries; the two last, though but small, are very grateful to the taste; but those woods are so rare (at least it has always appeared so to me) that few of the Highlanders are near enough to partake of the benefit.

I now set out on my last stage, of which I had gone about five miles, in much the same manner as before, when it began to rain below, but it was snow above to a certain depth from the summits of the mountains. In about half an hour afterwards, at the end of near a mile, there arose a most violent tempest. This, in a little time, began to scoop the snow from the mountains, and made such a furious drift, which did not melt as it drove, that I could hardly see my horse's head.

The horses were blown aside from place to place as often as the sudden gusts came on, being unable to resist those violent eddy-winds; and, at the same time, they were nearly blinded with the snow.

Now I expected no less than to perish, was hardly able to keep my saddle, and, for increase of misery, my guide led me out of the way, having entirely lost his landmarks.

When he perceived his error he fell down on his knees, by my horse's side, and in a beseeching posture, with his arms extended and in a howling tone, seemed to ask forgiveness.

I imagined what the matter was (for I could but just see him, and that too by fits), and spoke to him with a soft voice, to signify I was not in anger; and it appeared afterwards that he expected to be shot, as they have a dreadful notion of the English.

Thus finding himself in no danger of my resentment, he addressed himself to the searching about for the way from which he had deviated, and in some little time I heard a cry of joy, and he came and took my horse by the bridle, and never afterwards quitted it till we came to my new lodging, which was about a mile, for it was almost as dark as night. In the mean time I had given directions to my man for keeping close to my horse's heels; and if anything should prevent it, to call to me immediately, that I might not lose him.

As good luck would have it, there was but one small river in the way, and the ford, though deep and winding, had a smooth, sandy bottom, which is very rare in the Highlands.

There was another circumstance favourable to us (I shall not name a third as one, which is our being not far from the village, for we might have perished with cold in the night as well near it as further off), there had not a very great quantity of snow fallen upon the mountains, because the air began a little to clear, though very little, within about a quarter of a mile of the glen, otherwise we might have been buried in some cavity hid from us by darkness and the snow.

But if this drift, which happened to us upon some one of the wild moors, had continued, and we had had far to go, we might have perished, notwithstanding the knowledge of any guide whatever.

These drifts are, above all other dangers, dreaded by the Highlanders; for my own part, I could not think of Mr. Addison's short description of a whirlwind in the wild, sandy deserts of Numidia.

THOMAS PENNANT
(1726-1798)

❊   ❊   ❊

A zoologist by training, Thomas Pennant brought a scientific eye to his travels in Scotland. He has been recognised by no less than Dr. Samuel Johnson as 'the best travel writer' of his day.

Pennant attended Oxford and eventually made a name for himself in the natural sciences but he also possessed a naturally curious mind – he enjoyed the element of surprise and discovery that came with travelling to remote places.

In 1769 Pennant made his first tour of Scotland, which was so successful that he went on another three years later, in 1772. Accompanied by a small party, including an illustrator who sketched some of the earliest views of the islands, he boarded the Lady Frederick Campbell *and embarked on an eight-week journey to the Hebrides that took him from the Mull of Kintyre to Loch Broom. The voyage was considered the most thorough exploration of the region up to that time. 'For the next fifty years* Pennant's Voyage *was read by every visitor to the Hebrides,' notes historian Elizabeth Bray. 'It was brought out in three editions in his lifetime, as well as in a German translation.'*

Pennant had a tremendous eye for detail and his journals are full of fascinating commentary from the history of the islands and description of wildlife to sensitive observations of the often dire living conditions he witnessed.

❊   ❊   ❊

from PENNANT'S SECOND TOUR IN SCOTLAND

August 2. At seven in the morning take a fix-oared boat, at the east end of Loch-maree: keep on the north shore beneath steep rocks, mostly filled with pines waving over our heads. Observe on the shore a young man of good appearance, hailing the boat in the Erse language. I demanded what he wanted; was informed a place in the boat. As it was entirely filled, I was obliged to refuse his request. He follows us for two miles through every difficulty, and by his voice and gestures threatened revenge. At length a rower thought fit to acquaint us that he was the owner of the boat, and only wanted admission in lieu of one of them. The boat was ordered to shore, and the master taken in with proper apologies and attempts to sooth him for his hard treatment. Instead of insulting us with abuse, as a Charon of South Britain would have done, he instantly composed himself, and told us through an interpreter, that he felt great pride in finding that his conduct had gained any degree of approbation.

Continue our course. The lake, which at the beginning was only half a mile broad, now, nearly half its length, widens into a great bay, bending towards the south, about four miles in breadth, filled with little isles, too much clustered and indistinct.

Land on that called Inch-maree, the favoured isle of the saint, the patron of all the coast from Applecross to Loch-broom. The shores are neat and gravelly; the whole surface covered thickly with a beautiful grove of oak, ash, willow, wicken, birch, fir, hazel, and enormous hollies. In the midst is a circular dike of stones, with a regular narrow entrance; the inner part has been used for ages as a burial-place, and is still in use. I suspect the dike to have been originally druidical, and that the ancient superstition of Paganism had been taken up by the saint, as the readiest method of making a conquest over the minds of the inhabitants. A stump of a tree is shewn as the altar, probably the memorial of one of stone; but the curiosity of the place is the well of the saint, of power unspeakable in cases of lunacy. The patient is brought into the sacred island, is made to kneel before the altar, where his attendants leave an offering of money: he is then brought to the well, and sips some of the holy water: a second offering is made; that done, he is thrice dipped in the lake; and the same operation is repeated every day for some weeks; and it often happens, by natural causes, the patient receives some relief, of which the saint receives the credit. I must add, that if the visitants draw from the state of the well an omen of the disposition of St. Maree: if his well is full, they suppose he will be propitious; if not, they proceed in their operations with fears and doubts; but let the event be what it will, he is held in high esteem: the common oath of the country is by his name: if a traveller passes by any of his resting-places, they never neglect to leave an offering;

but the saint is so moderate as not to put him to any expence: a stone, a stick, a bit of rag contents him.

This is the most beautiful of the isles; the others have only a few trees sprinkled over their surface.

About a mile farther the lake again contracts. Pass beneath a high rock, formed of short precipices, with shelves between, filled with multitudes of self-sown pines, making a most beautiful appearance.

The south side of the water is bounded with mountains adorned with birch woods, mixed with a few pines: a military round runs along its length. The mountains are not very high, but open in many parts to give a view of others, whose naked and broken tops shooting into sharp crags, strangely diversify the scene, and form a noble termination.

Towards the bottom of the lake is a headland, finely wooded to the very summit. Here the water suddenly narrows to the breadth of a hundred yards, and continues to for near a mile, the banks clothed with trees, and often bending into little semilunar bays to the very extremity; from whence its waters, after the course of a mile, a continual *rapide*, discharge into a deep and darksome hole called Pool-Ewe, which opens into the large bay of Loch-Ewe.

The lake we had left is eighteen miles long: the waters are said to be specifically lighter than most others, and very rarely frozen: the depth is various, in some places sixty fathoms; but the bottom is very uneven: if ten feet of water were drained away, the whole would appear a chain of little lakes.

The fish are salmon, char, and trout; of the last is a species weighing thirty pounds.

Land; are received by the Rev. Mr. Dounie, minister of Gairloch, whom we attend to church, and hear a very edifying plain comment on a portion of scripture. He takes us home with him, and by his hospitality makes us experience the difference between the lodgings of the two nights.

EDWIN MUIR
(1887-1959)

❈   ❈   ❈

Edwin Muir was born in Orkney, on the island of Wyre, the son of a crofter. 'I'm not Scotch,' he once wrote, 'I'm an Orkneyman, a good Scandinavian, and my country is Norway, or Denmark, or Iceland, or some place like that.' When he was fourteen, the family moved to Glasgow, seeking a better life. It was not to be. The transition from rural to urban setting proved disastrous – within a few years his father had died of a heart attack, a brother of consumption and another brother of a brain tumour. Soon thereafter his mother succumbed as well. Not surprisingly, Orkney forever represented to him an Edenic ideal, a Paradise Lost and never found.

In 1925 Muir published his first volume of verse, First Poems. *Other works followed, including* Chorus of the Newly Dead *(1926),* Variations on a Time Theme *(1934),* Journeys and Places *(1937),* The Narrow Place *(1943),* The Voyage *(1946),* The Labyrinth *(1949),* New Poems *(1949-51), and* Collected Poems *(1952), as well as* Scott and Scotland *(1936) and* Essays on Literature and Society *(1949).*

In the early 1930s Muir set out alone in an old 1921 Standard car loaned by the Orcadian painter Stanley Cursiter, who was then director of the Scottish National Gallery. His intention was to offer his impression of contemporary Scotland, 'not the romantic Scotland of the past nor the Scotland of the tourist ... ' Today Scottish Journey *is considered a masterpiece of travel writing, as well as a subtle yet powerful rumination on Scottish identity, by one of Scotland's greatest modern writers of prose and poetry.*

❈   ❈   ❈

The Highlands

from SCOTTISH JOURNEY

I started rather late next morning and in a little while found myself definitely in the Highlands. I am not going to describe that beautiful country, so often described already, or catalogue the host of famous mountains that I passed on my way. The thing that impressed me most in the Highlands during my first day's run (apart from a small incident to which I shall come presently) was a thing which is common no doubt to all wild and solitary scenery: that is, the added value which every natural object acquires from one's consciousness that has not been touched by the human will. The larch woods, the streams, all of them noisy and active here because of the slant at which they run, the little mounds of turf: all had an exhilarating freshness which is absent from more cultivated places, and seemed to exist completely in themselves, as if they were their own end. The brooks seemed freer, the trees more naturally grown, and the silence that they filled with their presence almost a conscious thing. It may be simply that when one is alone with a hundred square miles of solitary nature one begins to become aware of its life as an independent mode of being. At any rate this awareness, whatever its cause, is refreshing. It seemed to me that the few solitary figures whom I passed on the almost empty road had a different look on their faces from the people I had grown accustomed to, and were a different race. The scent of birch and the light tinkle of streams filled the air all the forenoon, making it something different from ordinary air, something along with which one inhaled the fine essence of the free things growing round about: there was in it also a tincture of rock.

All the morning the air was warm and light, but towards one o'clock huge clouds began to collect to the south among the mountain crests; they overtook me; the sky darkened for the first time since I had set out from Edinburgh; and the atmosphere grew sick and heavy, with a faint touch of wetness. By the time I reached Kingussie, a summer holiday resort among the Cairngorms, the sun had made a deep cleft among the clouds again, and the main street was like a long empty baking oven. After enquiring in a tobacco shop which was the most reasonably cheap hotel, I went there for lunch and found the large dining-room already filled, and pretty dark-haired Highland waitresses flying from table to table. There seemed to be a great number of Glasgow-like ladies of late middle age in the place, with faces of formidable determination, who sailed into the room like miniature battleships, and bore down on their chosen tables as if they were enemies to be ruthlessly broached. These matrons had something of the air of invaders, too, and seemed conscious that here they were in foreign waters, but also that, as they had paid for these seas by private agreement, their presence was perfectly lawful. In their faces was that unscrupulous determination to enjoy themselves which is so common in people on the verge of old age, when the capacity for pleasure in outward things is about to shrink for ever. They flung themselves on their food with a greed which was touching and quite unconscious, and drove the waitresses as hard as they could, as if they took pleasure in setting this covey of pretty young girls in a ceaseless flurry of movement at their bidding. In such ways they enjoyed themselves so openly and scandalously that they made the younger people in the room look quiet and dejected. This demonstration, I felt, was probably repeated at every meal held in the huge dining-room. The men who attended these ladies were somewhat subdued. After the meal was over I found most of them in the lounge having a quiet smoke. There was one incident during lunch. Three severe middle-aged ladies entered and sat down at a table: they looked like schoolteachers. In a little while they began to fidget, and as this had no effect audibly complained. A waitress stopped apologetically at their table and spoke to them. They replied sharply and in unison, and a few minutes later left with loud complaints. I felt that I had seen a representative sample of Scottish hotel life, and resumed my journey.

When I stepped into my car the sky had darkened again and the air in my face was cool and wet. The mountains had shrunk, and their sides were inky-blue against the greyish-blue of the thunder clouds. Presently large drops began to fall, and I could hear a faint rumble of thunder behind the wall of hills. I drove on for a little, enjoying the rain in my face. Then with a long leap the thunder jumped the hills and seemed to be all around me. The rain beat down as if shot from the clouds in liquid bullets which fell with such force that they rebounded several inches from the road. I stopped the car, got out, and hurriedly pushed forward and secured the hood. The peals of thunder were coming fast now, and every one of them was flung about between the mountain peaks for quite a long time, producing an effect of a bombardment from every side. During my short stop a score of cars seemed to have passed me, racing at top speed to get out of the thunder zone. I had not noticed more than three or four on the whole route up to then; but now the road seemed to be alive, and the black glistening shapes rushing past one after another reminded me of a furious host of cockroaches scuttling away at some disturbance. I got into the car again and drove on. Suddenly, as I got up speed, the hood flew back over my head again, and the rain poured down solidly into the car. I stopped, got out, hauled forward the hood once more and firmly screwed it down. Then I settled myself in my seat and pressed the self-starter. Nothing happened; for the first time since I had begun my journey the little car refused to act. The thunder was louder than ever; cars were now racing past in hundreds; I got out in exasperation and began to tinker with the plugs, without knowing much about them. The car looked extraordinarily forsaken amid the pouring din, but the thunder was gradually rolling away to the north; I had seen only one or two flashes of lightning. Suddenly the storm was over and I was standing in a thin gentle rain, which did not seem so much to fall as to settle down in small feathery drops. The air was saturated with odours that rose all round in such a thick cloud that I felt I could almost touch it. The car stood contentedly by the side of the road. I got in, somewhat drenched, and pressed the self-starter. The engine responded at once.

I drove on through gentle rain which steadily grew thinner till it faded to a mere veil, a nothing; and in an hour's time I was able to unscrew the hood again and drive in the open air. Gradually the hills sank, fir-woods enclosed me on both sides, big country houses with winding red gravel drives appeared, then farms, and presently as I drove along a long straight road I found myself on a crest with the sea before me and far away the mountain peaks of Caithness. The sky was still covered by a thin curtain of cloud, but the light was perfectly limpid and pure; and outlined in it everything, far and near, was both soft and distinct, almost colourless and quite without shadow. The sea looked as clear as a great rain-pool and at the horizon ran away without a break into the sky.

As I drove down into Inverness I passed a by-road marked Culloden, but remembering my lack of instinct for battlefields I held straight on. Inverness gave me the impression I have always had on visiting it; that is, of being inconveniently crowded with vehicles of all kinds, most of them stationary. I reached it about five o'clock and asked the first man I met where I could get tea. He directed me to a luxurious tea-room somewhat in the Princes Street style, but in better taste and with fewer subdued lights, where a great number of young people, all of them startlingly good-looking, were sitting. In my dusty and oily state I felt disinclined to intrude into such a place, but I did not want to go out again and search for another, and to see so many handsome people in one room was a pleasure which I had not had for a long time. Also I wanted to inhale the atmosphere of Highland life at first in this qualified solution before I came to the real thing, which I hoped to find in my later journeyings.

Even in that little bourgeois tea-room in Inverness I felt that I was in a different land from the one I had been wandering through till then. It is difficult to say why I should have felt this. My first impression was of something absent from the atmosphere, something to which I had become used in the tea-rooms of Edinburgh and Glasgow, and which I thought of as a sort of charged thundery heaviness composed of unresolved desire from which the lightning of an aggressive or a provocative glance might flash at any moment. The tea-room was furnished with subdued lights in the Lowland style, it was true, but they did not have the effect for which they were designed, that is to create a vague sensuous twilight in which the floating desire of a Calvinistic people might unfold in safety, making a profit for the proprietor. This device, which must be as old as venereal science itself, though undiscovered and unpopularised by the Scottish tea-room proprietor until less than a century ago, simply did not work here; for the young men and women sat about like a well-bred company in a drawing-room where the blinds had been lowered to keep out the glare. There was in this atmosphere a strange lack of insistence, after Glasgow and Edinburgh, something contained and yet free, detached and yet spontaneous, which seemed so impervious to all desire to draw attention to itself that it conveyed a faint sense of defeat. I suddenly remembered a very strong impression I had had one still summer day in Monte Carlo during the weeks when the Casino was shut. The gardens were deserted, but on the benches a few constant visitors were idly sitting in the sun, visibly glad that they had found a refuge in that emptiness from the congested hell of gambling. As I sat watching these little groups of released souls Blake's lines came into my mind:

> 'And though all eternity
> I forgive you, you forgive me.'

I felt that I had strayed into a curious modern version of the isle of Avilion

> 'Where falleth neither sleet nor snow nor any rain,'

and I had somewhat the same feeling, though less intensely, in that little tea-room in Inverness. I was to have it more strongly later on, when I reached the Western Highlands. There Avilion is overrun by tourists in kilts, but I always felt that underneath these decorations the old life went on unchanged or almost unchanged, though the tourist could on more see it than he could see a dream.

I wanted to spend the night in a smaller town than Inverness, so I turned the nose of the car westwards towards Beauly. It was a clear evening full of watery lights, and the surface of the long narrow firth along whose south bank the car ran had the full smoothness of water continuously flowing over a sluice. The black road glistened, and drops were still falling from the thick woolly branches of the firs, as if they were trying already to blot out a little of the summer. The houses and fields at the opposite side of the strait had the peculiar teasing intimacy of things which are both near and inaccessible, reawakening in my mind one of the most persistent illusions of childhood: that everything can be easily reached, no matter what obstacles may lie between one and it. In the wet light the near bank, the far one and the firth itself seemed to flow past with the transparent motion of water. Presently a thin soft rain began to fall, enhancing still more of the watery softness of the landscape, the firth fell behind, and the road wound through wooded inland country.

It was still raining when I reached Beauly and found myself once more in a hotel. In this little town the pleasant sensations which I had begun to feel in Inverness grew stronger, and crystallised into a sense of having a great deal of time and space to do what I liked with, a common feeling in the Highlands. The room I was shown into was large and bright, and the main street on to which it looked out was about six times the width of an ordinary street, resembling more than anything else a continental market square set down in the country, with a few low houses to define with studied carelessness its outline. Why this street should have been built on such spacious lines I don't know: probably it is used or was once used as a weekly market for the farming community round about; in any case the effect is very pleasant. At the end of this wide street, abutting into it and producing still more convincingly the impression of a square, is a low red church which, I found out from the guide-book 'was founded in 1230 by Sir John Basset of Lovat for Cistercians from Val des Choux near Chatillon-sur-Seine' and was 'handed over at the Reformation to the 6th Lord Lovat, whose descendants forfeited the estates.' Probably the presence of this church determined the shape of the street which stretches in front of its gates, and makes it still look, in spite of its breadth, exactly what it ought to be. I spent a pleasant hour after the rain had stopped in wandering through the church and the churchyard looking at the tombs of the Clan of Mackenzie, and following from the inscriptions the moral fortune of families through three or four centuries, an occupation which gives existence a quietude and simplicity which it certainly does not have in reality.

❊   ❊   ❊

It was through a perfectly waste area of the Highlands that I drove next day on my way to Ullapool on the West Coast. A soft rain had set in and it accompanied me for the whole breadth of Scotland. After the first stretch of pleasant green wooded country that lies inland from Beauly the landscape grew more and more wild. All that

I could see of it was the little circle of visibility, a circle with a diameter of about half a mile, that travelled on with me. As the road mounted the rain thickened into low clouds – cold, clammy, and indeterminate shapes that seemed to rotate slowly in a circular plateau hemmed in by peaks which I could not see but only feel by a sixth sense. I stopped the car once or twice to get relief from the peculiarly lonely and foolish sound that it made in this amorphous solitude; and then a silence so oppressive set in that I felt that I could almost hear the rubbing of the clouds against the wet grass and rock and heather. It was as if a vast hand were clumsily pressing down this silence; the density of the clouds kneading everything together with a soft enclosing movement. Heavy drops lay on every blade of grass like a cold sweat, and yet the little circle of visibility remained, as though a pocket of light had slipped down here and were continuously bracing itself and making a fragile vault. In that circle blunt-looking rocks appeared and disappeared now and then, producing an effect as abrupt as if they were living things that had stepped out of the cloud and stepped back again. But except for them there was nothing but the black glistening road, the tangled heather, and the perpetual almost inaudible drip-dripping of the bodiless rain, falling slowly from just overhead.

After a long but busy imprisonment in this circle (for the car was running quite well), I saw with relief that I was going downwards; the clouds slowly settled a little higher against the invisible hills; and soon I was passing bright green larch woods, lodge gates appeared, and one or two figures, apparently bent on errands of their own, materialised on the road. Presently, looking downwards, I found that the car was running high above Loch Broom. The drip-drop of the rain in the woods gave a peculiar secrecy to this new landscape, and seemed to make even the clear waters of the loch more immobile, so that I felt they would lie there without a ripple until something unimaginable happened. The air was drenched in the wet scent of larch and fir; the road wound up and down through woods so bright that they seemed new-made; and it was almost a shock when I caught sight of the white walls and black roofs of Ullapool at a sudden bend, for they seemed to have no relation to the green watery world through which I was still passing. The town looked like a woodcut hung in a garden bower. I found when I reached it that it was a very pleasant little place.

It was only one o'clock when I arrived, but as there seemed no prospect that the rain would stop I decided to stay for the day. The hotel was full, mostly of English people, and I should have had the sense to change from my oily and mud-stained flannels before I went into the dining-room. However, I was hungry and in my own country, and still so much under the influence of the scenes I had passed through that for quite a long time I could not understand the glares that greeted me from the surrounding tables. I found out later in the afternoon that a code of etiquette had been established in the hotel by the southern visitors, and that I had unwittingly violated it. The Scottish boarders, I discovered, had obsequiously adopted it, and no doubt I would have adopted it too had I stayed long enough; for once a tone is set in any place one requires almost a dash of moral perversity not to fall in with it. A part of the code in this particular hotel, I found out by the evening, was to meet in the drawing room before dinner for sherry or cocktails; and this convention was so inviolable that even those among the Scottish contingent who were teetotallers piously attended the ceremony. By this time, having changed my clothes and proved myself amenable in other ways, I had been forgiven and even invited to take a hand at bridge. But one stout and gruff old gentleman with a public-school tie and a kilt was still not quite reconciled, and in a timid way, for I fancy he was quite kind-hearted, did his best to snub me.

I am always at a loss when I find myself among public-school boys, old or young, and one of the most disconcerting experiences I have ever had happened one Saturday at Twickenham, when I chanced to plunge right into a cloud of them in my wish to see a Rugby International between England and Wales. The best way in which I can describe my sensations is that I felt myself in the centre of an overwhelming unanimity the terms of which I could account for by no conceivable exercise of my mind, a unanimity which found expression in saying at every moment exactly the right thing. I was immensely impressed, somewhat downcast, and quite astonished by this mechanical perfection of response, this unquestioning assurance that the game of life can be played only in one way, and that that way is known to everyone who has been to public school. There were public-school girls there too, for one of them kept shouting 'Go through him, Smith' to one of the English three-quarters whenever he was tackled by a Welshman; and this too, surprisingly enough, turned out to be the right thing to say. It is the ability to say such things as 'Go through him, Smith', 'Well played, sir', or 'Ramsay MacDonald is a fine fellah' at the right moment that creates the tone I have been trying to give some idea of, and I have described my own inability to cope with it because I feel sure that that is shared by the majority of Highlanders, who have never been to public schools and do not know whether they are saying the right thing or not. 'The gillie is so nice' was the most popular of these sentiments in the North; at least I heard it in all the Highland hotels I stopped at, uttered in every case by middle-aged Englishwomen. As a sentiment it was understandable enough, for the Highlanders are a polite people; but most of the rest of the conversations over the cocktails was quite incomprehensible to me, and when a remark was accepted as peculiarly right I honestly could not tell why.

This habit of the English upper middle-classes of immediately establishing a code of manners whenever a few of them are gathered together, and of requiring everybody else to subscribe to it, is very queer. A Scotsman, in spite of his angularity of character, will adapt himself to the customs of any foreign country he may be in, and try to fit himself into the picture out of a feeling of propriety. But there is a type of Englishman (and Englishwoman) who reacts in exactly the opposite way, and it is impossible to say whether he does it out of arrogance, or of uneasiness, or of a mixture of both, or of a mere mechanical response to habit. From the piety with which these sherry and cocktail ceremonies were observed one might have thought that behind them was a sacred idea, such as the greatness of the British Empire; but there seemed to be a faint tinge of anxiety in them too, as if something were threatened and these harmless drinks washed the invisible danger away. I became aware of an extraordinary watchfulness; it may have been merely that those English people assembled fortuitously in a strange hotel did not know each other's addresses and clubs. But there was also that nervously maintained unanimity; and one felt that if it were shattered something terrible, or at least extremely unedifying, would happen, something almost like an exposure of nakedness. I felt relieved when the cocktails were safely drunk and I could retire to my solitary table.

In the afternoon I went for a stroll through the soft rain. The streets lay empty in their wet whiteness. On the dripping pier a young Highlander with a waterproof apron tied round his kilt was waiting beside a motor-boat. The waters of the loch were quite smooth. I walked up and down the pier for some time until I found a run of wooden steps leading down to an underground gallery almost level with the sea. There, protected from the rain, I walked about for a long time, listening to the drip of the water from the planks overhead and the murmur of the tide as it slugglishly flowed round the rotting piles. Innumerable star-fish, living and dead, were glued to the glistening black baulks, and shoals of little fishes skimmed over them every now and then as heedlessly as if they belonged to a different world. The water dripped, filling the little gallery with tiny echoes that sounded like shivering glass. I do not know why, but soft rain in the Highlands makes them seem twice as remote, so that one cannot imagine they are within reach of anywhere. A boy and a young woman presently appeared with a collection of suit-cases and got into the motor-boat along with the young Highlander. The engine started and in few minutes they had all been swallowed up in the mist.

I went to bed early to escape a threatened hand at bridge. When I tried to start the car next morning I could make nothing of it. A young mechanic belonging to the hotel tinkered gravely with the plugs for a while. The garage attendants in the Lowlands had always shown a sympathetic, humorous interest in my conveyance; but this young Highlander treated it with as much respectful concern as if it had been a Rolls-Royce, and did not give the faintest sign that he saw its comic possibilities. He was not really any kinder than the Lowland mechanics had been, but he showed a different consideration for my feelings, or rather for what I might conceivably have felt; for the garage happened to be filled with a dozen cars, all of which looked splendid beside mine, and it would have been easy for any hard-pressed garage hand to regard my engine troubles with impatience. But nothing of the kind happened, and I felt again that I was in a different country.

Up to Ullapool I had been driving over good and moderately level roads. From now on I was to find myself climbing up and down mountain sides over surfaces little better than a cart-track.

There must have been something wrong with the plugs, as the young mechanic had said; at any rate I noticed that on the first gradient the car seemed to be complaining more than usual. Then I came to a long, rough, steep rise. I got up full speed and covered a little stretch of it in third gear, then switched to second, and finally to first. The car went more and more slowly, seemed to waver for a moment, and stopped. I was only two-thirds up the hill, hanging precariously at what seemed to me an angle of forty-five degrees. I started the engine again, speeded it up until it roared, slipped the clutch into first gear, jerked the car up a few yards, and then rested it. In this way, by a series of jerks, I got the car up to the top, hoping that this was the worst hill I would have to climb. About a dozen powerful easy-moving cars from the hotel passed me while I was in the middle of this grass-hopper act. My hopes that I had survived the worst, however, were soon dashed; for I presently found myself jerking up a still worse mountain. If I had known more about the car I might have saved myself a great deal of distress for the next few days, for I am certain that there must have been something wrong with the plugs. As it was I was doomed to jerk myself up all the hill roads of the western and northern Highlands from Ullapool to Tongue, and sweat and curse among the strangest and most magnificent scenery. At one point in this curious journey I jerked off without knowing it a suit-case containing all my clothes; the engine was making too much noise for anything else to be heard. But I shall come to that later; and this is all I intend to say about my troubles with the car. They filled my mind in the most curious way, nevertheless, creating a sort of little private hell from which I looked like Dives on to the heavenly beauty of the north-western Highland mountains.

The thing which impresses me most about the wild scenery in this part of the Highlands is its strangeness. Geologists give the explanation that the mountains here consist of two formations which have piled up in confusion, so that the summits belonging to one of them sometimes burst through the surface of the other. One's actual impression of these peaks is that they do not belong to the world we know at all, but to a much older one; I had this feeling before I knew the geological explanation of it. The ordinary sensations which mountains arouse do not fit these extraordinary rock shapes; and yet they are not terrifying in any way, but merely strange beyond the power of the mind to fathom. Part of their strangeness may, no doubt, be explained by the abruptness with which they start up out of places which seem to have no connection with them. The movement of wild mountain scenery is generally a tossing movement as of waves. On the surface the scenery of West Sutherlandshire has this tossing movement, but the summits of which I have been speaking rise out of these billows like rocks out of a sea and seem to have a different consistency and to belong to a different order. They are bold and regular and yet unexpected in their shape, as if they were the result of a wild kind of geometry. One sees huge cones with their tops smoothly sliced off to form a circular plateau, gigantic pyramids, and even shapes that seem top-heavy, so that one cannot understand on what principle they remain upright. Round about these isolated peaks rools in large even swells a sea of lower mountains, from whose shapes one can perceive that they have been moulded by time, for they have its rise and fall and its continuity of rhythm. But these older cones and pyramids seem to have no connection with time at all; they are unearthly not in any vague but in a quite solid sense, like blocks of an unknown world scattered blindly over a familiar one. The thoughts they evoke are neither heavenly nor terrifying, but have a sort of objective strangeness and give one the same feeling one might have if one could have a glimpse of an eternal world, such as the world of mathematics, which had no relation to our human feelings, but was composed of certain shapes which existed in complete changeless autonomy.

Having jerked myself up several hills I landed at last at Kylesku Ferry, where I found I had to wait three hours for the tide. By this time the sun had come out again and the sea in the little inland loch was bright blue against the purplish-grey mountains. I found that I had done six miles an hour and that my right arm was sore with changing gears and pulling the brake. When I arrived I found a family of Australians, a father and two daughters, who had been at the hotel in Ullapool, and they told me that they too had been quite overawed by the cocktail ceremony, so that they had not dared to open their mouths. They told me also that they found it much easier to talk to people in Scotland than in England. They had begun their holiday in London, but during the fortnight they had stayed in a hotel where they had not spoken to a single human being except for the hotel servants. We talked of this and of the Highland deer forests, one of which took up all the hills and valleys we were looking at. With the incoming tide jelly-fishes in great numbers began to float past the little point where we sat. Except for two or three huts beside the ferry there was not a human habitation in sight. Nor in all the expanse of tree-less deer forest could I see a single movement to betray the presence of a living creature.

North from Kylesku I escaped the steep hills for a time, and the landscape in general became lower and more ordinary. As I reached the sea the car wound in and out among rocky gorges for a time. Then I suddenly found myself looking down on a bay filled with small rocky islets, and far beyond them, on the horizon, the long misty outline of Lewis. I stopped for a while to enjoy the unexpectedness of the sight, for these little islets had the strangeness which I had felt in the high geometrical peaks, and seemed to belong to the same world, reproducing it on a small scale. Whether I was right in thinking this, I do not know; it is difficult to tell which world one is in as one passes through these landscapes, especially if, like myself, one has little or no knowledge of geology. Or that little drove of islands – they seem to be nothing but rock, and yet an odd tree or two grew from them – may have belonged to a private world of their own. All I know is that they seemed as remote from human life as the huge peaks, and as impervious to all the sentimental associations which nature usually evokes in one's mind. There were one or two cottages on the shore overlooking this tiny archipelago, and smoke was rising from their chimneys in the calm evening air, a sight which for no reason I know of always awakens in me a host of sentimental memories; but here it awakened none at all; the impression of strangeness given by the little islands was too strong.

One could imagine oneself being so deeply influenced by this scenery, if one lived close to it for a long time, that one's most simple feelings about human life would be changed. I think something of this kind must have happened in the little town of Scourie, to which I presently came. In its very formation it seems to be in two minds, like the landscape around it. The houses that make it up are planted at the most abrupt intervals; one finds two or three quite close together, then a few fields, another house, fields again, a hotel on a little rise, a row of houses beyond it that have the air of belonging to a suburban avenue, a farm to one side, and at a good distance from all these, as if it existed in itself, a pier and harbour at the head of a neat and narrow little firth. Not very far from the pier, and away from the village, is a beautiful old house such as one would expect to find in the more cultivated parts of the Borders, and immediately behind it rises a wild hill of bare rippling rock. Beyond the hotel, at a little distance, rises another hill of the same rippling black rock, at whose foot lies a loch, black as ink, and by its look very deep. The village shop adjoins the hotel, and a group of well-set-up young men were standing talking and laughing in front of it when I arrived. It was Saturday evening.

The hotel was comfortably filled with English anglers, a peaceful set of men whose dreamy voices filled the dining-room with dim and watery reminiscences, in which one could hear the lapping of lake water and the day-long purling of streams. They drank a great deal of beer in a quiet hypnotic way, and their voices never rose and never stopped, but babbled on in the most tranquil way imaginable, so that one soon began to feel sleepy. I went for a walk along a cart-track leading up to one of the hills, from which I could look down into the black loch. The ripples running under the surface of the hill looked exactly like those that break the smoothness of a big wave. The light was quite clear, though it was ten o'clock, and I had definitely for the first time the feeling of being in the real north. I turned back again, for the blackness of the loch was a little frightening, wandered past one or two houses, crossed a foot-bridge over a little stream lined with tall irises, passed through a green field, and found myself at the pier, where a young man and a young woman were washing nets. The youths who had been standing outside the shop were dispersing in groups along the roads, and I returned to the hotel and to my bed.

❊   ❊   ❊

The evening I spent at Melvich was the pleasantest of all my journey. The hotel was unexpectedly comfortable and well-run, and the walls were quite without the usual bleeding array of pictured carcasses. I had actually dreamt of a frieze of such walls one night in a hotel unusually well furnished with them; so that the relief with which I saw the clean walls of the Melvich Hotel, though it may seem excessive, was quite understandable to myself. I arrived long after dinner was over, but the lady who ran the place provided me with a better meal – cold chicken and dessert – than I had had in any of the other hotels. As I had only a drive of a dozen miles over a fairly level and good road next day, and this evening solemnised the end of my jerks, I decided to allow myself a bottle of wine, and was provided with a very good one. When I finished my dinner about half-past nine the light was still perfectly clear, so I went for a walk past the straggling houses of the little village until I came to the shore. The outlines of the Orkney hills were still distinct, and the evening had that perfect tranquillity which I have always associated for some reason with Sunday evenings, when the very quality of the light seems different. I wandered about the shore for some time in this strangely distinct and yet dream-like clarity. I stayed there until about eleven o'clock; watched the shadows of the cliffs motionlessly reflected in the sea, the Orkney hills blown like bubbles against the colourless sky, the horse and cattle near-by cropping the grass – the tearing of their teeth and the pounding of their hooves sounding strangely loud in that stillness and at that hour – and a few silent couples scattered here and there over the soft turf along the cliff-tops. When I turned in the outline of everything had become softer, but was still perfectly clear, and the windows of the houses gleamed brightly, appearing still to hold the fullness of the light after it had faded from the walls. At twelve o'clock as I was going to bed I looked out through the window of my room and saw some horses in a field still moving about restlessly in the light, and occasionally pawing the ground with their hooves. The outline of the Orkneys had almost faded away, and was like a dark breath on the horizon.

JAMES CAMPBELL

❋   ❋   ❋

Born in Glasgow in 1951, James Campbell was editor of the New Edinburgh Review *between 1978 and 1982. His short stories, reviews, and essays have appeared in numerous publications on both sides of the Atlantic. He now works at the* Times Literary Supplement *and lives in London.*

Campbell has long had an interest in alternative lifestyles, especially the literature of the Beats. Among his books are Talking at the Gates: A Life of James Baldwin; Paris Interzone: Richard Wright, Lolita, Boris Vian, and Others on the Left Bank, 1946-60 *and, most recently,* This Is the Beat Generation: New York – San Francisco – Paris. *He also edited* The Picador Book of Blues and Jazz.

In Invisible Country, *Campbell returns to his native Scotland, inspired by – but not following in – the footsteps of fellow traveller and fellow Scot, Edwin Muir. The result is a 'record of a journey from one end of Scotland to the other, during which I stopped in as many places as was feasible, without setting myself the impossible task of being comprehensive, reporting on encounters with places and people ... ' In this selection he visits the area around Kildonan in Sutherland, where the past and the present seem very much alike.*

❋   ❋   ❋

Stories in Stone

from INVISIBLE COUNTRY:
A JOURNEY THROUGH SCOTLAND

The Inverness to Thurso train picked me up at Helmsdale at nine minutes past nine in the morning.

Twenty miles on through the Strath of Kildonan, the train made a sharp turn to the right, then continued to Thurso. I was

122

going to Bettyhill, which was north-west of there, and so had to disembark at Kinbrace and hope for a lift to take me thirty miles on. The train would stop at Kinbrace only by special arrangement with the guard, and so I sought him out once we started and he assured me that the engine would pause long enough for me to step down.

It was a weirdly beautiful journey through the heights of Kildonan, and once again I gladly would have extended it long beyond the time it lasted. Vestiges of steadings and lazybeds lay as bumps in the land along the length of the glen, here and there betrayed only by changes of shading in the earth. Very occasionally, a slightly grander house showed signs of continued habitation.

Sitting opposite was an old man with white hair and a weather-coloured face, his two walking sticks hooked on to the edge of the table which separated us. I made some remark on the landscape and he nodded his head in agreement, attaching his eyes to me. He was a Strath Naver man, who had lived there all his life, and his business was crofting. The night before he had been to Inverness and this morning he was travelling to Thurso to consult with a relative on some business matter. He lifted one of his walking sticks and, smiling for the first time, shook it at me.

'It's not as easy as it used to be.'

He asked why I was travelling this way and I mentioned an interest in the Clearances.

'Have you seen the museum at Bettyhill?'

'No, but I know about it and will see it when I'm there.'

'They should close it down, that's what they should do with it!'

'Why do you say that?'

'Because evictions is a thing of the past and they should leave them there. It's all finished with now and there's no use in talking about it all the time – evictions, evictions, evictions!'

I replied, somewhat feebly, that I could see no point in forgetting about it either.

'That's what they *should* do, forget about it. We have good proprietors up here now, that's the thing that matters, not the past, the past!'

For the remainder of the journey we talked about other things and then, as the train approached Kinbrace, I said goodbye and went to stand by the door. The train slowed and finally paused. I pulled down the window but the platform was not in sight and it was a long way to the ground, so I waited.

Then I heard a cry which was plainly meant for me:

'KIN – BRA – ACE!'

Since it was clear that the train was going to move no further along the track, there was only one thing to do if I was not to end up in Thurso. I opened the door, dropped my bag about ten feet to the ground, and then, to the amusement of the passengers left behind in the carriage, jumped after it, stumbling and almost falling over as I hit the ground. When I stood up nothing was sprained. A second later, the train pulled off, revealing the platform on the other side.

A postman was lifting up the mailbag from the platform where it had been dropped. From underneath his cocked hat, he regarded me sternly, standing in the sidings among weeds and nettles, picking up my own bag.

'You could've broke yer bloody neck, boy!' he called across the rails, shaking his head. 'If it was me was the guard I'd come over there and break it for you!'

I thanked him for his concern, and, feeling slightly daunted by my welcomes, walked out of the station on to the road.

I had been warned by the manager of the Bridge Hotel that it was a quiet road. It was so quiet that after half an hour I hadn't seen a car. The first one to pass had fishing rods on the roof-rack and German registration plates. The driver and his companion regarded me coolly and disappeared.

I thought of walking, but it would have been hopeless. The temperature was high in the seventies, and with my bag, not a backpack but one with handles, I could have advanced no more than a mile or two.

To my left, across a burn, the fields ran upwards in a slight rise which the map told me was Tor na Craoibhe. On my left side, Tor du. Enveloped by earth and sky, a landscape of ineffable beauty and authority, I felt more lonely than at any time since I started out. I was conscious of only one sound: the irregular croaking of a frog, coming from the direction of a lazy burn guarding Tor na Craoibhe. At first I could not make out what it was, until I heard it again, and then again. Finally, I began to look for it, for company, but if I got close it stopped croaking. So I went back to the roadside, and after a few seconds heard it again, and had to be content with that.

It was at least another half-hour before a second vehicle appeared on the road. It was a red Land Rover – the post van. Somewhat hopelessly, I stuck out my thumb and met the eyes of the postman, and to my surprise he pulled to a halt and climbed out of his cabin.

'Didna know you was comin' wi' me, boy,' he said, and opened the back door of his van to let me in.

PAUL THEROUX

❊   ❊   ❊

One could say that Paul Theroux has lived a charmed life. After graduating from university in 1963, he travelled to Italy and then Africa. He worked as a Peace Corps teacher in Malawi and lectured at Makerere University in Uganda. In 1968 he joined the University of Singapore and taught in the English department for three years. At the same time he was publishing short stories and novels. In the early 1970s he moved with his wife and children to Dorset, where he wrote Saint Jack *and then moved to London. He lived in Britain for 17 years.*

Among his many books include Picture Palace, *which won the 1978 Whitbread Literary Award;* The Mosquito Coast, *made into a feature film starring Harrison Ford;* Riding the Iron Rooster *(1988 Thomas Cook Travel Book Award);* The Pillars of Hercules; The Great Railway Bazaar; The Old Patagonian Express *and* Sunrise with Seamonsters. *His most recent collection is* Fresh Air Fiend: Travel Writings 1985-2000.

Theroux has always been among the most prickly and opinionated of travel writers. He writes what he sees. In The Flyer to Cape Wrath, *we find him in an uncharacteristically charitable mood.*

❊   ❊   ❊

The Flyer to Cape Wrath

from **THE KINGDOM BY THE SEA:**
A JOURNEY AROUND GREAT BRITAIN

My Blue Guide's description of the northwest coast of Scotland suggested a setting that was straight out of Dracula or The Mountains of Madness. 'The road crosses a strange and forbidding mountain wilderness,' it began, 'of sombre rock-strewn glens, perched glacial boulders, and black lochs.' And then, 'after 8m. of lonely moor and dark bog ... the road from the ferry's w. end to Cape Wrath crosses a bleak moor called The Parph, once notorious for its wolves,' and at last, 'the road rises across a desolate moor ... '

It made me want to set off at once. It seemed the perfect antidote to the Presbyterian monotony of Dingwall. If the guidebook's description was accurate, it would be like traveling to the end of the world – in any case, the British world. Cape Wrath was not merely remote – the ultimate coastline – it was also such a neglected place and reputedly so empty that the method for getting there had not changed for eighty years or more. Baedeker's *Great Britain* for 1906 said, 'From Lairg, mail-cart routes diverge in various directions, by means of which the highly picturesque country to the W. and N.W. ... may be conveniently explored ... '

At Dingwall Station I asked the best way to Cape Wrath.

'Get the post bus at Lairg,' Mr. MacNichols said.

In other words, the mail cart. There was no train, there was no bus, there was hardly a road – it was paved the width of a wagon for fifty-six miles. There were people who still called the post bus 'the flyer', as they called tenant farms 'crofts' and porridge 'crowdie'.

The train to Lairg left Dingwall and passed along the edge of Cromarty Firth, which at this state of the tide was shallow water seeping into the mudflats. Not long before, the railway line was to have been shut down, but it had been reprieved. It passed along the bleakest, boggiest part of Caithness, where the roads were often bad, and in winter it was an essential service. But Mr. MacNichols had confided to me that in the off season there were sometimes only three or four people on board.

To save money on the line, some of the stations had been closed. The ruined, boarded-up station building at Alness resembled many I had seen in Ulster. A large aluminum smelter had just closed at Invergordon – nine hundred more people out of work and another building left to rot. Decrepitude was decrepitude – the fury of terrorists was indistinguishable from the willfulness of budget-cutters and accountants.

Beyond the village of Fearn there were farms and fields of a classic kind: long vistas over the low hills, quiet houses, and smooth fields of fat sheep. There were steeples under the soft gray sky at Tain – the Tolbooth, with a conical spire and turrets, and a church spire like a freshly sharpened pencil. Pink and purple lupins shook on the station platform.

People used this train for shopping, travelling to a place like Tain from miles up the line. Two ladies were sitting next to me. They were Mrs. Allchin and Mrs. MacFee. They were discussing the butcher.

'Duncan is very obliging,' Mrs. Allchin said. 'We often give him a lift on stormy days.'

'I think it's an ideal place, Tain,' Mrs. MacFee said.

Mrs. MacFee had two large bags of groceries, and she had also managed to find a packet of 'toe-spacers' at the chemist's shop. It eased her mind to know that she had these for pedicures and nail-varnishing. Kenneth had mentioned a dinner-dance at the Lodge, and she did not want to fuss at the last minute.

Mrs. Allchin had been very lucky in Tain. Ian's lad, wee Colum, was having a birthday, and she had found a box of something called 'indoor fireworks'. Apparently, you just cleared a space on the table and set them off. Apparently, they were perfectly safe. Chinese.

'What won't they think of next,' Mrs. MacFee said.

But Mrs. Allchin's mind was elsewhere. The indoor fireworks reminded her that she was chain-smoking again. She often chain-smoked in trains. It worried her, like nail-biting.

'I dinna drink, at any rate,' Mrs. Allchin said.

We travelled inland, toward the hills at Culrain, which had a ruined look. And the roof was off the station at Invershin. Some other stations had clearly been sold off to be turned into common bungalows or holiday homes. There were cabbages growing where the platform had been.

We went through Acharry Glen – the River Shin on the left. I had settled down to watch the mountains passing, but soon we came to Lairg and I had to get out.

There was something very disconcerting about leaving a train in the middle of nowhere. It was all activity and warm upholstery, and then the clang of a carriage door and the train pulled out and left me in a sort of pine-scented silence. Lairg Station was two miles from Lairg, but even Lairg was nowhere.

I saw a man throwing mailbags and bundles of newspapers into the back of an old-fashioned vehicle. It was a cutdown version of a bus, about the size of a hearse. Still the man went on loading it with the bags and bundles the train had left.

I cleared my throat. He looked up. I said I was going to Durness on the post bus.

'This is the post bus,' he said. 'We can leave as soon as I get these bags loaded.'

His name was Michael Mathers. He pronounced it 'Maithers'. His accent was not Scottish. It was fairly Gaelic and very Scandinavian, a soft Norse whirr in every syllable. Later, I discovered that everyone in his part of Sutherland had the same accent, a legacy of the Vikings. This accent was all that remained of the local dialect, Norn.

We set off for Lairg and picked up more mail and an old couple on their way to Scourie. Michael said that this was a Bedford bus, only ten years old. It had gone 400,000 miles.

'When I took over,' he said, 'we had an Albion. Made in Glasgow. That one went 650,000 miles in fifteen years.'

He had been driving for twenty-one years. He was forty-four and had the solemn, kindly face of a fisherman. He had once tried working on a fishing boat. He said, 'You need a strong stomach for that.' It was cold, it was hard, there wasn't much money. At midnight on a pitching boat, struggling with nets, he would look into the distance and see the lights of Durness: the lucky people indoors. So he had chucked it.

We headed out of Lairg and were almost immediately in a bog. It was a wide dark landscape, with rocks and grass and heather close by, and mountains ahead.

There was no better glimpse into the life of remote Sutherland than through the smeared windows of this eight-seater. The post bus was a lifeline and Mr. Mathers much more than a driver. He not only picked up mail and dropped it off, and ran with it to houses in the rain, and carried scribbled messages from house to house; he also drove along a single-track road for the whole of the way north, which meant he had to stop when a car approached from the opposite direction – eighty or ninety times in a single trip – because the road was only wide enough for one car. He carried milk. He carried newspapers. He carried shapeless bundles labeled *For Graham*.

He stopped the bus at the Reeks, in the middle of a peat field, and with the mist flying sideways he hurried to the door with a pint of milk, the *T.V. Times*, today's *Scotsman*, and a birthday card for Mrs. Campbell. Farther down the road, at Fernside, it was two pints and a *Mirror*, and then a five-minute trot up a muddy path to deliver a junk-mail Sunglasses Special Offer from the Automobile Association (though Mr. Innes was expecting a long-overdue letter from his daughter in Australia), and then a copy of the *Sun* to Hope Cottage, and another favor – fifteen pounds of wet fish in a plastic shopping bag for a householder who had asked for it over at Kinloch. And more newspapers. Such effort and expense to bring people copies of the gutter press! But that was Mr. Mathers' job. And he was never abrupt. Whenever he handed something over, he exchanged a greeting. 'How's your mother feeling?' and 'The sheep are looking well' and 'It feels like rain.'

We came to an unearthly, gigantic landscape along Loch More in the Reay Forest. The fields looked bitter and brown and the loch very cold, and the mountains were vast shrouds of rock. One of these silver mountains was the most beautiful I had so far seen in Britain – a great bulge glittering with cataracts of scree. It looked as if it had just frozen in that carbuncular shape the day before.

'That's Arkle,' Mrs. MacGusty said. She wasn't local. Her accent was amused and tentative, like someone nibbling shortbread, the tones of Morningside – the genteel landlady accent of Edinburgh. 'It's Icelandic, you see.'

What did that mean?

'It's all turned over. These high mountains' – she seemed to be describing babies, her voice was so affectionately savoring the words – 'Ben Stack and Arkle – what should be on the bottom is on the top, they reckon, the geologists. You look at them and you think, "They all look duffrent!" '

Mr. MacGusty said, 'They're also very beg.'

This was Achfary, 'the Duke of Westminster's estate,' Mrs. MacGusty said.

'Does he farm here?' I asked.

'Oh, no. It's an estate. He keeps it for the shooting and the fishing. Prince Charles comes here in a helicopter sometimes, for the shooting. Och! I expect you're a republican!'

We were sitting by the roadside in the post bus as the rain came down. Mr. Mathers was bringing a copy of yesterday's *Express* to a cottage behind a high wall.

I said, 'So it's all gamekeepers here?'

'Aye,' Mr. MacGusty said. 'The duke owns a good butt of Sutherland.' He thought a moment. 'It's the old way of life.' He thought again. 'It's very unfair, in a way.'

It was more a shrug than a protest. But he was resigned. After all, we were talking about feudalism.

The past was accessible here as a present fact. Not only in ducal estates and private game reserves, but also in ancient names. The MacGustys got off the bus at Laxford Bridge. It was a Norse name – *lax* meant salmon (and of course the Yiddish *lox* for smoked salmon was a cognate). Then Mr. Mathers told me how his parents had both been fluent Gaelic speakers and that he spoke it fairly well. And peat-cutting was part of the past, too. The peat was free, but cutting it was backbreaking work. It was cut and left to dry in stacks, so everything depended on good weather. Even present-day crime sounded outdated – sheep rustlers and squatters and poachers.

We drove up the narrow track to Rhiconich. This was actually the coast, a muddled maze of islands and lochs. We went to Kinlochbervie, which was a busy fishing port on a sea loch, dealing in whitefish and lobsters.

We stopped twenty more times. Mr. Mathers did this twice a day on this small windy corner of Scotland. When he stopped and parked, the wind shook the bus and rattled the cottage gates and moaned against the telegraph wires. A pint of milk, a *Scotsman*, and a printed postcard saying *This is to acknowledge your communication of the 13th inst.* to Mrs. Massey at Drumbeg.

'Cape Wrath doesn't mean "angry",' Mr. Mathers said. 'It's from a Norse word that means "turning point". This is where the ships turned south. Sutherland is another Norse name – it was south for them.'

Then he smiled. 'Don't be disillusioned,' he said.

'The weather can be hellish here. In 1952, when I was still at school, we had a January storm. The winds were a hundred and twenty miles an hour – roofs were torn off houses. The Irish ferry was lost that night. It's often bad weather – horrible weather. I pity the lads in those wee fishing boats.'

We came to Durness. He said, 'This is it. There aren't more than three hundred people here. It's the work problem, you see. There's no employment.'

The village was empty, but the wind was a presence – wild gusts flew in from the direction of the Faeroes.

I walked back through the sandy cliffs, among the rabbit holes, to Keoldale and the Cape Wrath Hotel, and had my first good meal for days. There were a number of English anglers at the hotel. They blustered when the national news came on. They were all Tories. They called the Prime Minister 'Maggie'. Her nonsense suited their nonsense. One said he wanted to shoot the man being interviewed, who claimed he had known all along that the Falklands were going to be invaded. 'Too many bloody people giving advice!' Another said that half the Labour Party should be shot for treason. One thing about anglers, though. They went to bed early.

The next day I crossed the Kyle of Durness and walked seven miles to Kearvaig, which was like the end of the earth. But this was Cape Wrath proper and had peaty soil – it was crumbling cliffs and sand at Durness.

I saw a seal take a salmon. People told me that seals did not really eat them – that they just took bites of a fish's shoulders and threw the rest away. But this seal lay on his back with the eight-pound salmon in his mouth, and he tossed his head and snapped his jaws and ate the whole thing.

Then on my way back I saw a flock of sheep crossing a sandbar in the Kyle of Durness. The tide was coming in. The sheep started moving. Soon they were swimming, the big horned sheep in front, the lambs behind, with their noses out of the water. They were North Highland Cheviots. They moved very slowly, for the tide was still rising and they were still far from the bank. Fifteen minutes later the Kyle was filled, there were fewer sheep visible, and then there were none. They had all drowned, about nine of them, under the gray torn sky.

Some fantasies prepare us for reality. The sharp steep Cuillins were like mountains from a storybook – they had a dramatic, fairy-tale strangeness. But Cape Wrath was unimaginable. It was one of those places where, I guessed, every traveller felt like a discoverer who was seeing it for the first time. There are not many such places in the world. I felt I had penetrated a fastness of mountains and moors, after two months of searching, and I had found something new. So even this old, overscrutinized kingdom had a secret patch of coast! I was very happy at Cape Wrath. I even liked its ambiguous name. I did not want to leave.

There were other people in the area: a hard-pressed settlement of sheep farmers and fishermen, and a community of drop-outs making pots and jewelry and quilts at the edge of Balnakeil. There were anglers and campers,too, and every so often a brown plane flew overhead and dropped bombs on one of the Cape Wrath beaches, where the army had a firing range. But the size of the place easily absorbed these people. They were lost in it, and as with all people in a special place, they were secretive and a little suspicious of strangers.

Only the real natives were friendly. They were the toughest Highlanders and they did not match any Scottish stereotype I knew. They did not even have a recognizably Scottish accent. They were like white crows. They were courteous, hospitable, hard-working, and funny. They epitomized what was best in Scotland, the strong cultural pride that was separate from political nationalism. That took confidence. They were independent, too – 'thrawn' was the Lowlands word for their stubborn character. I admired their sense of equality, their disregard for class, and the gentle way they treated their children and animals. They were tolerant and reliable, and none of this was related to the flummery of bagpipes and sporrans and tribalistic blood-and-thunder that Sir Walter Scott had turned into the Highland cult. What I liked most about them was that they were self-sufficient. They were the only people I had seen on the whole coast who were looking after themselves.

It was a shire full of mountains, with spaces between – some valleys and some moors – and each mountain was separate. To describe the landscape it was necessary to describe each mountain, because each one was unique. But the soil was not very good, the sheep were small, the grass thin, and I never walked very far without finding a corpse – loose wool blowing around bones, and the bared teeth of a skull.

'Look,' a shepherd named Stephen said to me on one of these hillsides.

A buzzard-sized bird was circling.

'It's a hooded crow,' Stephen said. 'They're desperate creatures. In a place like this – no shelter, no one around for miles – they find a lamb and peck its eyes out. It's lost, it can't get to its mother, it gets weak. Then the hooded crows – so patient up there – dive down and peck it to pieces. They're a terrible bird.'

He said that it was the predatory crows, not the weather, that killed the lambs. It was a cold place, but not excessively so. In winter there was little snow, though the winds were strong and the easterlies were usually freezing gales. There were always birds in the wind – crows and hawks and comic squawking oystercatchers with long orange bills and singing larks and long-necked shags and stuttering stonechats.

It could be an eerie landscape, especially on a wet day, with all the scattered bones gleaming against the dun-colored cliffs and the wind scraping against the heather. It surprised me that I was happy in a place where there were so few trees – there were none at all here. It was not picturesque and it was practically unphotographable. It was stunningly empty. It looked like a corner of another planet, and at times it seemed diabolical. But I liked it for all these reasons. And more important than these, my chief reason for being happy was that I felt safe here. The landscape was like a fierce-looking monster that offered me protection; being in Cape Wrath was like having a pet dragon.

On one of my walks I met a veterinarian, Doctor Pike, who was making the rounds of the Cape Wrath farms, trying to persuade the farmers to dip their sheep. An ailment called sheep scab had been brought over from Ireland and had endangered some of the flocks.

Doctor Pike was a fluent Gaelic speaker. He was self-assured and well read, and though he did not boast, he did imply a moral superiority in the Highlander – and in the Scots in general – and he suggested that there was something lamentable and decadent in the English.

'Take the colonies,' he said. 'The Scots who went out were very hard-working and idealistic. But for a lot of the English families the colonies were the last resort. They sent the black sheep of the family – the rubbish, the drunkards, the layabouts.'

We were walking around Balnakeil Bay; he was headed for a farmhouse. We passed a shepherd driving a flock of sheep to be shorn.

Doctor Pike said, 'You might take that shepherd to be a fool or a rustic. But most of these shepherds are sensible men. I mean, they read. I go to many of these shepherds' wee cottages and – do you know? – I find lots of books in some of them. They take books with them out on the hillsides.'

We had a good view of the sea – the mouth of the bay was wide. There were no boats out there. I seldom saw boats, at any rate. It was one of the roughest areas on the British coast, and the scarcity of boats added to the feeling of emptiness I felt on shore. It was like the world after a catastrophic bomb.

Doctor Pike was still talking about shepherds. He said, 'There was a man here from Edinburgh. He saw a shepherd in the hills and said how wonderful it was to get so much fresh air and exercise. "But how does it feel to be so far from the center of things?"

'The shepherd stared at him and smiled. "That depends what you mean by the center of things." You see, he felt that it was just a matter of perspective. Who was this city man to say that the shepherd was not at the center of things?'

I told Doctor Pike that I had seen nine sheep drown in the incoming tide at the Kyle of Durness. He said it was a pity but it sometimes happened. Although sheep could swim, the horns of a ram made it hard for the creature to keep its head up, and the lambs were too frail to swim very far. But he said that he loved sheep – he loved working with them.

'They have very keen instincts. They have a wonderful sense for forecasting the weather – they know when a gale is coming. They begin leaving the hills many days before it begins to snow.'

The next day I went with Doctor Pike to Loch Eriboll. It was a sea loch piercing ten miles of Sutherland, and it was deep enough to take the largest ships. In the storms for which this part of

Scotland was notorious, ships found a quiet anchorage here.

'I wanted you to see something,' Doctor Pike said.

We rounded a bend, turning south toward Laid, along the shore of the huge loch.

'Look at this hillside,' he said.

It was a rough, steep slope, covered with small white boulders. Patches of the slope had been plowed, but most of it was covered with glacial rubble and humps, and the grass was blackish and sparse. Some sheep stood on it and looked at us with their characteristic expression of indifference and curiosity. The grazing land was very bad.

'Now look over there, across the loch,' he said.

It was like a different country, a different climate. It was not bouldery – it was soft and green. There were grassy meadows and gentle slopes over there. It was sheltered by the mountains behind it, and pleasant streams ran through it. There were trees over there! There were no houses; there were no sheep.

But this windswept side of the loch – the western shore, on which we stood – was lined with tiny whitewashed cottages. They were surrounded by broken walls and fences and some bushes. And there were gnarled trees, none higher than the cottage eaves. The roofs fitted the cottages in an irregular way, like lopsided caps, and made the cottages pathetic.

'These people once lived over there, on the good side of the loch.They were cleared off the land and moved here. They were crofters then – they're crofters still. They were given the worst land.'

He was talking about the clearances, the evictions by the chiefs and landlords who wanted to cash in on the land. It had taken years, but the Highlands were eventually emptied – that is, the fertile parts. Enormous sheep farms replaced some crofts, and others were turned into playgrounds – grouse moors and baronial estates. This was also a major reason for the tremendous number of Scottish emigrants, dispersed across the world between 1780 and 1860. So what had seemed to me no more than an early chapter in a history of Scotland, or a melodramatic painting by Landseer, was a lingering injustice. The cruelty of the clearances was still remembered, because many people who had been made poor still remained where they had been dumped.

'Is it any wonder that some of them are poachers?' Doctor Pike said.

He was fairly passionate on the subject. He said the land ought to be nationalized and divided into smaller units. The land could be made productive – people would have jobs.

I said he was the first left-wing veterinarian I had ever met. He denied that he was left wing. He said most radicals were devils. Then he said, 'Want to meet one of the victims of the clearances?'

We stopped at a small white cottage near the edge of the loch and were greeted by an old man. This was Davey McKenzie. He wore a tweed hat and a threadbare jacket and loose trousers. His shoes were cracked and broken. He had a healthy face and good color, and he was sinewy. He was about seventy or a bit more. He raised some sheep and he grew vegetables and he was always followed by a black terrier with a pleading face that lay down and snored whenever Mr. McKenzie sat down.

'We can't stay,' Doctor Pike said.

'You'll have a cup of tea,' Mr. McKenzie replied. He had the same Norse whirr in his accent that I had been hearing for days.

We entered the cottage and were introduced to Jessie Stewart, Mr. McKenzie's sister. She was perhaps a year or two younger than he, but she was pale and rather feeble. Doctor Pike whispered to me that she had recently had an operation, and he added, 'She's far from well.'

'Sit down in front of the fire,' she said. 'I'll put the tea on.'

It was the end of June – a few days from July – and yet a fire burned in the cottage hearth, and the wind made the rosebushes scratch at the window.

Doctor Pike said, 'Don't trouble yourself, Mrs. Stewart.'

'It's no trouble,' she said. 'And don't call me Mrs. Stewart. No one calls me that. I'm Jessie.'

The cottage was comfortable but austere – a few potted plants, pictures of children and grandchildren, a calendar from Thurso and some Scottish souvenirs, a glass paperweight showing Arthur's Seat, and a little doll in a tartan kilt.

Doctor Pike said his piece about sheep scab and then turned to me. 'You know you're in the Highlands when people make you welcome like this. No one is sent away. If you come to the door of a

Highlander, he lets you in.'

'That's very true,' Davey McKenzie said softly.

'I know a rune about that in Gaelic,' Doctor Pike said. 'Translated, it goes like this:

"I saw a stranger yestreen.
I put food in the eating place,
Drink in the drinking place,
Music in the listening place –
And the lark in its song sang!

"Often, often, often, often,
Comes the Christ in the stranger's guise." '

'That's very beautiful,' Davey said.

'Some people come,' Jessie said. 'But these days there are vandals about. We never locked our doors before, but now we lock them. People come – they look so strange, some of these hikers and campers, and the women are worse than the men.'

She went for the tea. Doctor Pike said, 'I was telling Paul about the crofters here, how they were moved from the other side – from that good land.'

He did not say that it was over a century ago.

'It was unfair, aye,' Davey said. He blinked at me. He had wet, red-rimmed eyes. 'There's so much good land lying idle. Aye, it's hard land where we are.'

He was a quiet man. He said no more. It seemed to me terrible that he had spent his whole life trying to feed his family by digging this stony ground, and always in sight of the green fields under Ben Arnaboll across the loch.

But the bad land had turned many people into wanderers. Jessie Stewart's life was proof of that.

'So you come from America,' she said to me. 'I've been to America myself. I spent eighteen years there.'

I asked her where exactly.

She said, 'In Long Island and Virginia. New York City. Bar Harbor, Maine.'

'The best places.'

'I was in service,' she said. 'The people were wealthy, you see.'

Her employers had moved from house to house, according to the season, and she had moved with them. Perhaps she had been a cook. Her scones were wonderful – she had brought out a whole tray of scones and shortbread and sandwiches with the tea.

Why had she left America?

'I got very ill. For a while I couldn't work, and then I started getting doctors' bills. You know how expensive hospitals are in the United States. There's no National Health Service – '

And she had no insurance; and the family she worked for wouldn't pay; and she needed major surgery.

' – I could never have afforded it there,' she said. 'It would have taken all my savings. I came back home here and had my operation on the National Health. I'm feeling a wee bit better now.'

So she had left the poverty trap in the Highlands and emigrated to the United States and become a servant and fallen into the American poverty trap. And now she was dying on the croft where she had been born. Most of the crofters here were old people whose children had moved away.

I continued to Caithness alone. The farther east I went, the greener it was, the more fertile the land. There were high mountains near the sea. The sheep were fat. They winced from the ditches where they crouched to get out of the wind. I went on to Coldbackie, Bettyhill, and Swordly. They were small cold places. I went to Brawl and Bighouse. The grass was better here. Caithness was a milder, more sheltered place, with sweet-smelling grass. But I liked it much less than Sutherland – its mountains streaming with pale scree, its black valleys of peat, its miles of moorland and bog, its narrow roads and surfy coast, and its caves. It was like a world apart, an unknown place in this the best-known country in the world. No sooner had I left it than I wanted to go back.

DAVID McFADDEN

❊   ❊   ❊

David McFadden has published over twenty books of poetry and prose,
including Great Lakes Suite *(1997)*, An Innocent in Ireland *(1995)*,
There'll Be Another *(1995)*, Anonymity Suite *(1992)*, Gypsy Guitar
(1987), Canadian Sunset *(1986)*, The Art of Darkness *(1984)*,
Animal Spirits *(1983)*, My Body Was Eaten by Dogs *(1981)*, On the
Road Again *(1978)*, A Knight in Dried Plums *(1975), and* Intense
Pleasure *(1972)*. He lives in Toronto.

    *As 'An Innocent Flirtation in Tongue' so indicates, McFadden could
very well be the perfect travelling companion — full of wit and devilish good
fun, he brings a poet's sensitivity to his subject and a journalist's acute eye. He
gets himself into all kinds of strange and entertaining adventures. Here, he
follows in the footsteps of the prolific travel writer H. V. Morton. But
somewhere along the way, McFadden leaves Mr. Morton behind. What is left
instead is his own singular voice — at once quirky, wry, and affectionate,
bouyed by an insatiable curiosity and a love of the absurd.*

❊   ❊   ❊

An Innocent Flirtation in Tongue

from **AN INNOCENT IN SCOTLAND:**
MORE CURIOUS RAMBLES AND SINGULAR ENCOUNTERS

Wednesday, June 26. The northeastern chunk of Scotland is fairly
flat and reminiscent of the southeastern chunk of England. But
when you get to the pretty village of Bettyhill, a couple of houses
and a pub, you're approaching the entrance to the amazing
Northwest Highlands – that is, if you're travelling westwards. Way
off on the southwest horizon are dozens of pale blue mountains,

each presenting its own perennial profile to the world. Some are rounded and high, some severely peaked and relatively low, one looks like the letter M, with straight sides and a V out of the top, another like the letter N – in fact there's probably at least one for every letter in the alphabet – and then off in the distance there's an irregular ridge that looks like a long word in Arabic script. The road takes a dip and the entire range sinks beneath the horizon: the faster you're driving the faster they sink. Roadside houses are festooned with spherical fishing buoys of all colours and sizes. Sparkling rivers pour down from great looming but somehow friendly peaks, and across yellow-brown banana-coloured sandy beaches into the grey sea under a grey sky.

Mr. Morton was enthused about Tongue. He doesn't talk at all about the area we've been through the past day or so, he saves it up for Tongue, which comes from the Gaelic *tunga*, meaning 'tongue'. If you believe Morton, when you approach Tongue you enter a whole other world. I don't quite see it, though there are some charming white beaches, with rocky coves and little islands offshore. A cheery little tidal river, probably called the River Tongue, flows out into Tongue Cove, and perched on the Tongue Promontory, sitting above the river, is an old wrecked castle that has an aura around it that seems to be saying, *I know I'm in ruins but I don't mind one little bit.* The Tongue Hotel looks as if it might cater exclusively to retired cabinet ministers and manufacturers of computerized showers.

There's a Bank of Scotland in Tongue, and I'm the only customer. The manager, a large man with a loud voice and dressed in a black suite, white shirt, black tie, and black shoes, barks out, 'Jenny!' moments after I walk in. Then he looks at me. I have a sweet little smile on my face. He looks a bit embarrassed for having yelled so loudly in a small room.

'Good morning,' I say, softly.

'Good morning,' says he, even more softly.

Then Jenny came trotting out.

She gave me the cash I was after. But then she noticed the manager glaring at her meaningfully and getting ready to bark again. So she remembered to ask for some identification. I decided against embarrassing her by saying, Sorry, I've already got the money. I handed her my passport, and she looked at my photo and signature and said, 'Lovely day, izzen tit?'

'Yes,' said I. 'Is it always like this in Tongue?'

'Oh no, it's up and down,' she said.

Our eyes met and we both blushed. The manager went into his office with a sigh and closed the door softly.

'Up and down, that's the way I like it,' I whispered.

'Och, me too,' she said.

'What time do you get off work?' I queried, admiringly.

'Och, if this was last week it'd be an entirely different story, y'see, but my husband's home from his job on the oil rigs.' She reached out and lightly ran her pinky over the back of my hand.

'Nice guy?'

'Och, y'know. Nothin' I do pleases him.'

'Sounds like the bank manager.'

'Aye, an' I wish *he'd* git a job on the oil rigs, I do.'

❊   ❊   ❊

A magnificent sky-hugger looms south of Tongue and it's called Ben Loyal, the summit of which is only 2,509 feet above sea level, but transplant it to the Alps and it'd make the Matterhorn look like a molehill. It's nicely pointed, like a dunce's cap, and it's surrounded by lesser peaks. It's green with grass on the lower slopes and green with lichen on the upper, with plenty of white and black rocks interconnected. The birds are singing as I drive along, up and down, and the landscape is like a fugue, with the rolling countryside reaching up into higher rolling countryside and then bursting forth into great arpeggios of mountains rising up into the sky from not much above sea level.

This is the road Morton took. I could have taken the new causeway, but I wanted to be loyal to the old boy, and also to find out why he felt he had entered a new world. He was so glad the ferry of the time only took foot passengers, no vehicles, because that meant he had to motor along this interesting route. But Morton, not only does he never talk about the roads he travels on, he never talks about why he never talks about them. He was too wily not to be aware that he wasn't talking about the roads, in my opinion. Maybe his editor insisted he not talk about the roads. But the simple fact is that Morton was a born promoter: he was inventing automotive tourism, and if he talked about how bad the roads were, everybody would have stayed at home – or taken the train.

How many photographs of Ben Loyal would there be in existence right now? I bet there are photos of Ben Loyal buried in boxes or pasted in albums in every country of the world. It's a wonderful mountain, and it still will be long after all those photographs are dust. And maybe someday a fleck of dust, that was once a part of a photograph of Ben Loyal, will float around the top of the mountain and land right on its topmost peak.

Morton seems to be breathing down my neck. He's sitting quietly, reliving his experiences. His spirit is right here in the car with me.

'I don't even know your first name, sir.'

'Call me Henry, or call me H.V.,' he says.

'Is it okay if I call you Mr. Morton? After all, you're so much older than I am.'

'Yes,' he says, 'but when I took this route I was younger than you.'

'Much smarter, too,' I declared.

'I was more professional than you. I knew what the public wanted,' said he. 'You're a bit out with the fairies, to use Jock's expression.'

'You were *there*, too?'

'I'm not letting you out of my sight for the entire trip.'

I gave it to him straight. 'Maybe I'm a rank amateur by your standards, but by mine you were a cliché-monger, a promoter, and a stereotype artist. Look at what you say about Ben Loyal: 'Ben Loyal is a hill on which Norse gods might have sharpened their swords.' I mean, yech! And you never visited the prehistoric sites at all.'

'They're boring. You shouldn't visit them either.'

'I don't find them boring.'

'Your readers will. And look, my books outsold yours a thousand to one.'

'This is true. But listen to yourself: "Thor must have come from Thurso to use Ben Loyal as his whetstone." '

'Oh, don't worry about it, young feller. No need to be jealous.

It was a different world then.'

'Thanks, Mr. Morton.'

'And if I were alive today, I'd have a hard time making money as a writer, believe you me.'

'You did a heckuva good job with those books, Mr. Morton. We don't talk like that any more, it's true, but nevertheless your books are still an enjoyable read, even if you do go on a bit about Ben Loyal.'

'Thanks, partner.' Yeah, he actually called me *partner.* 'I think it's known nowadays as being market-driven, of having a sincere desire to give the readers what they want. If you don't have a taste for that, you're wasting your time writing.'

'I know, but what isn't a waste of time anyway? Making money can be said to be a waste of time. You gotta follow your bliss, man.'

'Now who's the cliché-monger?'

After entering the stratosphere of mytholinguistic ecstasy over Ben Loyal, Mr. Morton couldn't find a place to stay in Durness (probably still couldn't), so they sent him to a crummy old fisherman's hotel, which, of course, turned out to be exactly to his liking, and he wasn't too shy to tell us. He had an interesting chat with a fisherman in the evening and an enormous breakfast in the morning.

I stop to check my map, and a car pulls up behind me. The loveliest young lady with the prettiest smile gets out of the car and proceeds to take a picture of Ben Loyal. She has a good shot, too, with a lovely little loch in the medium foreground, and a small herd of Highland cattle in the immediate foreground. The entire mountain, with a wisp of mist at the peak, was framed so naturally it would seem like one of those lucky, spontaneous snapshot master-pieces. She thanked me profusely for helping with the focusing.

Dun Dornaigil Broch sits on the shore of the fast-running River Hope, which flows into Loch Hope. Dwarfed by Ben Hope (3,004 feet), the broch looks like a bishop's hat, one of those ridiculously tall hats thirty-five feet high at the front and only about twelve feet high at the sides or back. A little drawing was carved into a stone by a visitor in 1772 – at which time, before radiocarbon testing, it was thought the brochs were built by Vikings: they even thought Stonehenge was built by the Druids. It might be interesting to adapt those miniature cameras used in medical procedures for inspecting the interior of these hollow walls. It might be amazing what could be found, and without any need to excavate. Not only was this broch meant to provide protection, it was also built to be admired. Looking closely at the walls, one can only be amazed at the delicate and thoughtful stonework, and the artful use of stacks of thin loose chippings to plug up narrow fissures in the wall, in a manner identical with Pictish walls all over Scotland.

Loch Eriboll is a sea loch with a splendid array of islands in it – whaleback islands, pyramid-shaped islands, and so on. The water is green, the beaches are white, and rocks stick up out of the sand in a manner reminiscent of the Zen gardens of Kyoto. Numerous young people are running along the beach, enjoying the warm sun. And there is one older fellow in a swimsuit, and sporting a huge belly, lying on his back on the sand, trying to heat up his metabolism a bit. Directly above him is a large basalt rock that is loose and almost wobbling in the gentle breeze.

A shepherd, four dogs, and a vast herd of sheep appear on the road. Some of the sheep are chocolate brown. The shepherd is wearing a pair of blue trousers splattered with white paint, a beige cardigan, a pale-yellow suit jacket, and he's bald on top, but his sandy-grey hair shoots out in all directions. He's got a pair of binoculars around his neck, for locating stragglers along the strand and up the side of hills. A bottleneck in the flow of traffic has ensued, and, as I drive up, the driver stalled in front of me quickly puts his camera away. Could he have been embarrassed to have been caught taking pictures of sheep?

Cars and lorries are lining up onboth sides, causing the transportation of the sheep to slow down immeasurably, since the shepherd is forced to funnel the flock along the painfully narrow gap between the cars and the side of the hill. Oh, what a headache this is becoming for him! How was he to know there'd be an unprecedented upsurge in tourist traffic just as he tries to take a short cut along the road? We all seem to know we're going to be here for a good chunk of time, so all engines are turned off. In almost every car now, tourists are taking pictures of sheep in all directions. One fellow can't be bothered getting out of his car or turning around, so he's firing off pictures through his rear-view mirror.

We are now entering SIX MILES OF ENCHANTED LOWLIFE COUNTRY. It had been 'gnome-like' (whatever that means), but some spray-bomber preferred 'lowlife'. I stop to take a shot of Ben Arkle (2,580 feet, with peak wreathed in cloud) with the old stone Laxford Bridge in the foreground (f22 and 1/30 with camera propped against arm of the new bridge, further back and at a higher level than the old one). After getting the shot, I stepped back onto the silent road while admiring Ben Arkle's twin sister, Ben Stack (2,356 feet), and almost killed a speeding cyclist. He swerved all over the road, but finally managed to come to a stop without falling – and then he actually apologized for not having given me a warning, rather than scream at me for not watching the road. He said he was drifting when he should have been whistling. He said it was great cycling around here. You can go as slow as you want up a hill and as fast as you want down a hill. But you have to carry lots of spare parts just in case. He was from Glasgow.

Ullapool, the major town on the northwest coast, is where you get the ferry for Stornoway, on the Isle of Lewis (where I'm not going on this trip), and it has the largest expanse of tacky North American-style residential and commercial architecture imaginable. Tourists drive slowly down the main street along the harbour, trying to figure out what to do, and perhaps looking for a parking spot. Tourists already parked seem reluctant to leave their cars: they sit there taking pictures of the surrounding mountains, such as Beinn Eilidea (1,830 feet) and Benn Ghobhlach (2,082 feet). Those without parking spots drive to the end of the waterfront street, where there's a running circle, and they turn around and creep slowly back.

It's 5:30 and all the tea wagons are being towed home. There's a big football game tonight between England and Germany, but the BBC is doing a desperately hyperbolic, Mortonesque job of promoting it. They keep saying things like, 'The whole nation will grind to a halt tonight' – which is definitely not true. At least the Scotland part of the nation certainly has no intention of grinding to a halt. Nobody up here – not even the English incomers – gives a hang about who wins. It's that kind of attitude on the part of the BBC that riles the Scots and makes them consider England even more of a foreign country than they ordinarily would. Also, the sleazy English tabloids have been doing their best to whip up anti-German feeling among the British fans. The German football reporters are being interviewed, and they're being noble about it all, saying the press should be ashamed of itself for trying to exploit outdated ethnic animosities.

A couple of ancient Buddhist manuscripts have been unearthed at the British Museum. They've been dated to AD 200 and are thought to be copies of verbatim transcriptions of the Buddha's words. A phone-in show host mentions this on the air, and immediately some fellow named Martin phones in from Dundee.

'Before we get deciphering those scrolls,' he says, 'I'd like to offer a few thoughts of my own.'

'Would these thoughts be on a par with the Buddha's?' queries the announcer.

'Why not?' says Martin.

'Do you think in centuries to come we'll be talking about the thoughts of Martin of Dundee?'

'Well, you won't know till you hear them, will you?' says Martin.

'Okay, go ahead.'

Martin clears his throat, then intones dramatically: 'If you can answer your own questions truthfully, then you know you're being honest with yourself.'

For some reason the announcer didn't consider that remark to be all that philosophically profound. 'Thank you, Martin,' he said, a bit sarcastically. 'I think I'll take a relaxing tablet after that one. Bye-bye.' *Click.*

After a long, winding drive down the northwest coast, with plenty of stops to gawk at mountains and read historical plaques, I made another sweep around Glengarry, then stopped for the night in the good-sized town of Invergarry, which the people of the glen refer to as 'the village', and where they go for supplies. The night clerk and the bartender at the Invergarry Hotel are both tall, skinny, intellectual-looking fellows with long, skinny noses. Do they get many customers from Glengarry?

'I've been here six years,' says the bartender, 'and we used to get a good crowd in here some nights from Glengarry, but no more.'

'What's the story?'

'The story is they've pretty well all been killed in car accidents.'

He then proceeds to tell me the news that Dion Alexander kindly spared me when he was lamenting the dwindling population of the glen: about one horrible car crash after another, grisly details of the deaths of Glengarry residents returning to the valley after a boozy evening in Invergarry.

'All men in their thirties. They used to come down, but there have been so many car accidents they drink at their own pub they have up there. In all of Britain, if you're a male motorist in your thirties, the Highlands is the worst possible place to be. And it's not on the single-track roads either. The big crashes are always on the A roads. The A82 is apparently the worst road in Britain for fatal accidents.' He mentioned one crash a few years ago in which two guys were killed and one survived. Then the one who survived was in another accident about two years later, in which he and two friends were killed. 'So, we don't get people from Glengarry in here any more. There's hardly anybody left up there of that age. They've all been wiped out. What a tough-luck place.'

As for the crashes, he suspects it might have something to do with the shift in traffic patterns from season to season. In the summer it can take you an hour to get onto the A82 (the main road from Inverness southwest to Fort William and beyond) from a side road, but in the winter you don't even bother stopping because there's never anyone there – or almost never.

THE
WESTERN
ISLES

MARTIN MARTIN
(c.1660-1719)

❊   ❊   ❊

A native of Skye and a Gaelic speaker to boot, Martin Martin wrote one of the earliest accounts of a visit to the Hebrides. In 1698 he penned A Description of the Western Islands of Scotland circa 1695, *reportedly the first book on the Hebrides to be published, based on a series of voyages he made in the 1680s and 1690s. A companion piece,* A Voyage to St. Kilda *was also published in the same year.*

He belonged to a new generation of islanders who received their education in English in the Lowlands. Martin studied at Edinburgh University and eventually became tutor to the heir of the Macdonalds of Skye. He also studied medicine at the University of Leyden in the Netherlands.

Martin, though a man of science, had little patience for narrative or anecdotes, the very stuff of modern travel writing. Instead, in his writings on the Hebrides, we get a rather disjointed collection of observations and impressions based on the habits, customs, beliefs, folklore, and anything else that captured his attention and imagination. Generations of travel writers owe a huge debt to Martin, including such well-known travellers as James Boswell and Samuel Johnson. They carried a dog-eared copy of Martin's book with them and referred to it frequently in the account of their famous journey.

❊   ❊   ❊

Jura

from A DESCRIPTION OF THE WESTERN ISLANDS OF SCOTLAND, CIRCA 1695

The isle of Jura is by a narrow channel of about half a mile broad separated from Islay. The natives say that Jura is so called from Dih and Rah, two brethren, who are believed to have been Danes, the names Dih and Rah signifying as much as without grace or prosperity. Tradition says that these two brethren fought and killed one another in the village Knock-Cronm, where there are two stones erected of 7 feet high each, and under them, they say, there are urns, with the ashes of the two brothers; the distance between them is about 60 yards. The isle is mountainous along the middle, where there are four hills of a considerable height. The two highest are well known to sea-faring men by the name of the Paps of Jura. They are very conspicuous from all quarters of sea and land in those parts.

This isle is twenty-four miles long, and in some places six or seven miles in breadth. It is the Duke of Argyll's property, and part of the Sheriffdom of Argyll.

The mould is brown and greyish on the coast, and black in the hills, which are covered with heath and some grass that proves good pasturage for their cattle, which are horses, cows, sheep, and goats. There is variety of land and water-fowl here. The hills ordinarily have about three hundred deer grazing on them, which are not to be hunted by any without the steward's licence. This isle is perhaps the wholesomest plot of ground either in the isles or continent of Scotland, as appears by the long life of the natives and their state of health, to which the height of the hills is believed to contribute in a large measure, by the fresh breezes of wind that come from them to purify the air; whereas Islay and Gigha, on each side of this isle, are much lower, and are not so wholesome by far, being liable to several diseases that are not here. The inhabitants observe that the air of this place is perfectly pure, from the middle of March till the end or middle of September.

❊   ❊   ❊

Several of the natives have lived to a great age. I was told that one of them, called Gillouir MacCrain, lived to have kept one hundred and eighty Christmasses in his own house. He died about fifty years ago, and there are several of his acquaintances living to this day, from whom I had this account.

❊   ❊   ❊

Between the north end of Jura, and the isle of Scarba, lies the famous and dangerous gulf, called Cory Vrekan, about a mile in breadth; it yields an impetuous current, not to be matched anywhere about the isle of Britain. The sea begins to boil and ferment with the tide of flood, and resembles the boiling of a pot; and then increases gradually, until it appears in many whirlpools, which form themselves in sort of pyramids, and immediately after spout up as high as the mast of a little vessel, and at the same time make a loud report. These white waves run two leagues with the wind before they break; the sea continues to repeat these various motions from the beginning of the tide of flood, until it is more than half-flood, and then it decreases gradually until it hath ebbed about half an hour, and continues to boil till it is within an hour of low water. This boiling of the sea is not above a pistol-shot distant from the coast of Scarba Isle, where the white waves meet and spout up: they call it the Kaillach, *i.e.*, an old hag; and they say that when she puts on her kerchief, *i.e.*, the whitest waves, it is then reckoned fatal to approach her. Notwithstanding this great ferment of the sea, which brings up the least shell from the ground, the smallest fisher-boat may venture to cross this gulf at the last hour of the tide of flood, and at the last hour of the tide of ebb.

This gulf hath its name from Brekan, said to be son to the King of Denmark, who was drowned here, cast ashore in the north of Jura, and buried in a cave, as appears from the stone, tomb, and altar there.

❊   ❊   ❊

There is a church here called Killearn, the inhabitants are all Protestants, and observe the festivals of Christmas, Easter, and Michaelmas; they do not open a grave on Friday, and bury none on that day, except the grave has been opened before.

The natives here are very well proportioned, being generally black of complexion and free from bodily imperfections. They speak the Irish language, and wear the plaid, bonnet, etc., as other islanders.

SETON GORDON
(1886-1977)

✻   ✻   ✻

Naturalist, writer, and wildlife photographer Seton Gordon was one of the best nature writers that Scotland has produced. Born in Aboyne, Aberdeenshire, he studied natural sciences at Exeter College, Oxford. During his long career, he wrote nearly 30 books spanning almost 70 years on life and work in rural Scotland. In particular the daily life and customs of the Hebrides provided inspiration for most of his writings. He lived in various places thoroughout Scotland over the years before settling with his wife Audrey Pease in 1915 near Duntulm in Skye.

In Hebridean Memories, *first published in 1923, he discusses subjects that he held dear to his heart: birds and animal life, the crofting and fishing communities. This selection takes place on the flat, windswept island of Tiree.*

✻   ✻   ✻

A Sea-girt Home of the Peregrine

from HEBRIDEAN MEMORIES

From the extreme south-western shore of the lonely Hebridean isle of Tiree rises a storm-swept hill, Ceann a'Bharra. On its eastern side the hill is gently sloping, with grassy banks where hardy sheep graze and where, in April and May, many primroses and wild hyacinths bloom. Seaward, great cliffs descend sheer into the Atlantic, and on these dark, menacing rocks the peregrine falcon, the raven, and many kittiwakes, guillemots and green cormorants make their spring and summer home.

During the March of which I write few, very few, fine days cheered the western islands. Storm clouds almost constantly raced across the sodden land from the open spaces of the ocean, and the air was laden with salt spray and watery vapours.

But at length came a day when the sun shone brightly and the sky was clear, though a strong southerly wind swept across this island of little shelter.

During winter the lochs of the isle are peopled with many wild swans, from Iceland and the Siberian steppes. But today each loch was deserted, although upon that sheet of scarcely-moving water known as the Faodhail fed three Bewick's swans – two parents with their only youngster of the previous season. A mile from them, where the stream has its source in an extensive bog, three whooper swans could be seen. The two Bewick's swans were, I think, lingering here beyond their season for the sake of their young, for when they rose from the water to fly, with musical cries, backward and forward overhead, the immature swan did not accompany them, though in its direction they cast many an anxious glance. The youngster had apparently received some recent injury, for its power of flight must have been unimpaired when, in autumn, it journeyed south from distant Siberia.

Above the 'machair', or level grazing land, lapwings rocked and swayed in impulsive flight, furiously pursuing any of the gull tribe that unwittingly trespassed overhead. Upon the short-cropped grass a flock of golden plover fed warily. In the clear air were many larks, each singing his hardest as he rose until he became a mere speck against a background of deep blue. From each ditch snipe rose, with curious scraping cry and arrow-swift swerving flight.

A nine-mile walk from the little village of Scarinish brought me to the slopes of Ceann a'Bharra, and for the first time for a week I was for a brief space in shelter from the wind.

But although that spring had been boisterous beyond the average it had been mild, and already in mid-March the grass, even upon the hill slopes, was of that verdure which one associates with April and May. In the warm sunshine moths fluttered, and one sensed clearly the coming of the tide of full spring, and of the summer which would shortly follow.

As I commenced the short climb to the hill-top the wind veered round a little, and from the Atlantic swept a heavy, though short-lived, squall of hail and rain. In the warm sunshine which followed there was in the air the pleasant scent of growing grass and awakening life.

From a low, sandy shore half a mile to the westward came the deep booming sound of a heavy surf breaking without pause upon the white sands, and above the shore a cloud of salt spray hung. In summer the hill of Ceann a'Bharra, as I have said, is the home of many birds. Today only the outposts of these summer birds had arrived, but the peregrine throughout the year, has its home on these wild rocks. As I looked from the hill-top down upon the grim precipice with the troubled ocean beneath, the falcon darted from her inaccessible nesting ledge and, with harsh and oft-repeated cries, mounted into the air in the teeth of the breeze. It seemed curious that her anxiety should have been so acute, for the time of her nesting was as yet almost a month ahead. On at least three occasions she returned to the same ledge. Once, as she sailed swiftly across the cliff face, a great black-backed gull pursued her in deter- mined manner, but the falcon heeded him not and easily outdis- tanced him.

Immediately beneath the ledge of the peregrine a green cormorant stood beside her half-completed nest. In the nest there lay a large, green pine branch, picked up, presumably, from the water's surface, for the nearest fir tree – on Tiree itself no tree of any kind can exist – was distant at least twenty-five miles from the cliff.

Few herring gulls has as yet arrived at their nesting ledges, but I was interested to see that numbers of kittiwakes – the latest of the gull tribe to nest – were floating buoyantly upon the sea near the cliffs and that some of them were already standing beside their old nests. The guillemots had not as yet come in from the open ocean, nor had the puffins arrived; but rock pigeons darted from their gloomy caves, and I was astonished to see a blackbird flit across the face of the cliff. This bird of sweet music was apparently a migrant, for no blackbird nests upon Tiree. Upon the hill-top a dead sheep lay; from it a raven rose, poised against the wind, and soared steadily high above the rocks.

There are but few hills, even in the romantic country of the Hebrides, with so wild and magnificently grand an outlook as Ceann a'Bharra. Here is the home of the tireless spirit of the Atlantic. Here are great caves, where the ocean swell thunders, and great rocks smoothed and polished by the constant action of wind and tide, and to the ear is ever present the deep boom of the surf.

Today, over the ocean, were spread many drifting showers, so that everywhere sun and rain strove for mastery, and blue skies and grey, misty squalls contended together.

Southward, far into the Atlantic, rose the lonely light house of Skerryvore, the home of almost constant storms. Midway between where I stood and the lighthouse, ponderous waves were breaking leisurely on that submerged rock known in Gaelic as Bogha na Slighe, or in English, the Rock of the Passage. It is a deadly obstacle for any ship out of her course in darkness or in thick weather.

About Skerryvore itself was a curious misty patch on the ocean. So bright was it that it seemed as though the sun shone here continuously, but the glass showed it to be caused by the surf from the great waves as they crashed, one after the other, upon the smooth-worn sides of the rock, their spume hanging in white fog around the lighthouse and causing the unusual effect. Here on Ceann a'Bharra I seemed to be midway between two distinct types of weather. From east to south the horizon was dark with heavy clouds of rain. The Island of Mull was invisible, though nearer at hand the heavy swell might be seen leaping high against the dark, rocky sides of the small island known as Bac Beag, or the Little Dutchman.

From time to time, through drifting rain squalls, Iona showed; but away to the west, and especially towards the north-west, the sky was blue and the air clear. On Barra Head the sun shone brightly, and the lighthouse, although quite forty miles distant, was distinct. Then, bearing more northward, one could see other islands of the Outer Hebrides – Mingulay of the many cliffs, Barra Island with its conical hill, and even the lesser height of Easaval in South Uist.

Midway between Tiree and Barra the mailboat threaded her course. There is a fascination in watching the Atlantic waves as they play about rocks that are just showing above the tide. With each long wave the water, with slow and unhurried motion, engulfs the whole rock in a white flood of foam. No part escapes. And with the coming of the wave the air-filled waters show so many different colours – palest green, deepest blue, and all the shades of these colours, but each one perfect in itself. The wave passes. Down the steep sides of the rock there stream innumerable cascades of snow white water, contrasting sharply with the amethystine depths beneath them.

In its unhurried majestic speed, its tremendous strength, the Atlantic swell has its especial charm.

Above where the waves thundered rock doves darted to and fro, entering and leaving the gloomy caves where, in April, they would make their primitive nests. From the hill-top a curlew sprang with wild shriek of alarm.

Towards sunset the wind lessened. Over the sea there spread many lights of sun and shade, and the air had that clearness which foretells the near approach of rain.

Upon the southern horizon lay a minute portion of a rainbow of brilliant colours – a 'wind dog' fishermen call such a phenomenon – and near it hung a hail squall, transformed by the unusual light to a thing of pale, sea-green colour as it descended to the ocean's surface.

At sunset the western sky burned with the last rays of the sun, shining through a narrow window from the gateway of Tir nan Og, or the mythical Land of Youth.

An hour later, with the coming of night, the new moon, with Venus close beside her, shone palely upon this Hebridean island, and in the quiet of the evening the cries of many lapwing, active by night as by day, carried far across the machair.

JOHN McPHEE

❊   ❊   ❊

Without a doubt, John McPhee is one of the best journalists and storytellers of our day. Whether writing about oranges or basketball, McPhee makes every subject sound compelling. A long-time staff writer for the New Yorker, *his many books include* Oranges *(1967),* The Pine Barrens *(1967),* Encounters with the Archdruid *(1971),* The Deltoid Pumpkin Seed *(1973),* The Survival of the Bark Canoe *(1975),* Coming into the Country *(1976),* Basin and Range *(1980),* In Suspect Terrain *(1983),* Rising from the Plains *(1986),* Assembling California *(1993), and* Annals of the Former World *(1998), which was awarded the Pulitzer Prize in 1999.*

This Princeton, New Jersey, native has written frequently about Scotland and his Scottish ancestry in the likes of 'Pieces of the Frame', 'Josie's Well', and 'From Birnam Wood to Dunsinane'.

In the late 1960s he returned to the island of his ancestors, Colonsay, which, at that time contained about 140 inhabitants. McPhee is a thoughtful and perceptive writer, and The Crofter and the Laird *(1970) remains one of his most luminous pieces of writing. He is clearly impressed by the people that he meets on Colonsay – their quiet dignity and genuine kindness – especially by the beauty of the Gaelic language, which, in one particularly memorable passage, he describes as being 'so beautiful that one almost resents having to hear the language anywhere else.'*

❊   ❊   ❊

from THE CROFTER AND THE LAIRD

The air is calm, and the cuckoo sounds from the hills of Balaromin Mor. Below, on The Strand, the tide is low and the hill cows have positioned themselves on the wet flat sand, their forms indistinct in

the mist, and they slowly move their heads from side to side. The hill
cows are covered with golden hair that is so long it mats their faces
entirely and drips down their sides. They are woolly mammoths,
gigantic Saint Bernards, slow-moving hair farms. They are truly
unbelievable to any eye that has not seen them before. They are also
cattle, inside it all, and there is something mildly electrifying about
their presence on The Strand, evidence of intellectual stirrings in
those effigial heads, for they could have no other reason for being
there than curiosity. The sound of the cuckoo has not stopped. To
me it is a novelty – the actual bird's being there in the hills. With
every call, it compliments the Swiss, sounding, as it does, exactly
like the clock. I have counted, and the last call is No. 66. It is late in
the day – 66 P.M. From the cliff where the cuckoo apparently is, an
arm of rock reaches out. Centuries ago, a hole was drilled in the
outer edge of this projection, which has been known since then as
the Hangman's Rock. A great many people were hanged there, for
offenses against the interests of the clan.

Crossing Big Lookout Hill in Scalasaig, I met David Clark,
who had been cutting peat. He was replacing chunks of sod. 'You
replace the turf, like a good golfer,' he said. 'Not many people burn
peat on Colonsay anymore. Our peat is not of as good quality as the
peat of Islay. Everyone burns it there – ministers, doctors. But ours
makes a good glow. If you get good weather, it dries just as hard as
coal. And what's wrong with a good fire and a book, if it comes to
that?' David Clark and his sister Mary Clark share a house beside
the church in Scalasaig. They are the retired keepers of the inn
there. They are islanders, whose mother's family was of the original
clan, and they have shown me the now ruined house in Bonaveh
where they were born, with its long vista over the remnants of other
houses and then across the water east to the Strait of Corryvreckan,
and they seem to regard me as if I had been born in Bonaveh, too,
and were only now rising from decades of sleep. Four-year-old
Jenny was with me when David was cutting the peat. 'Bye, bye just
now,' he said to her as we left. 'I hope you'll manage back soon.'

The sky is royal blue, and below the blue, just above the
waves, is a layer of dusty red. Venus is twice as bright and, in this
sky, twice as large as Venus is supposed to be. Dusk is collecting,
and the stars will show through in a moment. The sun is just gone.

In half a minute's time, it will be tomorrow, the first of June.

Inside, I have lighted the usual driftwood fire. Enough driftwood collects on the shores of this island to build a roof over Scotland, and some is from North America. It makes a good glow, and in a bedroom grate it is something to stare into before sleep – an illusion of warmth before the cold of the night. Some recent days have been so fair that we have gone to the beaches, but the indoor temperature is forty-two at the moment. Donald Gibbie said a couple of things tonight that are now, somehow, there in the fire. He and Margaret invited us to their house for a dram, and that was followed by tea and pancakes. The manner in which an evening ends here is a model for the world to follow. When the Colonsay hostess feels that the day is over and there has been enough of talking, she heats the teakettle and opens the tin of pancakes she has prepared earlier in the day. She spreads butter on the pancakes and steeps the tea, then sets all before her guests, and when it has been consumed the visit is over: 'Good night and sleep well' – no obscurities about when things should end. Early in the evening, I had mentioned that I'd heard the laird would arrive soon, and I asked Donald if he still doffed his cap to him. He said that he could not help doing so. 'These class distinctions have to go. They're holding us back,' he said. 'But when I was a small boy, if I did not take off my cap before the laird I was severely punished by my parents for being disrespectful. It is too deep in me now for me to change, but I teach the children that it is unnecessary. Like the others, whenever I see the laird I say nothing unless he speaks to me. If he says something, I remove my cap and say, "Good morning, Milord," or "Good evening, Milord." I simply can't help it.' Later in the evening, Donald told me what he and other islanders thought would happen in the event of a thermonuclear war. What led to this was that he had been asking me for details of New York, and I told him that we had once had an apartment there in an unintelligibly large housing complex where thirty-two thousand people lived on seventy-five acres of Manhattan. Merely around our own elevator shaft – twelve floors, eight apartments per floor – lived three times the population of Colonsay. This brought the bomb to mind, because we had lived in that apartment during an era of nuclear crisis, and I told Donald and Margaret how we had expected from moment to moment that in the next instant we would be vapor, and how sometimes we would look out the window at the city at night and wonder if it would be gone by morning. Donald reacted without surprise and told me about Benbecula. There is, he said, a rocket range on Benbecula, which is one of the Hebrides, a hundred miles north-northwest of Colonsay. It is apparently not a missile installation – just a target range for small rockets. Nonetheless, almost since the beginning of the era of the hydrogen bomb the people of Colonsay have felt themselves to be living in the greatest of danger because of their proximity to Benbecula. Donald said, 'If the bomb ever does come, we shall be among the first to go.'

JOHN J. O RIORDAIN

❊ ❊ ❊

'The "Scotland" of which I write is not confined to the political entity of either today or yester-year. It is an indefinitely bounded spiritual country stretching from Lindisfarne to the Faroe Islands and from the Atlantic Ocean to the North Sea.' So says Irish priest John J. O Riordain in the Foreword to A Pilgrim in Celtic Scotland.

Iona has long been considered a sacred site, ever since Saint Columba, accompanied by twelve monks, set sail from Ireland in 563AD and landed on the tiny isle's southern end. Centuries later, it remains a favourite destination for spiritual pilgrims. John J. O Riordain is one of these latter-day pilgrims.

❊ ❊ ❊

Iona of My Heart

from A PILGRIM IN CELTIC SCOTLAND

While my pilgrimage to Iona began from our monastery in Dundalk, I consider it to have really got underway at Queen Street railway station in Glasgow. The platform where I awaited the morning train to Oban was crowded with the daily commuters although it was not yet eight o'clock. When the incoming Edinburgh train came to a standstill it disgorged a chaotic scurrying mass of humanity, but in the midst of the chaos I discerned a loosely cohesive group with a substantial amount of luggage. Could they possibly be bound for Iona? I watched them re-group on the platform and ultimately board the Oban train. I followed at a distance and took my seat in the same carriage though at the opposite end. Shortly after, the '8.12-for-Oban' was on its way, due allowances having been made for Celtic time-keeping.

The question remained: were they going to Iona? They were certainly in holiday mood and their picnic supplies indicated that preparations had been made for a long journey. The focus of that happy little party was a beautifully featured gentle lady with a subdued but obvious charm, whom I later came to know as Mary Lauden. She was in the company of her husband, Bill, their children, and their neighbour, Joyce Cairns. Joyce was conspicuous by her dazzling white hair and artistic mien. Well, I thought, if these are going to be among my companions for a week on Iona, things are looking good.

The three-hour journey to Oban occasioned an uninterrupted feast of Highland scenery as the train sped northwards along the shores of the Clyde, Gare Loch and Loch Long to Tarbet and Loch Lomond. From Tarbet to Crianlarich, Ben Lomond on the far side of the lake and Ben More to the north of it dominated the skyline. Then at Crianlarich the train took a westward route through Glen Lochy, past the southern entrance to Glen Lochy and on towards the Pass of Brander, leaving Loch Awe to our left and majestic Ben Cruachan to our right. The narrow Pass soon opened up to a panoramic view of romantic Loch Etive.

It is on the shores and hinterland of this lovely expanse of water that the folk tradition has set the most romantic portion of the tragic Celtic saga concerning the elopement of Deirdre of the Sorrows and Naoise son of Uisneach. Here, the two lovers are said to have survived on summer berries and winter mast together with the hunt of the hill and fish from the loch. The couple had eloped because King Conor McNessa of Ulster had planned to marry Deirdre who was said to have been the most beautiful woman in Ireland. But Deirdre wanted none other than Naoise, the handsome young warrior in the king's service. With false assurances of safety, the envoys of the king coaxed the lovers back home to Ireland where Naoise was promptly murdered. Deirdre, not willing to give herself to the king, jumped to her death from a speeding chariot.

The story of Deirdre and Naoise is not the only romantic tale associated with Loch Etive. At the Connel end of the loch we were able to catch a fleeting glimpse of Dunstaffnage castle where, in 1746, the celebrated Flora MacDonald spent ten days as a prisoner on her way to trial and jail in London for her part in the escape of

Bonnie Prince Charlie. And it was to Dunstaffnage at the dawn of history that the Irish brought a stone of great significance (probably the *Lia Fail*, or 'Stone of Destiny', but perhaps a coronation stone from Dunadd), which was removed to London and kept at Westminster Abbey for use in the coronation of English monarchs and which has now been returned to Scotland.

The Oban train came to a standstill right at the pier where the noon ferry was waiting to take its quota of passengers to Mull. By this time I had exchanged a few smiles and nods of recognition with the Edinburgh group. I had also surreptitiously glanced at their luggage tags and, sure enough, 'Iona' was clearly marked on each item. All I had to do then was to collect my ticket at the Caledonian MacBrayne office right there on the quayside and trail the Edinburgh pilgrims up the gangway of *The Island of Mull* without further care for travel arrangements.

If the scenes from the Glasgow-Oban train were beautiful, the loveliness that surrounded us for the forty minute crossing of the Firth of Loarn [sic] between Oban on the mainland and Craignure in Mull was truly intoxicating. Weather conditions were particularly favourable and wherever the eye fell in any direction, be it on sea or sky, distant mountains or shore-line hills, it fell on azure forms. Besides, we were never so far from land as to be denied some sight of historic and folkloric locations on the mainland and islands.

First, there was Oban's chief landmark, McCaig's Folly. It had dominated the town for a century. One may well wonder was it folly or grace, because McCaig, after whom the folly is named, was a generous and good man who spent his personal fortune in providing employment to alleviate the condition of his less fortunate townspeople. An Oban banker with family background in neighbouring Lismore, McCaig, in 1897, undertook the building of this magnificent granite rotunda modelled on the Colosseum in Rome. Money ran out during the construction phase and he never realised his dream of having within its walls an art gallery and museum.

Down at the shore, on the starboard side of the ferry, was another striking granite building: the Catholic cathedral of St. Columba. Said by many experts to be the finest modern Gothic building in all of Britain, it measures no more than a hundred and fifty feet in length and is fronted by a ninety-foot tower. The architect, Sir Gilbert Scott, chose pink granite from Peterhead and artistically set it off against blue granite from Inverawe. The roof is of magnificent Kentish oak beams and the yellow and brown tints in the slate blend in with the stone work. The overall result is a building of beauty, simplicity and elegance.

Rising up behind the cathedral was the green hill of Dunollie, the ancient capital from which Loarn, son of Erc, and his descendants ruled. A short distance beyond the cathedral and on the right of the road that winds by the sea is 'The Dog Stone.' It is a huge natural pillar of granite which folk tradition identifies as the very stone where Fionn McCool, the semi-mythical Celtic hero, used to tie up his dog, Bran. Next, a little higher on the slopes of the wooded hill are the ruins of a castle which for centuries was the court of the MacDoughals, Lords of Loarn. No sooner has the ferry passed the MacDoughal stronghold than a long green and almost treeless island comes into view. This is the illustrious Lismore of St Moluag which boasted the cathedral church of Argyll and the Isles in pre-Reformation times. On the port side is the sheltering Island of Kerrera, and thereafter the coast of Mull with the thirteenth-century Dewart Castle of the MacLeans as its most prominent feature.

We disembarked at Craignure, ('the cliff of the yews'), on the Island of Mull. A fleet of buses was at the service of passengers to take them to their various destinations. Most were taking the 38-mile journey through Glenmore, down the Ross of Mull to Fionnphort and Iona. Mull is a large, beautiful island with more than three hundred miles of coastline. Not least among its attractions are its lakes, mountains, cliffs, ocean scenery, stone circles, standing stones, cairns and crannogs, together with its many thousands of deer and the eagles that make their home around the 3,171-foot Ben Mor, the island's highest mountain.

❈　　❈　　❈

It was somewhere on the far side of Bunessan village, in the Ross of Mull, that I caught my first glimpse of Iona. This was the '*mons gaudi*' (the hill of rejoicing) so longed for by mediaeval pilgrims. From there I could see the gleaming white sands of Iona and my heart beat faster. The last leg of the journey was the seven-minute

ferry trip from Fionnphort across the Sound of Iona to St Ronan's
Bay. Ahead of us was Martyr's Bay on the port side, Dun I (the
highest point on the island) on starboard, and between both, on the
site of Columcille's original foundation, stood the restored
thirteenth-century Benedictine abbey.

✻   ✻   ✻

After Colmcille's death, the monastery flourished for two centuries.
Then, because of the Viking terror, monastic life became virtually
unsustainable on the island. Raids are recorded for AD 795, 802,
806, 825, 976, 986. For this reason, at the beginning of the ninth
century, the entire Columban administration moved to Kells in the
Irish Midlands. With the decline in Celtic monasticism in the
twelfth century, the remaining monks in Iona were ousted in favour
of a community of Benedictines from Durham. These were the
builders of the fine stone abbey and the nearby convent for the
Canonesses of St Augustine. Despite the official passing of the
Celtic community, it is probable that some of the remaining Irish
monks were accepted into the new community. Certainly, there is an
Irish architectural stamp on much of the stonework in both
buildings. For a long time the community of religious women was
predominantly Irish, albeit under the rule of Norse superiors. The
ruins of the convent are among the finest that remain in Scotland
and, in time, who knows but another George MacLeod may restore
them.

During the late mediaeval period, prior to the Reformation,
life went on as in most other monastic communities, except that on
Iona conditions continued to be grim. The archaeological excava-
tions of what is thought to have been the nuns' graveyard reveals
that this was the burial place of a large number of people, mostly
women, none of whom had children, none of whom had died
violently and none of whom had lived beyond about the age of forty.

From its devastation during the sixteenth-century
Reformation down to George MacLeod's restoration in the
twentieth, the monastery on Iona lay in ruins.

Did Colmcille foresee it all? A prophesy attributed to him,
says tht he did:

In Iona of my heart, Iona of my love, where monks' voices were, shall be lowing of cattle. But ere the world shall come to an end, Iona will be as it was.

❊   ❊   ❊

For the Catholic community at least, Iona is not yet 'as it was.' But there are signs of movement in that direction. At *Cnoc a Chalmain* a new Catholic house of prayer with a small chapel is being officially opened this year, the 1400th anniversary of the saint's death, while the ecumenical *Iona Community* is in existence for more than half a century. In a sermon at Iona, Cardinal Winning of Glasgow said: 'The path to further reconciliation ... cannot lie in brooding over our wounds, or in mutual recriminations, but in a continued series of creative experiments born of good will.' Iona today is conducting such an experiment and it was to participate in it, for a week at any rate, that I stepped ashore.

Most Celtic holy places in Scotland and elsewhere are, nowadays, little more than archaeological sites. Iona is different. Under God, the Very Rev George MacLeod (1895-1991), is primarily responsible for changing the fortunes of this 'holy of holies' in the Celtic world. Govan, the area of Glasgow where he ministered in the 1930s, had high unemployment. George hadn't money to assist his people but if it was work they wanted then he had no shortage of it, because he was determined to restore the ruined thirteenth-century Benedictine abbey on the Isle of Iona in the Inner Hebrides. And so, shortly before the outbreak of World War II, he and his band of unemployed volunteers set out on what must have been seen at the time as one of the craziest undertakings imaginable.

On Iona, having provided themselves with temporary accommodation and whatever essential facilities were required, they set to work. While establishing an adequate food-chain for his team, George, being a man of God, ensured that the spiritual food-chain was also in order. Day by day, as well as taking off his coat to shovel and pick, he prayed for some considerable time with his closest associates. Observing this, his volunteer force inquired if they, too, might be allowed to share payer with him; and so there came into being the Iona Community and the main structures of their daily life. Ever since, at a certain time in the morning and in the late evening, the entire staff repairs to the abbey church for prayer.

The workers donated their labours. Would others perhaps donate the necessary money and materials for the restoration? George wrote letters, begged and cajoled; and as in the gospel story, if people didn't give from the sheer generosity of their hearts, they gave to get peace from George. Not only individuals were approached but companies and governments. The most spectacular response was from the Norwegians, who sent a ship-load of timber in reparation for the destruction wrought on Iona by their Viking ancestors over a thousand years previously. If you ever happen to be in the abbey dining room, observe the ceiling and roof and see for yourself what a fine act of reparation it was!

Work for youth was very much in the mind and heart of MacLeod. Side by side with the restoration of the abbey, which continued from 1938-67, he ran summer camps, accommodating the young people in old wooden cabins. In the late 1960s, when work on the abbey was nearing completion, and the wooden cabins were deteoriating by the year, he turned his thoughts to the idea of a purpose-built centre which would cater for youth, for families, and for the disabled. It would also be a centre for international reconcil-iation. Today it stands, relatively unobtrusive on the Iona landscape, and named appropriately The MacLeod Centre.

About three miles from the abbey, on the Ross of Mull, at a spot called Camas (Gaelic for a *small bay* or *cove*), the Iona Community manages another property devoted to the service of youth. The buildings there were originally constructed as a salmon fishing station owned by the Duke of Argyll. The duke leased them to MacLeod at a nominal rent. In the course of time, this venue has become more and more a centre for delinquent youngsters from Borstals. Here, in a beautiful setting, the young people have an opportunity of experiencing outdoor activities on land and sea, as well as engaging in discussion, and worship too, if they so wish. For many youngsters, the holiday in Camas is the moment of grace that has changed their lives.

The pilgrimage to Iona has also been a source of grace for myself. During my stay in 1992, I became friendly with the then wardens, Philip and Alison Newell, who invited me back to lecture on Celtic spirituality. This offer I gladly accepted, and through it I have made a lot of friends across the religious divide, thus in a small way realising some of the hopes of George MacLeod. Unfortunately, I never had the pleasure of meeting the man himself as he passed away some weeks before I became involved with the community. During my stay I learned that the Joyce Cairns whom I had first seen on the Oban train had done the last sketch of the nonagenarian MacLeod, a work later purchased by the National Gallery in Edinburgh.

Pilgrims who book into the abbey are not just paying guests; they are part of the establishment for the duration of their stay; in a sense they become 'the Iona community.' They are assigned various chores relating to house maintenance as well as participating actively in the morning and evening church services. Every Wednesday a designated person from the Iona Community is deputed to lead a pilgrimage to the holy places of the Island, starting at the 8th-century St Martin's Cross, and including the Convent (Nunnery), the Hill of the Angels, the Machair, *Port a Churraic* (Columba's Bay), the Hermit's Cell, Dun I, and St Oran's Chapel where the final prayer is recited.

As well as being a religious exercise the Wednesday pilgrimage is a community-builder. It is relaxed and rural, with plenty of fresh air, beautiful scenery and a welcome picnic lunch on the Machair about half way through. At the end of the four or five hour outing, one can always enjoy a swim in the clear blue waters that surround Iona, or join a friend in the pleasant atmosphere of the coffee shop which is a small unobtrusive *refugium peccatorum* which would surely meet with the whole-hearted approval of St Columcille.

On a personal note, the highlight of my own pilgrimage was having my feet washed at the end of the journey. It wasn't simply the fact that the kind act was performed by Jean Matthews, a Southern Baptist from the U.S.A., nor indeed the gospel symbolism of the gesture, but the foundation of that symbol: the sheer luxury of having one's feet washed after walking without shoes for several hours.

SIR ALASTAIR DUNNETT
(1908-1998)

✳   ✳   ✳

Born in Kilmacolm, Sir Alastair Dunnett was educated at Hillhead High School in Glasgow. He joined the head office of the Commercial Bank of Scotland at age 17. In the early 1930s he turned his back on a lucrative career in banking to start his own magazine for Scottish boys. Dunnett and his partner in crime James ('Seumas') Adam co-founded a short-lived Scottish adventure magazine called The Claymore *which Dunnett described as 'a tuppeny weekly adventure paper for Scottish boys'.*

Dunnett was the chief press officer to Tom Johnston, the Secretary of State for Scotland from 1940 to 1946, editor of the Daily Record *from 1946 to 1955, and editor of* The Scotsman *from 1956 to 1972. He also held a variety of posts in government, broadcasting, the arts and industry. In 1995, he served as Chairman of Thomson Scottish Petroleum and was knighted in the same year, an honour which amused him greatly. He said at the time, 'Her Majesty has done herself a great honour!' Sir Alastair lived in Edinburgh and was married to the author Dorothy Dunnett.*

The idea for The Canoe Boys *came as a result of the pending demise of* The Claymore. *Left with no work and a huge printer's bill, Dunnett and Adam arrived at an ingenious solution: the duo would earn enough money to repay their debts by writing dispatches for* The Daily Record, *Scotland's self-proclaimed national paper, of their journey north from the Clyde by way of the West Coast to the Hebrides by canoe. This excerpt captures the essence of that trip as they land on the 'forbidden' isle of Rhum.*

✳   ✳   ✳

The Forbidden Island

from **THE CANOE BOYS:**
FROM THE CLYDE PAST THE CUILLINS

Eigg rides the inner Minch like a ship. The island's unmistakable shape can be seen from mainland peaks far into the heart of Scotland. Five miles long, it lies as if travelling from south to north, with a trawler bow almost 1000ft high, a dip down to a central well-deck, and a battlemented poop rising to 1300ft. This galleon shape is the central spine of the island, breaking in cliffs along the middle of the land, and shielding, at their feet, green fields and crofts. The 'poop' is the splendid peak, the Sgurr, and it was for the harbour at its base, in the south of the island, that we were making.

We had six miles of open water to cross, but once into the swing of the great swell we found the passage easy. We got a squall of rain half-way over which blotted out the island for many minutes, and chilled us more than the gouts of the sea. As we came up to the red cliffs of the south shore, the caves there opened their mouths at us. The sea was hammering the reefs off Castle Island, sending white streaks out back into the channel. Where the channel narrows we rounded the point of the pier suddenly, seeing below us the yellow sand of the shallows.

We were very fresh, and it was no more than midday, when we came aground on the concrete slope of the pier. There was no one to be seen at the sheds, or around any of the trim houses in sight. We bundled into some bushes, flinging off our bleached paddling clothes, and spreading them into the air. In a few moments we were kilted and shod, and on the road towards the centre of the island.

We had a dashing encounter with two small Eigg citizens, at an intersection of roads which puzzled us about our proper direction. A small girl of about six appeared, leading a tiny infant by the hand. It was an infant at that stage when, seen walking, they look even tinier than a babe in arms, and the pace it was setting was an almost imperceptible forward stacher. Here was an opportunity to have a neutral verdict on our Gaelic. We approached the pair gently, not to frighten them, and the following conversation went through in Gaelic without a hitch:

'Which is the road to the post office?'

'That's it yonder.'

'Great thanks to thyself, O little girl.'

We went forward in terrific gratification, glowing in the tribute paid by our little pathfinder, who, unlike her older relatives, could not have been tempted to help us out in English, as she had probably a very hazy knowledge of that language. We turned back to wave to her, and she waved without shyness, and also revolved the incredibly small child on its axis, so that he was looking eventually in our direction and could wave too. These two made a brave little picture on the down side of the brae from us, with 60 miles of the Scottish coast for their backcloth.

It was a post office and grocery store combined: indeed, a cooperative store, with the isles folk shareholders, and dividends going at the end of the year. I had the melancholy first task of wiring home for £3, by way of an advance against the newspaper fees we would eventually get. This was a delicate piece of telegram compilation, to find an economical and yet not too disturbing form of words.

Incoming mail awaited us in the form of letters and a packet or two. The packets had been forwarded through Mallaig post office, where Mrs Watt the postmistress (we did not know her yet) had printed heavily across one of them: 'Canoe Boys! Weary waiting for you! Hurry up and give us a call! P.O. Mallaig.' It was a friendly shattering of the post office rules, and our hearts warmed to the knowledge that we had a following.

We also failed to buy any bread, as the steamer was not due until the next day with a consignment of Glasgow-made loaves. But 'Mrs MacDonald down at the shore will make you a baking of scones'. This news we announced to Mrs MacDonald herself who heard it bravely at the door of her beautiful cottage. She had a family of sons, and was accustomed to hungry emergencies. By the time we had the tent up and the tea going, the scones were ready, a biscuit tin full of treacle and soda scones, and she filled our bonnets with eggs too.

It wasn't hard to find business in Eigg which kept us five days there. Everybody had to paddle the canoes round the bay, and some of the folk came from the bigger settlement, at Cleadale on the west side, to get their turn. There was the Sgurr to climb, caves to explore, the minister, the priest, and the doctor to visit. The Muck boys came one day in their boat on ferry affairs, and they had to see the canoes again. There was also the hope that the wind, now round dead to the west, would die a little and let us get to Rhum. For it was essential that we take in Rhum on our way. We wrote some things, and mended our clothes; and as the thickets at our tent door abounded with the ripest brambles, we bought sugar in the store and made a great boiling of jam, which went onwards with us on the trip, in an aluminum pot which never thereafter got rid of the purple dye.

The church, the school, and the post office are strung out along the top of the ridge where the road, rising from the hamlet at the harbour, crosses the spine of the island to reach Cleadale on the far shore. Here they provide a centre for spiritual, mental and bodily services within energetic reach of all the homesteads of the island. The siting of these common buildings exposes them, of course, to heavy weather up there on the middle heights. The Roman Catholic church and the priest's house have a cosier setting among the croft houses of Cleadale, looking over to the Outer Isles.

But on the day we attended the parish church, the Sunday, it was in a brilliant atmosphere, with the sun polishing the scene out of all recognition by artists or photographers. The church has clear windows, and as we stood to sing the psalms our eyes stared round, and our breath caught, at the immense glory of the scene. For the church, on its height, forms as it were a pulpit on the Western Isles, and dominates them all. From window after window there are views to move the soul of man. On that Sunday the sky was an endless blue, and the sea that wind-dark colour we have not yet managed to translate from the Greek. In spite of the seascapes over towards the islands, it was the mainland views that held us, starting up towards the Sound of Sleat and the low hills before Loch Alsh, and sweeping in a great purple offering east and southwards to Ardnamurchan and beyond to Caliach Point, in Mull, with ranges away inland to the Grampian Hills. In the sea, Muck and Coll were mere foreground fragments. The man who preaches a sermon yonder has a rich start in the samples of God's handiwork under the eye.

The man who preached the sermon was as unusual as his parish. The Reverend Mr MacWhirter would announce the psalms from his pulpit, and then sweep out of the perch in his black robes like a bat, to huddle over the small harmonium, pounding and pedalling the uncertain melody. He was no islesman, having recently come from an industrial parish of Lanarkshire, and he was shortly to leave the Small Isles and move on.

In the meantime he was enjoying himself. Each time it was necessary for him to voyage to another of the islands to take a service there, or perform some pastoral office, he donned a white yachting cap and placed himself in the bow of the Muck launch, gulping enormous rations of sea-air as they hammered solidly through the Atlantic. Upon the glebe, which ran for many green acres about the huge manse house, he was engaged in some stock-rearing experiments, and we learned from himself of a recent hitch in this planned husbandry.

At a sale on the mainland he had bought and shipped home a stallion Highland pony, arranging also for the vet to arrive in a day or two and make the beast a gelding. In the meantime the pony had been put into a meadow occupied by the minister's mare, and while there had made unexpected use of his opportunities. In the course of nature, and long after the vet had come and finished his fell work, the mare dropped a splendid foal; and the pony was still to be seen scrutinising, perhaps with a knowing eye, this leggy pledge of his erstwhile virility.

Mr MacWhirter had tackled the problem of his bachelor housekeeping by engaging an ex-R.N. manservant, and when we visited the manse one evening we found the pair busy at a gallant scone-baking. The results fell short of perfection, and the blae scones were fed to the hens, a flock of which was developing about the door, as another stock side-line.

Our own taste in scones had again been grossly flattered by the productions of Mrs MacDonald. Our slightly replenished purse enabled us to call for more. On each occasion we battled for the right to make a little payment. I understand this to be another of the differences which distinguish exploration in our countryside from that carried out in foreign parts. It is the custom, one reads, to haggle with the foreign native over the price to be paid, with a flurry of bidding and bargaining on both sides. The same practice is common with us, although, in the Highlands, it is the seller who is bidding down, or even refusing payment, and the purchaser who is bidding up. It is a situation often exploited by the stranger, perhaps unwittingly, and one hears of advice given: 'You musn't offer payment for anything they give you. They're very offended if you don't take it for nothing.' One would hope that the traveller with a decent appreciation of modern conditions will not go too far in applying to his case the ancient standards of hospitality.

Between the soda and the treacles scones, we were in as great a dilemma as with the scones and the pancakes at Calve. It was a ceaseless anxiety to decide which were best to eat. With all the electric ovens and aluminum girdles and fancies of today, how many people know how to bake scones like these? One morning we got the biscuit tin filled for the last time, and packed for an afternoon departure.

Rhum was the next stop, and its mere appearance on our schedule meant the making of a little piece of history. Our best route there was to be northwards up the east coast of Eigg, and then out north-west and straight up Loch Scresort, the port where the only houses lay. The wind had gone more northerly too, but we hoped that this would die.

No one had seen us arrive in Eigg, and there was no one to watch us go. We paddled along out through the familiar channel between the two perches north of the harbour, came round the huddle of reefs off Rudha na Crannaig, and kept into the shore for the pull up the coast. There was plenty of shelter inshore, for the cliffs fall sheer almost to the sea, the only shore at most points being mere rock debris weathered and fallen off the face. Over this face, nearly 1000ft high for most of its length, spout a succession of waterfalls, trailing downwards like moving lace. They are merely the normal hill burns, which start in the wet high ground, and on their way to the sea suddenly lose their footing and make the endless drop. In an east wind they fold back on themselves as they reach the cliff edge, and are scattered back inland upon the grass of the plateau, where they rise to gather in their little moor channel and struggle seawards vainly again. This day the wind was from the other direction, but it was strong enough to search down over the precipices to our level, promising a harder greeting when we should leave the lee.

The shore bent away eventually towards the north-west and into the wind's eye. A muffled belt appeared ahead like a harbour bar, streaming free past the end of Eigg through the water where we were going. We drove into it, and knew we were in real weather again. There was a sudden chill in the late September wind too, which even the heat of our effort could not thaw. We bent and dipped to a long grind to clear the north end of Eigg and reach the Sound of Rhum. There were two miles to cover, and they took us over two hours.

It was necessary that we should reach Rhum, and land and stay on it. It is an island with a dark history, and its name had followed us like a challenge since we had left the Crinan Canal. 'You won't be landing on Rhum anyway?' we had repeatedly been told. 'They don't allow anybody on the island.' This we had heard so often that we had come to reply at last that, if we got nowhere else, we should certainly land on Rhum.

The whole island is preserved as a private estate, and it is official information to yachtsmen, mountaineers, geologists, as well as mere travellers and tourists, that visitors are not encouraged. It is a phrase which can cover a variety of discouraging practices, and its modern story starts badly with the undeniable episode of the Clearances in the 1820s, when the 400 inhabitants were evicted in a body, and shipped to somewhere overseas. Memories are alive, and I judge them authentic, of the terrors of that time. One can pore with pleasure over the scale-map of the island, peppered with place-names, and discern something of the love with which a happy community dowered in apt descriptive Gaelic names their peaks and passes, the seal rocks and the cave bays, the upland lochs and mosses, the sea and inland cliffs, the rivers, the burns, the braes. All this in a noble, small land-mass in the sea, six miles square, with a tumultuous skyline. It is not that Rhum has no modern challengers. The adjacent townships and villages, on isle and mainland, seethe with stories of indignation and reprisals. Raids on the deer are frequent, although perhaps more frequent in story than in performance.

There are those in Mallaig who will claim, unofficially, to have seen poached stags unloaded from boats returned after a Rhum foray. It is an unhappy atmosphere, mingling banditry and restriction. And it exists. We had pledged ourselves, in print and to a countless acquaintance, to land and spy out this strange land, and to report. It was utterly essential that we should reach Rhum.

At the time of which we speak, however, it was becoming doubtful if the hour for the visit had arrived. Beyond the north point of Eigg we had another seven miles of open water to face, and we had seldom seen water so open and gaping. The wind was coming hard from the direction of Loch Scresort, Rhum's only harbour, and from the whole Atlantic, which was situated just round the corner. It brought not only the broken waves which rode the main mass of the water, but also the waves which it lifted from the sea and flung at us. Eigg fell away on our left as we pulled on. To stop paddling meant the losing of a great deal of way, so that it was impossible to bale, and the canoes were filling uncomfortably. A point came when we ceased to make headway at all. About two miles out from Eigg we simply sat, flailing on at the sea, and making no forward progress. The wind had no pity, and felt as if it would blow for ever. Very little more of this and we should be too tired to keep control. So we did what we had never yet done on the trip – turned round about and ran for where we had come from.

The wind and seas took us swiftly towards the shore. We surf-rode as we chose. A shout back and forward between us settled for a landing-place on the north-west, the nearest shore of Eigg, so that our next stage back towards Rhum would be the shortest possible distance. Nearer the shore, we picked up the small island called Eilan Thuilm, and aimed to land behind it, to lessen the onrush which would bear us heavily on the rocks. We worked strenuously towards this lee, baling hard at intervals, to lighten the load of the canoes and keep them from damage by reducing the solid weight which would strike. Because it was clear that we were going to strike, and that heavily.

Nearer in, we saw that the shore was large boulders, and surf was spouting among them. It was too late to back out and try another place. Slowing down as much as we dared by the dangerous process of back-paddling, we struck. I rested for a moment on a round brown boulder which ran suddenly dry and punched me jarring on the thighs through the slats and fabric of my keel. I was half-way out and up to the waist, in the hope of running the canoe up among the rocks, when the next wave took us both, canoe and me. I lost it, and went bundling up among the boulders, got to my feet some yards on, and floundered, battering my bare feet, grabbing after the painter. I got it before the next wave, and we went in this time hand in hand, as it were, bumping painfully; myself wincing over my shin-bones, and agonising as the canoe's ribs cracked. Eventually the canoe wedged close inshore, and, water-filled, would not be moved even by the successive waves which submerged us. Seumas, who had made a more adept if not a drier landing, splashed through to heave us both ashore, myself and canoe. Presently the paddle also came in.

At this stage we were certain that the trip was finished. In skin and ribs the canoes had taken such a damaging that they should have been unrepairable. And we were so soused and bruised ourselves as to delay the post-mortem until the morning. There was a strip of green here, good camping site save for the endless wind to which it was exposed, and we tented up, managing to build a low wind-break of stones round our walls before the darkness came down.

A miraculous healing fell upon us all during the night. A cold sunlight washing the tent roof woke us, and we stretched, feeling no more than surface wounding. A sortie to the canoes revealed a similar condition. By a freak of their fragile strength they had no ribs sprung and no rents, although we could still hear, knelling in our ears from the time of the landing, the sounds with which they had crashed ashore, tossing and crunching like flotsam tea-chests. One or two holes punched in the fabric were the only damage we could find, although a survey of the shore at low tide showed almost every rock in sight smeared with the blue paint rasped from our keels, to say nothing of other blotches we fancied could be our blood. A few strips of sticking-plaster patched up our ocean-going craft and ourselves, and we began to get ready again for the attempt on Rhum.

It was the same kind of day; perhaps a little slacker in the wind, but bitter cold, with a steep sea making ashore and promising a soaking launch. We were now beginning to reckon exposure among our potential handicaps. Yesterday had shown that, with the wind northerly, the heat of paddling was not enough to eliminate over very many hours the fangs of the wind, nor could our bodies be sure of warming up to a tolerable temperature the inevitable shipped water in which we sat. So we tried a new launching trick in the hope of getting dry away. Normally we pushed off straight into shore breakers, wading until we had two feet of depth, slipping aboard and sitting, to paddle out through the broken water. The essential pause when the canoe was taking our weight meant a brief loss of headway and control, and by the time the canoe was driving well offshore the cockpit had swallowed some inches of water, a nucleus of which remained for the rest of the day.

For today's launch we donned bonnets and oilskins against the wind. Running the canoes out through the nearest shallows, we shielded the cockpits with the skirts of our oilskins against the first few breakers. Then, each man watching for his wave lull, we stepped in and paddled off standing up, so that the canoes were never halted, and we hitched and jumped them over the waves rather than through them, until fairly into the Sound. Only then did we take time to get squeezed down into the sitting position, finding negligible water there compared with our normal intake. This is perhaps an advanced form of canoe handling. We used it several times later in similar conditions, finding that our bare feet planted on the canoe bottom gave us an enormously stronger and more urgent control of balance, in spite of the much higher centre of gravity in the standing position.

And then the long slog to Rhum, although we were inside the grand pillared entrance of Loch Scresort before we could feel assured that the wind would not beat us back. Every mile of the seven took us a full half-hour, heads down and eyes three-quarters shut. Only when we were well in towards the loch end could we look up, in the lee, and see round. Ahead was Kinloch Castle, a red sandstone pile, distinguished among fine trees, with a hamlet scattering of houses about. We turned aside and landed below a small plantation of trees which promised camping shelter, splashing ashore with more noise than we were used to making, and intoning 'Rhum, Rhum! Here we come!' or some such exuberance.

This time we brought up the canoes and laid them in a V to enclose the tent. A stag came up to the fence and leaned his Royal head over, coughing at us in the bronchial signal of the rut. He came to visit us frequently in the next hours.

A large man, in tweeds, with a gun and two dogs, arrived scrambling round a shore path and came over towards us. As we continued with the arrangement of our camp site, there was a short conversation:

'Have you got permission to land here?'

'Yes.'

'Who from?'

'Ourselves!'

It was an almost casual opening, but complete. In the stiff ensuing silence Seumas and I conversed normally as we unpacked. There was an adjacent throat-clearing and – 'You can't stay here without permission.'

'We're here!'

'You'll need permission!'

'We're staying!'

Our contribution to this was of an offhand character. The tent was now out of its bundle and the pole was assembling. The visitor drew nearer.

'You'll have to see Lady Bullough before you put that tent up, Just leave the tent here and come to see Lady Bullough.'

'The tent is going up!' This was said with some volume, and the tones may well have reached the castle. Short as the conversation was, it took place at a backcloth which was the rising tent. Its off-white weathered shape was already erect and pegged. Now we ripped out our bundles with the dry clothes and towels, and, as if the man with the gun had no existence, we stripped and dried ourselves upon the grass, standing and flexing and towelling with the shiver of cold delight this moment always gave us. It was a naked insult, and on the horizon of our casual view – for we didn't even look at him – we could see the man's face flame as red as the sunset. This was from no physical embarrassment, but because he was ignored – treated like a paid convenience, a situation with which, in his present service, he was doubtless familiar. There was a sense, indeed, in which we pitied the man for our behaviour. He was a Highlander, but he was in the wrong setting, and we were at no pains to hide our contempt. In a moment or two we were kilted and clothed and well shod, glowing against the chill of the night. As we started to make a meal, the man with the gun and the dogs went off by the way they had come.

Some time later he was back, with a new opening:

'Would you gentlemen like to come and see Lady Bullough?'

'Certainly! We should very much like to see Lady Bullough.'

Our little procession wound round to the head of the loch, and we chatted on such topics as might be allowed to be of common interest. The island well knew of our voyage, and, indeed, of our intention to make Rhum a port of call. But the conversation was heavy with an overlay of the proprietorial principle, that no part of this island moor could under any circumstances offer a welcome, or perhaps even a foothold, to the visitor.

At one point, our guide related, pathetically ingratiating: 'When you were paddling up the loch this evening Lady Bullough phoned me down and said, "There are poachers in the loch. Don't allow them to land!" And I said: "These aren't poachers. They're sports." "Well," she said, "they musn't land anyway!" But I said ... '

Arrived at the castle, our guide went in to announce us. He was back soon, with apologies.

'Lady Bullough is very sorry, she can't see you now. But you have her permission to camp on the island, and we have to give you a haunch of venison with her compliments.'

We accepted the explanation, and the promise of the tribute, gravely, and strolled off about our business upon the forbidden ground. Not another hint of hostility came into the air again, although we have not heard that subsequent excursions have fared as lavishly. We were indeed received with kindness on all sides, as if the people of the place were relieved to be able to break away from a forbidding routine. In one of the houses we were invited to a sumptuous supper of roast venison, and the lady of the house prepared a packet of sandwiches to take us over the Sound of Sleat on the next day. For a long time we retained the memory of a child of this house – a girl at least 12 years of age, yet so unused to new faces on this desert island that she crouched all the evening shyly behind a chair, peeping and giggling like a four-year-old.

Crossing a courtyard in the late darkness, we came on an unforgettable scene. Lamplight streamed from a deep door, and we stepped into a butcher's workshop. Four stags, the day's kill, were being dismembered by a group of young Skyemen, who went at the job with bloody hands, making enormous shadows on the walls. As we watched them, they ripped the venison apart – the hands with their antlers on a side bench, the carcasses slung up to chained hooks, the hides off like cheese-cloth, and the knives and saws going with inhuman skill. These were apparently gillies brought to the island for the shooting season. It was a vivid picture – a strong and simple scene – one to put on canvas.

There is a post office on the island, although the traffic is trifling. It was a Cockney voice which served us here – indeed, we discovered only one Gaelic speaker among the two dozen or so of permanent residents. He was the chief stalker, and he had little opportunity of using his native language. While the post-mistress went into the rear premises for some telegraph forms, we took from the counter the dated franking stamp and imprinted it plentifully upon our log, so as to authenticate our visit. And, oddly, this landing and camping affair of ours still seems to be most rare. We also stamped the backs of our wrists, and even, I think, our palms, with 'Isle of Rhum'.

Having landed, there was nothing else to be done here. We had hoped to include also in our Small Isles circuit a visit to Canna, lying still farther to the west, but decided to abandon this in favour of a push north, via Mallaig. Accordingly we were packing by early morning, with the wind still westerly, and fresher than we cared to have it. Our course was to be due east to Mallaig, and this 20-mile passage would be the longest yet in open water, with only a passing glance, midway, at the shore of Sleat, in Skye. Anyway, the wind was right for us, and we packed. Also, we took delivery ceremoniously of the haunch of venison. It weighed 26lb, professionally bagged and sewn, and it dangerously upset all our stowage technique. Rather than refuse it on any ground of sailing safety, we should have abandoned our most needful possessions. After a deal of experiment, however, we lashed the mighty thing on the top of Seumas's stern section, with the shank bone pointing aft, and the red meat of the haunch snugging up to the small of his back. I took over bundles of his stuff to spread out the weight, and in this way we got trimmed and afloat at last.

On the way out of Loch Scresort towards the east we had enough smooth water to see how Seumas was riding. He was truly weighted, with precariously little free-board left; and this persuaded us not to use the sails, although we were to have the wind with us. There was a fine wind, too, for the direction we were taking. But paddling would have to do. Sailing, although giving us a good deal more speed and ease, would have forced the freighted canoe much too low.

It was a six-hour pull at the paddles, in heavy sea all the way. Once clear of Rhum coast there was no shelter whatsoever, and we took more water aboard than normal because the sterns were too heavy to come up fast to the following sea. However, the venison was a good breakwater on Seumas's poop, and it was well brined before we had gone far. It was not a passage which could be forced. We went on at our own pace, stopping the paddles for not more than five minutes in the six hours. It was too cold, indeed, to stop, and much rain blashed in showers that looked like smoke columns as they came up astern, and felt like lances.

We had hoped to encounter on the way some of the great fleet of steam herring drifters then fishing out of Mallaig, many of whose crews we knew. But for four-fifths of the way there were none in sight, and that for a reason which was later to cause us modestly to preen. The weather was too bad for them! Of course, we had the wind more or less astern. At no point of the passage could we conceivably have turned round and attempted to go back. Only one vessel passed us on the route. It was later than our half-way stage, when we seemed to be close to the Point of Sleat, Skye's most southerly mark, and felt a sense of comfort that here was a solid place to make for if things should get worse. The white houses of Aird were quite clear in the occasional sunshine. Then the upper works of a small ship appeared between us and the land. She was throwing water over her mast, but, what made for more unease, she was hull down, which meant that the land beyond her was even miles away.

For the second part of the trip we needed no compass, as the great white pillar of smoke rising above Mallaig fattened out of the sea ahead, and we watched it grow for 10 miles, until the roofs of the high kippering sheds appeared, where it comes from. When we were so far past the Point of Sleat that we could no longer see it on our left without turning to look, we had a few miles only to go. They were long, but they passed.

A mile or two off Mallaig we could see the houses and the harbour easily. One or two herring drifters came out – the only ones, we learned later, to make a fishing that day – and turned southwest for the Coll banks. This pointed them into the weather, so that they shortly looked like Shetland sea-ponies, throwing ragged manes of spray out of their eyes, and bucking skittishly.Soon we were near enough to see people on the pier, and to be seen ourselves. Nearing still, we watched the whole silent and busy pantomime of arrival excitement – the pointed arms, the beckonings and runnings, the training and passing of binoculars, the climbings on to railway wagons – until the outer quay wall was a black spectating mass, which moved with us shouting round the end of the pier. The mass fringed the harbour edge with our progress all the way, and eventually milled below the end of the road to watch us bump ashore. Then the active fragments sprayed off from the edges and ran towards us, and they were men and boys helping to lift us and our canoes ashore. This was a kind welcome, the more so because the people had dignity themselves. As we chatted and chaffed with them in a first passage of words, the news spread back that we had come from Rhum, and this was satisfying in the highest degree, being both a joke and a wonder as well. As the crowd continued to grow and press around, we left the canoes to them at last and slipped off to see to our livelihood at the post office.

Here we found a certain shyness, as we sent off our Press wires, for the ladies of the official service had urged our arrival, and here we were! Nor were we prepared to be fobbed off; as was their ruse, by being attended at the grill by the junior staff. We had Mrs Watt, the postmistress, and her daughter Ethel haled from the back premises to answer for themselves, and there was a hilarious session of mock-complaint and counter-charge, until passers-by came in to discover what the laughter was about, and another concourse formed. One thing, as the saying goes, led to another, to such effect that we were shortly installed in the parlour of the Watts' house, which was handily affixed to the post office. Here, still in our tattered and salt-bleached paddling flimsies, we went at a substantial tea, and held occasional court as friendly heads came round the door incessantly. Everybody, I think, felt better after this.

ALEXANDER SMITH
(1830-1867)

❊   ❊   ❊

Poet, essayist, and novelist, Alexander Smith was born in Kilmarnock in 1829. Although he followed in his father's trade as a lace pattern designer, he spent much of his free time writing poetry, which would eventually bring some fame and fortune. He was editor of Glasgow Miscellany *magazine until 1854 when he became Secretary of Edinburgh University. He published several volumes of poetry, which failed to garner much attention, before switching almost exclusively to prose.*

Alexander Smith died of typhoid fever in early 1867. Among his works include A Life Drama and Other Poems *(1852),* Sonnets on the Crimean War *(with Sydney Dobell, 1855),* City Poems *(1857),* Edwin of Deira *(1861),* Dreamthorp *(1863), and* Alfred Hagart's Household *(1866).*

In 1864 Smith spent six weeks on Skye. The result, A Summer in Skye, *is a prose poem to the island.*

❊   ❊   ❊

Riding through Skye

from A SUMMER IN SKYE

AFTER SPENDING ANOTHER ten days or thereabouts with Mr. M'Ian and at my bothy, I intimated my intentions of paying a visit to my friend the Landlord – with whom Fellowes was then staying – who lived some forty miles off in the north-western portion of the Island. The old gentleman was opposed to rapid decisions and movements and asked me to remain with him yet another week. Now his speech was as old-fashioned as he was himself; ancient matters turned up on his tongue just as ancient matters turned up on his farm. There might be an old grave or an old implement on the one, so would be found an old proverb or an old scrap of Gaelic poem on the other.

When he found I was resolute he glanced at the weather-gleam and the troops of mist gathering on Cuchullin, muttering as he did so, ' "Make ready my galley," said the king, "I shall sail for Norway on Wednesday." "Will you," said the wind, who, flying about, had overheard what was said, "you had better ask my leave first." '

As M'Ian had predicted, I could only move from his house if the weather granted permission; and this permission the weather did not seem disposed to grant. For several days it rained as I had never seen it before; a waterspout too had burst up among the hills and the stream came down in mighty flood. There was a great hubbub at the house. Mr. M'Ian's hay, which was built in large stacks in the valley meadows, was in danger and the fiery cross was sent through the cotters.

Up to the hay-fields every available man was dispatched with carts and horses, to remove the stacks to some spot where the waters could not reach them; while at the bridge nearer the house women and boys were stationed with long poles and what rudely-extemporised implements Celtic ingenuity could suggest, to intercept and fish out piles and trusses which the thievish stream was carrying away with it seaward. These piles and trusses would at least serve for the bedding of cattle.

For three days the rainy tempest continued; at last, on the fourth, mist and rain rolled up like a vast curtain in heaven and then again were visible the clumps of birch-wood and the bright sea and the smoking hills and, far away on the ocean floor, Rum and Canna, without a speck of cloud on them, sleeping in the coloured calmness of early afternoon. This uprising of the elemental curtain was, so far as the suddenness of the effect was concerned, like the uprising of the curtain of the pantomime on the transformation scene – all at once a dingy, sodden world had become a brilliant one and all the newly-revealed colour and brilliancy promised to be permanent.

Of this happy change in the weather I, of course, took immediate advantage. About five o'clock in the afternoon my dog-cart was brought to the door; and after a parting cup with Mr.

M'Ian – who pours a libation both to his arriving and his departing guest – I drove away on my journey to remote Portree and to the unimagined country that lay beyond Portree, but which I knew held Dunvegan, Duntulm, MacLeod's Tables and Quirang. I drove up the long glen with a pleasant exhilaration of spirit. I felt grateful to the sun, for he had released me from my rainy captivity.

The drive, too, was pretty; the stream came rolling down in foam, the smell of the wet birch-trees was in the brilliant air, every mountain-top was strangely and yet softly distinct; and looking back, there were the blue Cuchullins looking after me, as if bidding me farewell! At last I reached the top of the glen and emerged on a high plateau of moorland, in which were dark inky tarns with big white water-lillies on them; and skirting across the plateau I dipped down on the parliamentary road, which, like a broad white belt, surrounds Skye. Better road to drive on you will not find in the neighbourhood of London itself! and just as I was descending, I could not help pulling up.

The whole scene was of the extremist beauty – exquisitely calm, exquisitely coloured. On my left was a little lake with a white margin of water-lillies, a rocky eminence throwing a shadow half-way across it. Down below, on the sea-shore, was the farm of Knock, with white outhouses and pleasant patches of cultivation, the school-house and the church, while on a low spit of land the old castle of the Macdonalds was mouldering. Still lower down and straight away stretched the sleek blue Sound of Sleat, with not a sail or streak of steamer smoke to break its vast expanse and with a whole congregation of clouds piled up on the horizon, soon to wear their evening colours. I let the sight slowly creep into my study of imagination, so that I might be able to reproduce it at pleasure; that done, I drove down to Isle Oronsay by pleasant sloping stages of descent, with green hills on right and left and, along the road-side, like a guard of honour, the purple stalks of the foxglove.

The evening sky was growing red above me when I drove into Isle Oronsay, which consists of perhaps fifteen houses in all. It sits on the margin of a pretty bay, in which the cry of the fisher is continually heard and into which the *Clansman* going to or coming from the south steams twice or thrice in the week. At a little distance is a lighthouse with a revolving light – an idle building during the day, but when night comes, awakening to full activity – sending now a ray to Ardnamurchan, now piercing with a fiery arrow the darkness to Glenelg.

In Isle Oronsay is a merchant's shop, in which every conceivable article may be obtained. At Isle Oronsay the post runner drops a bag, as he cries on to Armadale Castle. At Isle Oronsay I supped with my friend Mr. Fraser. From him I heard that the little village had been, like M'Ian's house, fiercely scourged by rains. On the supper-table was a dish of trouts.

'Where do you suppose I procured these,' he asked.

'In one of your burns, I suppose.'

'No such thing; I found them in my potato-field.'

'In your potato-field! How came that about?'

'Why, you see the stream, swollen by three day's rain, broke over a potato-field of mine on the hillside and carried the potatoes away and left these plashing in poll and runnel. The Skye streams have a slight touch of honesty in them!'

I smiled at the conceit and expounded to my host the law of compensation which pervades the universe, of which I maintained the trouts on the table were a shining example. Mr. Fraser assented; but held that Nature was a poor valuator – that her knowledge of the doctrine of equivalents was slighty defective – that the trouts were well enough, but no reimbursement for the potatoes that were gone.

Next morning I resumed my journey. The road, so long as it skirted the sea-shore, was pretty enough; but the sea-shore it soon left entered a waste of brown monotonous moorland. The country round about abounds in grouse and was the favourite shooting-ground of the late Lord Macdonald. By the road-side his lordship had erected a stable and covered the roof with tin; and so at a distance it flashed as if the Koh-i-noor had been dropped by accident in that dismal region.

As I went along, the hills above Broadford began to rise; then I drove down the slope, on which the market was held – the tents all struck, but the stakes yet remaining in the ground – and after passing the six houses, the lime-kiln, the church and the two merchants' shops, I pulled up at the inn door and sent the horse round to the stable to feed and rest an hour.

After leaving Broadford the traveller drives along the margin of the ribbon of salt water which flows between Skye and the Island of Scalpa. Up this narrow sound the steamer never passes and it is only navigated by the lighter kinds of sailing craft. Scalpa is a hilly island of some three or four miles in length, by one and a half in breadth, is gray-green in colour and as treeless as the palm of my hand. It has been the birthplace of many soldiers.

After passing Scalpa the road ascends; and I noticed as I drove along that during the last hour or so the frequent streams have changed colour. In the southern portion of the island they come down as if the hills ran sherry – here they are pale as shallow sea-water. This difference in hue arises of course from a difference of bed. About Broadford they come down through the mossy moorland, here they run over marble, Of marble the island is full; and it is not impossible that the sculptors of the twentieth century will patronise the quarries of Strath and Kyle rather than the quarries of Carrara. But wealth is needed to lay bare these mineral treasures. The fine qualities of Skye marble will never be obtained until they are laid open by a golden pick-axe.

Over past Scalpa, I approached Lord Macdonald's deer forest. I had turned the flank of the Cuchullins now and was taking them in rear and I skirted their bases very closely too. The road is full of wild ascents and descents and on my left, for a couple of miles or so, I was in continual presence of bouldered hillside sloping away upward to some invisible peak, overhanging wall of wet black precipice, far-off serrated ridge that cuts the sky like a saw. Occasionally these mountain forms open up and fall back and I saw the sterilist valleys running no man knows whether. Altogether the hills here have a strange weird look. Each is as closely seamed with lines as the face of a man of a hundred and these myriad reticulations are picked out with a pallid gray-green, as if through some mineral corrosion.

Passing along I was strangely impressed with the idea that some vast chemical experiment has been going on for some thousand of years; that the region is nature's laboratory and that down these wrinkled hill-fronts she had split her acids and undreamed-of combinations. I never think of verdure in connection with that network of gray-green, but only of rust, or of some metallic discolouration. I cannot help fancying that if a sheep fed on one of those hillsides it would to a certainty be poisoned. Altogether the sight is very grand, very impressive and very uncomfortable and it was with the liveliest satisfaction that, tearing down one of the long descents, I turned my back on the mountain monsters and beheld in front the green Island of Raasay, with its imposing modern mansion, basking in sunshine. It is like passing from the world of gnomes to the world of men.

I have driven across Lord Macdonald's deer forest in sunshine and in rain and am constrained to confess that, under the latter atmospherical condition, the scenery is the more imposing. Some months ago I drove in the mail-gig from Sligachan to Broadford. There was a high wind, the sun was bright and consequently a great *carry* and flight of sunny vapours. All at once, too, every half-hour or so, the turbulent brightness of wind and cloud was extinguished by fierce squalls of rain. I could see the coming rain-storm blown out on the wind toward me like a sheet of muslin cloth. On it came racing in its strength and darkness, the long straight watery lines pelting on rock and road, churning in marsh and pool. Over the unhappy mail-gig it rushed, bidding defiance to plaid or waterproof cape and wetting every-one to the skin.

The mail jogged on as best as it could through the gloom and the fury and then the sunshine came again, making to glisten, almost too brightly for the eye, every rain-pool on the road. In the sunny intervals there was a great race and hurry of towered vapour, as I said; and when a shining mass smote one of the hillsides, or shrouded for a while one of the more distant serrated crests, the concussion was so palpable to the eye that the ear felt defrauded and silence seemed unnatural. And when the vast mass passed onward to impinge on some other mountain barrier, it was singular to notice by what slow degrees, with what evident reluctance the laggard skirts combed off.

All these effects of rain and windy vapour I remember vividly and I suppose that the vividness was partly due to the lamentable condition of a fellow-traveller. He was a meek-faced man of fifty. He was dressed in sables, his swallow-tailed coat was thread-bare and withal seemed made for a smaller man. There was an uncomfortable space between the wrists of his coat and his black-thread gloves. He wore a hat and against the elements had neither protection of plaid or umbrella. No-one knew him, to no-one did he explain his business. To my notion he was bound for a funeral at some place beyond Portree. He was not a clergyman – he might have been a school-master who had become green-moulded in some out-of-the-way locality.

Of course one or two of the rainy squalls settled the meek-faced man in the thread-bare sables. Emerging from one of these he resembled a draggled rook and the rain was pouring from the rim of his pulpy hat as it might from the eaves of a cottage. A passenger handed him his spirit-flask, the meek-faced man took a hearty pull and, returning it, said plaintively, 'I'm but poorly clad, sir, for this God-confound climate.' I think often of the utterance of the poor fellow: it was the only thing he said all the way; and when I think of it, I see again the rain blown out towards me on the wind like a waving sheet of muslin cloth and the rush, the concussion, the up-break and the slow reluctant trailing off from the hillside of the sunny cloud. The poor man's plaintive tone is the anchor which holds these things in my memory.

The forest is of course treeless. Nor are deer seen there frequently. Indeed, only once did I get a sight of antlers in that place. Carefully I crept up, sheltering myself behind a rocky haunch of the hill to where the herd were lying and then rushed out upon them with a halloo. In an instant they were on their feet and away went the beautiful creatures, doe and fawn, a stag with branchy head leading. They dashed across a torrent, crowned an eminence one by one and disappeared. Such a sight is witnessed but seldom; and the traveller passing through the brown desolation sees usually no sign of life. In Lord Macdonald's deer forest neither trees nor deer were visible.

When once quit of the forest, I came on a shooting-box, perched on the sea-shore; then I passed the little village of Sconser and, turning the sharp flank of a hill, drove along Loch Sligachan to Sligachan Inn, about a couple of miles distant. This Inn is a famous halting-place for tourists. There are good fishing streams about, I am given to understand and through Glen Sligachan you can find your way to Camunsunary and take the boat from thence to Loch Coruisk as we did ...

From the inn door the ridges of the Cuchullins are seen wildly invading the sky and in closer proximity there are other hills which cannot be called beautiful. Monstrous, abnormal, chaotic, they resemble the other hills on the earth's surface as Hindoo deities resemble human beings. The mountain, whose sharp flank I turned after I passed Sconser, can from here be inspected leisurely and is, to my mind, supremely ugly. In summer it is red as copper, with great ragged patches of verdure upon it, which look by all the world as if the coppery mass had *rusted* green. On these green patches cattle feed from March to October.

I baited at Sligachan – dined on trout which a couple of hours before were darting hither and thither in the stream – and then drove leisurely along to Portree while the setting sun was dressing the wilderness in gold and rose. And all the way the Cuchullins followed me the wild irregular outline, which no familiarity can stale, haunts me at Portree, as it does in nearly every quarter of Skye.

Portree folds two irregular ranges of white houses, the one range rising steeply above the other, around a noble bay, the entrance to which is guarded by rocky precipices. At a little distance the houses are white as shells and as in summer they are all set in the greenness of foilage the effect is strikingly pretty; and if the sense of prettiness departs to a considerable extent on a closer acquaintance, there is yet enough left to gratify me so long as I remain there and to make it a pleasant place to think about when I am gone. The lower range of houses consists mainly of warehouses and fish-stores; the upper, of the main hotel, the two banks, the court-house and the shops. A pier runs out into the bay and here, when the state of tide permits, comes the steamer on its way to or from Stornoway and unlades.

Should the tide be low the steamer lies to in the bay and her cargo and passengers come to shore by means of boats. She usually arrives at night; and at low tide, the burning of coloured lights at the mast-heads, the flitting hither and thither of busy lanterns, the pier boats coming and going with illuminated wakes and ghostly fires on the oar-blades, the clatter of chains and the shock of the crank hoisting the cargo out of the hold, the general hubbub and storm of Gaelic shouts and imprecations make the arrival at once picturesque and impressive.

In the bay the yacht of the tourist is continually lying and at the hotel door his dog-cart is continually departing or arriving and on the evenings of market-days, in the large public rooms, farmers and cattle-dealers sit over tumblers of smoking punch and discuss noisily the prices and qualities of stock.

Besides the hotel and the pier, the banks and the courthouse already mentioned, there are other objects of interest in the little island town – three churches, a post-office, a poorhouse and a cloth manufactory. And it has more than meets the eye – one of the Jameses landed here on a visitation of the Isles, Prince Charles was here on his way to Raasay, Dr. Johnson and Boswell were here; and somewhere on the green hill on which the pretty church lands, a murderer is buried – the precise spot of burial is unknown and so the entire hill gets the credit that of right belongs only to a single yard of it.

In Portree the tourist seldom abides long; he passes through it as a fortnight before he passed through Oban. It does not seem to the visitor a specially remarkable place, but everything is relative in this world. It is an event for the Isles-man at Dunvegan or the Point of Sleat to go to Portree, just as it is an event for a Yorkshireman to go to London.

When I drove out of Portree I was in Macleod's country and I discovered that the character of the scenery had changed. Looking back, the Cuchullins are wild and pale on the horizon, but every-thing around is brown, softly-swelling and montonous. The hills are round and low and except when an occasional boulder crops on their sides like a wart, are smooth as a seal's back. They are grey-green in colour and may be grazed to the top. Expressing once to a shepherd my admiration of the Cuchullins, the man replied, while he swept with his arm the entire range, 'There's no feeding there for twenty wethers!' Here, however, there is sufficient feeding to compensate for any lack of beauty.

About three miles out of Portree I came upon a solitary-looking school-house by the wayside and a few yards farther to a division of the roads. A finger-post informed me that the road to the right led to Uig, that to the left to Dunvegan. As I am at present bound for Dunvegan, I skirr along to the left and after an hour's drive come in sight of Loch Snizort, with Skeabost sitting whitely on its margin. Far inland from the broad Minch, like one of those wavering swords which medieval painters place in the hands of archangels, has Snizort come wandering; and it is the curious mixture of brine and pasture-land, of mariner life and shepherd-life which gives its charm to this portion of the island.

The lochs are narrow and I fancy a strong-lunged man could shout across. The sea-gull skims above the feeding sheep, the shepherd can watch the sail of the sloop, laden with meal, creeping from point to point. Above all places which I have seen in Skye, Skeabost has a lowland look. There are almost no turf-huts to be seen in the neighbourhood; the houses are built of stone and lime and are tidily white-washed. The hills are low and smooth; on the lower slopes corn and wheat are grown; and from a little distance the greenness of cultivation looks like a palpable smile – a strange contrast to the monotonous district through which, for an hour or so, I have driven.

As I pass the inn and drive across the bridge, I notice that there is an island in the stony stream and that this island is covered with ruins, The Skye-man likes to bury his dead in islands and this one in the stream at Skeabost is a crowded cemetery. I forded the stream and wandered for an hour amongst the tombs and broken stones. There are traces of an ancient chapel on the island, but tradition does not even make a guess at its builder's name or the date of its erection. There are old slabs, lying sideways, with the figures of recumbent men with swords in their hands and inscriptions indecipherable now – carved on them. There is the grave of a Skye clergyman who, if his epitaph be trusted, was a burning and a shining light in his day. I never saw a churchyard so mounded and so evidently over-crowded. Here laird, tacksman and cotter elbow each other in death. Here no-one will make way for a newcomer, or give the wall to his neighbour.

And standing in the little ruined island of silence and the dead, with the river perfectly audible on either side, I could not help thinking what a picturesque sight a Highland funeral would be, creeping across from the moors with wailing pipe-music, fording the river and his bearers making room for the dead man amongst the older dead as best they could. And this sight, I am told, may be seen any week in the year. To this island all the funerals of the countryside converge. Standing there, too, I could not help thinking that this space of silence, girt by river noises, would be an *eerie* place by moonlight. The broken chapel, the carved slabs lying sideways, as if the dead man beneath had grown restless and turned himself and the headstones jutting out of the mounded soil at every variety of angle, would appeal in the ink of shadow and the silver of moonbeam. In such circumstances I would hear something more in the stream as it ran past than the mere breaking of water on stones.

After passing the river and the island of graves I drove down between hedges to Skeabost church, school, post-office and manse and thereafter I climbed the steep hill towards Bernesdale and its colony of turf-huts; and when I reached the top I had a noble view of the flat blue Minch and the Skye headlands, each precipitous, abrupt and reminding me somehow of a horse which has been suddenly reined back to its haunches. But the grand vision is not of long duration, for the road descends rapidly towards Taynlone Inn. In my descent I beheld two bare-footed and bare-headed girls yoked to a harrow and dragging it up and down a small plot of delved ground.

Sitting in the inn it began to remember me how frequently I had heard in the south of the destitution of the Skye people and the discomfort of the Skye hut. During my wanderings I had the opportunity of visiting several of these dwellings and seeing how matters were transacted within. Frankly speaking, the Highland hut is not a model edifice. It is open to wind and almost always pervious to rain. An old bottomless herring firkin stuck in the roof usually serves for a chimney, but the blue peat-reek disdains that aperture and steams wilfully through the door and the crannies in the walls and roof. The interior is seldom well-lighted – what light there is proceeding rather from the orange glow of the peat-fire, on which a large pot is simmering, than from the narrow pane with its great bottlegreen bull's-eye. The rafters which support the roof are black and glossy with soot, as can be seen by the sudden flashes of firelight. The sleeping accommodation is limited and the beds are composed of heather or ferns. The floor is the beaten earth, the furniture scanty; there is hardly ever a chair – stools and stones, worn smooth by the usage of several generations, have to do instead.

One portion of the hut is not unfrequently a byre and the breath of the cow is mixed with the odour of peat-reek and the *baa* of the calf mingles with the wranglings and swift ejaculations of the infant Highlanders. In such a hut as this there are sometimes three generations. The mother stands knitting outside, the children are scrambling on the floor with the terrier and the poultry and a ray of cloudy sunshine from the narrow pane smites the silver hairs of the grandfather near the fire, who is mending fishing-nets against the return of his son-in-law from the south.

Am I inclined to lift my hands in horror at witnessing such a dwelling? Certainly not. I have only given one side of the picture. The hut I speak of nestles beneath a rock, on the top of which dances the ash-tree and the birch. The emerald mosses on its roof are softer and richer than the velvets of kings. Twenty yards down that path is a well that needs no ice in the dog-days. At a little distance, from rocky shelf to rocky shelf, trips a mountain burn, with abundance of trout in the brown pools. At the distance of a mile is the sea, which is not allowed to ebb and flow in vain; for in the smoke there is a row of fishes drying; and on the floor a curly-headed urchin of three years or thereby is pommeling the terrier with the scarlet claw of a lobster. Methought, too when I entered I saw beside the door a heap of oyster shells.

Within the hut there is good food, if a little scant at times; without there is air that will call colour back to the cheek of an invalid, pure water, play, exercise, work. That the people are healthy, can be seen from their strong frames, brown faces and the age to which many attain; that they are happy and lighthearted, the shouts of laughter that ring around the peat-fire of an evening may be taken as sufficient evidence.

I protest I cannot become pathetic over the Highland hut. I have sat in these turfen dwellings, amid the surges of blue smoke received hospitable welcome and found amongst the inmates good sense, industry, family affection, contentment, piety, happiness. And when I have heard philanthropists, with more zeal than discretion, maintain that these dwellings are a disgrace to the country in which they are found, I have thought of districts of great cities which I have seen, of evil scents and sights and sounds: of windows stuffed with rags; of female faces that look out of a sadder Inferno than that of Dante's; of faces of men containing the debris of the entire decalogue, faces which hurt more than a blow would: of infants poisoned with gin, of children bred for the prison and the hulks.

Depend upon it there are worse odours than peak-smoke, worse next-door neighbours than a cow or a brood of poultry; and although a couple of girls dragging a harrow be hardly in accordance with our modern notions, yet we need not forget that there are worse employments for girls than even that.

I do not stand up for the Highland hut; but in one of these smoky cabins I would a thousand-fold rather spend my days than in the Cowgate of Edinburgh or in one of the streets that radiate from Seven Dials.

SAMUEL JOHNSON
(1709-1784)

❊   ❊   ❊

Born in Lichfield and educated at Lichfield Grammar School and Pembroke College, Oxford, Samuel Johnson was an essayist, critic, poet, and one of the most powerful and influential personalities of his day. He had already finished his famous dictionary by the time he was forty-six.

Johnson met James Boswell in 1763. Ten years later, in August 1773, they began their famous tour of Scotland ('a hundred days in all kinds of weather,' writes Frank Delaney). Johnson was 63, Boswell 32. What appealed most to Johnson was the ancient traditions of the Highlanders, their customs and habits. He went not for leisure but rather 'to see something different from what we are accustomed to see.'

Johnson and Boswell travelled through the Highlands using the services of a small pony. Over the years there have been many attempts to retrace their path; most recently, Moray Maclaren in 1948, Israel Shenker's In The Footsteps of Johnson and Boswell *in 1982, and Frank Delaney in 1993. None though, quite capture the spirit of the original journey.*

❊   ❊   ❊

The Highlands

from A JOURNEY TO THE WESTERN ISLANDS OF SCOTLAND

As we continue our journey, we were at leisure to extend our speculations, and to investigate the reason of those peculiarities by which such rugged regions as these before us are generally distinguished.

Mountainous countries commonly contain the original, at least the oldest race of inhabitants, for they are not easily conquered, because they must be entered by narrow ways, exposed to every power of mischief from those that occupy the heights; and every new ridge is a new fortress, where the defendants have again the same advantages. If the assailants either force the strait, or storm the summit, they gain only so much ground; their enemies are fled to take possession of the next rock, and the pursuers stand at gaze, knowing neither where the ways of escape wind among the steeps, nor where the bog has firmness to sustain them: besides that, mountaineers have an agility in climbing and descending distinct from strength or courage, and attainable only by use.

If the war be not soon concluded, the invaders are dislodged by hunger; for in those anxious and toilsome marches, provisions cannot easily be carried, and are never to be found. The wealth of mountains is cattle, which, while the men stand in the passes, the women drive away. Such lands at last cannot repay the expence of conquest, and therefore perhaps have not been so often invaded by the mere ambition of dominion; as by resentment of robberies and insults, or the desire of enjoying in security the more fruitful provinces.

As mountains are long before they are conquered, they are likewise long before they are civilized. Men are softened by intercourse mutually profitable, and instructed by comparing their own notions with those of others. Thus Caesar found the maritime parts of Britain made less barbarous by their commerce with the Gauls. Into a barren and rough tract no stranger is brought either by the hope of gain or of pleasure. The inhabitants having neither commodities for sale, nor money for purchase, seldom visit more polished places, or if they do visit them, seldom return.

It sometimes happens that by conquest, intermixture, or gradual refinement, the cultivated parts of a country change their language. The mountaineers then become a distinct nation, cut off by dissimilitude of speech from conversation with their neighbours. Thus in Biscay, the original Cantabrian, and in Dalecarlia, the old Swedish still subsists. Thus Wales and the Highlands speak the tongue of the first inhabitants of Britain, while the other parts have received first the Saxon, and in some degree afterwards the French, and then formed a third language between them.

That the primitive manners are continued where the primitive language is spoken, no nation will desire me to suppose, for the manners of mountaineers are commonly savage, but they are rather produced by their situation than derived from their ancestors.

Such seems to be the disposition of man, that whatever makes a distinction produces rivalry. England, before other causes of enmity were found, was disturbed for some centuries by the contests of the northern and southern counties; so that at Oxford, the peace of study could for a long time be preserved only by chusing annually one of the proctors from each side of the Trent. A tract intersected by many ridges of mountains, naturally divides its inhabitants into petty nations, which are made by a thousand causes enemies to each other. Each will exalt its own chiefs, each will boast the valour of its men, or the beauty of its women, and every claim of superiority irritates competition; injuries will sometimes be done, and be more injuriously defended; retaliation will sometimes be attempted, and the debt exacted with too much interest.

In the Highlands it was a law, that if a robber was sheltered from justice, any man of the same clan might be taken in his place. This was a kind of irregular justice, which, though necessary in savage times, could hardly fail to end in a feud, and a feud once kindled among an idle people with no variety of pursuits to divert their thoughts, burnt on for ages either sullenly glowing in secret mischief, or openly blazing into publick violence. Of the effects of this violent judicature, there are not wanting memorials. The cave is now to be seen to which one of the Campbells, who had injured the Macdonalds, retired with a body of his own clan. The Macdonalds required the offender, and being refused, made a fire at the mouth of the cave, by which he and his adherents were suffocated together.

Mountaineers are thievish, because they are poor, and having neither manufactures nor commerce, can grow richer only by robbery. They regularly plunder their neighbours for their neighbours are commonly their enemies; and having lost that reverence for property, by which the order of civil life is preserved, soon consider all as enemies, whom they do not reckon as friends, and think themselves licensed to invade whatever they are not obliged to protect.

By a strict administration of the laws, since the laws have been introduced into the Highlands, this disposition to thievery is very much represt. Thirty years ago no herd had ever been conducted through the mountains, without paying tribute in the night, to some of the clans; but cattle are now driven, and passengers travel without danger, fear, or molestation.

Among a warlike people, the quality of highest esteem is personal courage, and with the ostentatious display of courage are closely connected promptitude of offence and quickness of resentment. The highlanders, before they were disarmed, were so addicted to quarrels, that the boys used to follow any publick procession or ceremony, however festive, or however solemn, in expectation of the battle, which was sure to happen before the company dispersed.

Mountainous regions are sometimes so remote from the seat of government, and so difficult of access, that they are very little under the influence of the sovereign, or without power; and the sentence of a distant court could not be easily executed, nor perhaps very safely promulgated, among men ignorantly proud and habitually violent, unconnected with the general system, and accustomed to reverence only their own lords. It has therefore been necessary to erect many particular jurisdictions, and commit the punishment of crimes, and the decision of right to the proprietors of the country who could enforce their own decrees. It immediately appears that such judges will be often ignorant, and often partial; but in the immaturity of political establishments no better expedient could be found. As government advances towards perfection, provincial judicature is perhaps in every empire gradually abolished.

Those who had thus the dispensation of law, were by consequence themselves lawless. Their vassals had no shelter from outrages and oppressions; but were condemned to endure, without resistance, the caprices of wantonness, and the rage of cruelty.

In the Highlands, some great lords had an hereditary jurisdiction over counties; and some chieftains over their own lands; till the final conquest of the Highlands afforded an opportunity of crushing all the local courts, and of extending the general benefits of equal law to the low and the high, in the deepest recesses of obscurest corners.

While the chiefs had this resemblance of royalty, they had little inclination to appeal, on any question, to superior judicatures. A claim of lands between two powerful lairds was decided like a contest for dominion between sovereign powers. They drew their forces into the field, and right attended on the strongest. This was, in ruder times, the common practice, which the kings of Scotland could seldom control.

Even so lately as in the last years of King William, a battle was fought at Mull Roy, on a plain a few miles to the south of Inverness, between the clans of Mackintosh and Macdonald of Keppoch. Col. Macdonald, the head of a small clan, refused to pay the dues demanded from him by Macintosh, as his superior lord. They disdained the interposition of judges and laws, and calling each his followers to maintain the dignity of the clan, fought a formal battle, in which several considerable men fell on the side of Mackintosh, without a complete victory to either. This is said to have been the last open war made between the clans by their own authority.

The Highland lords made treaties, and formed alliances, of which some traces may still be found, and some consequences still remain as lasting evidences of petty regality. The terms of one of these confederacies were, that each should support the other in the right, or in the wrong, except against the king.

The inhabitants of mountains form distinct races, and are careful to preserve their genealogies. Men in a small district necessarily mingle blood by intermarriages, and combine at last into one family, with a common interest in the honour and disgrace of every individual. Then begins that union of affections, and co-operation of endeavours, that constitute a clan. They who consider themselves as ennobled by their family, will think highly of their progenitors, and they who through successive generations live always together in the same place, will preserve local stories and hereditary prejudices. Thus every highlander can talk of his ancestors, and recount the outrages which they suffered from the wicked inhabitants of the next valley.

Such are the effects of habitation among mountains, and such were the qualities of the highlanders, while their rocks secluded them from the rest of mankind, and kept them an unaltered and discriminated race. They are now losing their distinction, and hastening to mingle with the general community.

NEIL M. GUNN
(1891-1973)

❖   ❖   ❖

One of Scotland's best-known writers, novelist Neil Gunn was born in 1891 in Dunbeath, on the far north-east coast of Caithness, the son of a fisherman. He was educated at the local school, and passed the Civil Service examination in 1907. He worked in the Civil Service from 1911 as a customs and excise officer in Inverness and other locations in Scotland. Gunn married Daisy Frew in 1921.

His first novel, Grey Coast *(1926) was published to immediate acclaim. Subsequent novels include* Morning Tide *(1931),* The Lost Glen *(1932),* Sun Circle *(1933),* Butcher's Broom *(1934),* Highland River *(1937),* The Silver Darlings *(1941),* Young Art and Old Hector *(1942),* The Green Isle of the Green Deep *(1944),* The Silver Bough *(1948), and* The Well at the World's End *(1951). He continued to work as an essayist and broadcaster until his death in 1973.*

In 1937, Gunn gave up his job in the Civil Service, sold his house in Inverness, and bought a boat. It marked a turning point in his life, for that was the year he decided to become a full-time freelance writer. With wife Daisy and brother John, he began a three-month voyage around the Inner Hebrides and wrote about it in Out in a Boat. *In the following passage he feels overwhelmed by the beauty that surrounds him, as the crew winds its way toward Skye on a perfect day, 'so full of wonder.'*

❖   ❖   ❖

Out to Sea

from OFF IN A BOAT

On such a lovely morning the adventure seemed full of promise and in a very short time we were conscious of being in a new world. It is difficult to explain how deep the meaning in these last words. Two elements composed it, I think: the first, the novelty of being on the ocean making for anchorages we had never seen, assisted by small-scale charts we were unaccustomed to read, for the truth (as may have been gathered) was that neither of us knew anything about navigation or the handling of any craft beyond a row-boat; the second, the strangeness, the wonder, the beauty of the scene itself. We had both travelled in steamers and I still have a vivid memory of the mountains of North Africa rising out of the sea (with their suggestion of elephants and tropic jungles and hinterlands of burning sand), but never – and I had visited the Hebrides and traversed their length and breadth a few times – had natural features and atmospheric effects combined to make use of the world, as far as the eye could reach, a place of such still enchantment that at moments its beauty was profoundly sad.

The clear blue of the overhead sky passed into the haze of the horizon out of which the hills rose in dim purple, full of distance and legendary peace. I had never realised how mountainous Harris was, and I gazed at the Clisham, on whose steep road an insignificant buzzing figure on a motor bike had once nearly broken his neck. Southward the eye caught the saddle-back of Ben Lee and the cone of Ben Eval in North Uist. South of that, Hecla, Beinn Mhor, and the hills towards Loch Boisdale in South Uist. And finally, remote, out of the mist, a nipple against the sky, insubstantial, inclined to vanish, that could only be Heaval in Barra. Land outlines and sea inlets in between were guessed at or perhaps imagined, so uncertain were they in the opalescent haze.

Above these lands, at no great height, hung a continuous ridge of puffed-out cloud, like the angel clouds in Renaissance pictures. Their whiteness had an internal warmth, a suggestion of pink, that tinted the sea to a gleaming hue, and the water undulated slowly like sheeted iron. A similar cumulus formation hung over Skye, but there it was Arctic white, like puffed-out snow, while the land beneath faded away in sunbright haze.

The water changed continuously in colour, and over its vast waste birds worked singly or in little coveys, black guillemots, large guillemots, puffins, fulmars, while a single gull made us feel truly at sea by following us from side to side and sometimes passing overhead and throwing a startling shadow on our hands.

As we came abreast of the Ascrib Isles, we passed quite close to a school of basking sharks. Their triangular dorsal fins, showing full above the water, looked like the mainsails of miniature yachts, only the fins were black and moved to some other caprice than the wind's. They cut in and out in sudden swirling circles as if they were playing an amusing game or worrying some hidden life to death.

But within this visible world, I was haunted by my own particular worry, and every now and then I got up and felt the circulating pipes and cylinder heads. Occasionally new noises developed to my ear, thuds and thumps and queer irregular beats. Yet the engine was going steadily and I was afraid to experiment either by giving her more throttle or moving the ignition lever. We had left Duntulm at 10.30 a.m. and at 12.7 Waternish Point was abeam, so we were doing about six knots, and if in that time we had had the last of an ebbing tide in our favour, on the other hand we were towing a dinghy which though small was heavy. I was not dissatisfied. With the broad entrance to Loch Snizort behind us, the first step in our journey had been taken. It was a new anchorage now, whatever happened. At last we had won through the web of circumstance, with its decisions and clinging obstructions, for freedom. We set a course for Dunvegan Head, which lay in the sea like an immense squatting animal with its snub nose out of the water.

As we came abreast of Loch Dunvegan, still going steadily, I abandoned my half-formed plan of entering and anchoring between the islands of Mingay and Isay, where there is good shelter, as a Waternish man had told me, and where we could have devoted the rest of the day to getting things shipshape, particularly in the piled-up mess that was the cabin. To tell the truth, I did not care to let the Crew remain in the cabin while the enging was going. I did not feel like taking any chances until I knew my mechanism a bit better, for I could still see very vividly the flash of that naked tongue of flame over a wildly flooding carburettor when we had started her up in the morning. There was a hatch over the forecastle, through which one could push up on to the deck in an emergency, but in the event of such an emergency arising it might not be altogether wise to complicate its pattern with fore-hatch acrobatics.

Moreover the day was fine, and all that wild shore, with its towering basaltic cliffs, that forms the north-west coast of Skye, might be a good place to get round while the going was good, particularly as it is exposed on the south-west to the full force of the prevailing swells and provides no sheltering anchorage of any kind.

I asked the Crew how she felt about it. She smiled and turned away, and all in a moment I saw she was so sick with excitement that her dry lips refused to come adrift.

The sea's depth had got her, a depth so near that she could have leaned over and put her fingers into it; and nothing between her and it but thin planking upon which some hundredweights of defective metal beat its devil's tatoo. A sense of insecurity so awful, so imminent, that sheer sick apprehension kept her head up – lest she see the distant bottom too clearly. And for the rest, she had absolute reason to have confidence neither in the navigator nor the boat.

Some understanding of this came upon me in a wave, and I laughed. She had encouraged me in my mad courses! And I could see by that smile that she was not giving in now. It was faint perhaps, a trifle wan, but game. I rallied her, pointing out our perfect security. The day was so fine that if the boat sank under us, we could row ashore in the dinghy. But she moved my talk aside and pointed to a great dark-hulled steam yacht, her varnished lifeboats swung out on their davits, now coming out of Dunvegan Loch. We watched until we could clearly see three white caps on the bridge and the steady stare of faces that must have wondered and smiled. The Crew gave a salute, and three caps were lifted. The courtesy of ships that pass on the high seas!

The yacht disappeared towards the distant haze of Harris, and we settled back into our own world. The sun was very hot and we took off our jackets. I brought the compass into use for the first time. I had had to stand to see over the high deck of the cabin. I now got the bearing of Dunvegan Head on the compass and sitting in a corner of the low cockpit extended one arm along the tiller and the other along the rail. The Crew made herself comfortable in the other corner.

Never in my wildest dreams had I imagined so perfect a day, so full of wonder. It was as if we were floating on a coloured bubble. There was that air of the intangible, the incredible. And at odd moments it did bring a feather of something to the throat.

We played games at trying to name the colours of our enchanted world, but it was a difficult game that tended to pass into long silences. Every now and again I rose to see that nothing was in our way, then subsided.

Shortly after two o'clock we were abreast of Dunvegan Head; then laying our course on Meall a Veg Head, I decided the time had come when we must make up our minds where we were going.

We settled on Loch Bracadale, in the west of Skye, and for anchorage on Portnalong at the entrance to Loch Harport. The name Portnalong was quite new to me, and our decision here, as in all other cases, was reached after a study of the chart and the *Sailing Directions*. Never had either of us any personal knowledge to go upon. A rough calculation showed that we could not hope to arrive much before six o'clock. I increased the oil drip-feed of the engine for luck. Neither of us worried about a set meal. The Crew spread out biscuits, cream cheese, and a cupful of milk in the cockpit. I ate with relish and she with deliberation, while the rocks moved slowly past and the sound of the engine was almost forgotten.

The sun beat down upon us and upon the sea yet not glaringly but, as it were, modified by the distant sombre haze. There was induced, too, an insidious lightness of the head, not unpleasant, a sort of etherialised intoxication due in some measure, I suspect, to eddying whiffs from the engine! The roar of the engine in that world of ineffable quietude became itself a comment of the purest fantasy – for which there could be no acknowledgment but a smile.

JAMES BOSWELL
(1740-1795)

❧   ❧   ❧

Born in Edinburgh, the eldest son of a judge, Boswell studied law at the University of Edinburgh. A precocious young man, he began jotting down notes in his journal at the age of eighteen. In 1760 he journeyed to London, where he briefly flirted with Catholicism. Between 1765 and 1766 he travelled in Europe, making the acquaintance of such prominent figures as Voltaire and Rousseau. He returned from the Continent in 1766 and was admitted as an advocate. His Account of Corsica in 1768 and its sequel brought him a goodly measure of fame. But he is best remembered, of course, for his masterpiece, The Life of Johnson (1791), a biography of Samuel Johnson.

Boswell first met Johnson on his second visit to London, in May 1763, at Tom Davies' bookshop in Russell Street. They became friends and when Boswell invited the great man to accompany him on a journey to the Hebrides, the good doctor heartily agreed. The Journal of A Tour to the Hebrides was not published until 1785, a year after Johnson's death.

When Boswell and Johnson went to the Hebrides, he was only thirty-three. His writing style is chatty, at times self-serving, but always entertaining. In love with the very notion of fame – one suspects he would have done exceedingly well in today's celebrity-saturated culture – Boswell revelled in being in the company of great men. His ability to persuade Dr. Johnson to make this rather treacherous journey was considered nothing less than a grand literary coup.

In the following passage, Boswell has left Dr. Johnson behind to explore the island of Raasay (which he spells Rasay) on his own, accompanied by Malcolm Macleod, an elderly Highland gentleman.

❧   ❧   ❧

from the JOURNAL OF
A TOUR TO THE HEBRIDES

Friday, 10th September

Having resolved to explore the island of Rasay, which could be done only on foot, I last night obtained my fellow-traveller's permission to leave him for a day, he being unable to take so hardy a walk. Old Mr Malcolm M'Cleod, who had obligingly promised to accompany me, was at my bedside between five and six. I sprang up immediately, and he and I, attended by two other gentlemen, traversed the country during the whole of this day. Though we had passed over not less than four-and-twenty miles of very rugged ground, and had a Highland dance on the top of Dun Can, the highest mountain in the island, we returned in the evening not at all fatigued, and piqued ourselves at not being outdone at the nightly ball by our less active friends, who had remained at home.

My survey of Rasay did not furnish much which can interest my readers; I shall therefore put into as short a compass as I can, the observations upon it, which I find registered in my journal. It is about fifteen English miles long, and four broad. On the south side is the laird's family seat, situated on a pleasing low spot. The old tower of three stories, mentioned by [Martin] Martin, was taken down soon after 1746, and a modern house supplies its place. There are very good grass-fields and corn-lands about it, well dressed. I observed, however, hardly any inclosures, except a good garden plentifully stocked with vegetables, and strawberries, raspberries, currants, &c.

On one of the rocks just where we landed, which are not high, there is rudely carved a square, with a crucifix in the middle. Here, it is said, the lairds of Rasay, in old times, used to offer up their devotions. I could not approach the spot, without a grateful recollection of the event commemorated by this symbol.

A little from the shore, westward, is a kind of subterraneous house. There has been a natural fissure, or separation of the rock, running towards the sea, which has been roofed over with long stones, and above them turf has been laid. In that place the inhabitants used to keep their oars. Thare are a number of trees near the house, which grow well; some of them of a pretty good size. They are mostly plane and ash. A little to the west of the house is an old ruinous chapel, unroofed, which never has been very curious. There was a heelbone, in particular, which Dr Macleod said was such, that if the foot was in proportion, it must have been twenty-seven inches long. Dr Johnson would not look at the bones. He started back from them with a striking appearance of horrour. Mr M'Queen told us, it was formerly much the custom, in these isles, to have human bones lying above ground, especially in the windows of churches. On the south of the chapel is the family burying place. Above the door, on the east end of it, is a small bust or image of the Virgin Mary, carved upon a stone which makes part of the wall. There is no church upon the island. It is annexed to one of the parishes of Sky; and the minister comes and preaches either in Rasay's house, or some other house, on certain Sundays. I could not but value the family seat more, for having even the ruins of a chapel close to it. There was something comfortable in the thought of being so near a piece of consecrated ground. Dr Johnson said, 'I look with reverence upon every place that has been set apart for religion'; and he kept off his hat while he was within the walls of the chapel.

The eight crosses, which Martin mentions as pyramids for deceased ladies, stood in a semicircular lie, which contained within it the chapel. They marked out the boundaries of the sacred territory within which an asylum was to be had. One of them, which we observed upon our landing, made the first point of the semicircle. There are few of them now remaining. A good way farther north, there is a row of buildings about four feet high; they run from the shore on the east along the top of a pretty high eminence, and so down to the shore on the west, in much the same direction with the crosses. Rasay took them to be the marks for the asylum; but Malcolm thought them to be false sentinels, a common deception, of which instances occur in Martin, to make invaders imagine an island better guarded. Mr Donald M'Queen, justly in my opinion, supposed the crosses which form the inner circle to be the church's land-marks.

The south end of the island is much covered with large stones or rocky strata. The laird has enclosed and planted part of it with firs, and shewed me a considerable space marked out for additional plantations.

Dun Can is a mountain three computed miles from the laird's house. The ascent to it is by consecutive risings, if that expression may be used when vallies intervene, so that there is but a short rise at once; but it is certainly very high above the sea. The palm of altitude is disputed for by the people of Rasay and those of Sky; the former contending for Dun Can, the latter for the mountains of Sky, over against it. We went up the east side of Dun pretty easily. It is mostly rocks all around, the points of which hem the summit of it. Sailors, to whom it is a good object as they pass along, call it Rasay's cap. Before we reached this mountain, we passed by two lakes. Of the first, Malcolm told me a strange fabulous tradition. He said, there was a wild beast in it, a sea-horse, which came and devoured a man's daughter; upon which the man lighted a great fire, and had a sow roasted at it, the smell of which attracted the monster. In the fire was put a spit. The man lay concealed behind a low wall of loose stones, and he had an avenue formed for the monster, with two rows of large flat stones, which extended from the fire over the summit of the hill, till it reached the side of the loch. The monster came, and the man with the red-hot spit destroyed it. Malcolm shewed me the little hiding-place, and the rows of stones. He did not laugh when he told this story. I recollect having seen in the *Scots Magazine*, several years ago, a poem upon a similar tale, perhaps the same, translated from the Erse, or Irish, called *Albin and the Daughter of Mey*.

There is a large tract of land, possessed as common, in Rasay. They have no regulations as to the number of cattle. Every man puts upon it as many as he chooses. From Dun Can northward, till you reach the other end of the island, there is much good natural pasture unincumbered by stones. We passed over a spot, which is appropriated for the exercising ground. In 1745, a hundred fighting men were reviewed here, as Malcolm told me, who was one of the officers that led them to the field. They returned home all but about fourteen. What a princely thing is it to be able to furnish such a band! Rasay has the true spirit of a chief. He is, without exaggeration, a father to his people.

There is plenty of lime-stone in the island, a great quarry of free-stone, and some natural woods, but none of any age, as they cut the trees for common country uses. The lakes, of which there are many, are well stocked with trout. Malcolm catched one of four-

and-twenty pounds weight in the loch next to Dun Can, which, by the way, is certainly a Danish name, as most names of places in these islands are.

The old castle, in which the family of Rasay formerly resided, is situated upon a rock very near the sea: the rock is not one mass of stone, but a concretion of pebbles and earth, so firm that it does not appear to have mouldered. In this remnant of antiquity I found nothing worthy of being noticed, except a certain accommodation rarely to be found at the modern houses of Scotland, and which Dr Johnson and I fought for in vain at the Laird of Rasay's new-built mansion, where nothing else was wanting. I took the liberty to tell the laird it was a shame there should be such a deficiency in civilized times. He acknowledged the justice of the remark. But perhaps some generations may pass before the want is supplied. Dr Johnson observed to me, how quietly people will endure an evil, which they might at any time very easily remedy; and mentioned as an instance, that the present family of Rasay had possessed the island for more than four-hundred years, and never made a commodious landing place, though a few men with pickaxes might have cut an ascent of stairs out of any part of the rock in a week's time.

The north end of Rasay is as rocky as the south end. From it I saw the little Isle of Fladda, belonging to Rasay, all fine green ground; and Rona, which is of so rocky a soil that it appears to be a pavement. I was told however that it has a great deal of grass, in the interstices. The laird has it all in his own hands. At this end of the island of Rasay is a cave in a striking situation. It is in a recess of a great cleft, a good way up from the sea. Before it the ocean roars, being dashed against monstrous broken rocks; grand and aweful *propugnacula*. On the right hand of it is a longitudinal cave, very low at the entrance, but higher as you advance. The sea having scooped it out, it seems strange and unaccountable that the interior part, where the water must have operated with less force, should be loftier than that which is more immediately exposed to its violence. The roof of it is all covered with a kind of petrifications formed by drops, which perpetually distil from it. The first cave has been a place of much safety. I find a great difficulty in describing visible objects. I must own too that the old castle and cave, like many other things, of which one hears much, did not answer my expectations.

People are every where apt to magnify the curiosities of their country.

This island has abundance of black cattle, sheep, and goats; a good many horses, which are used for ploughing, carrying out dung, and other works of husbandry. I believe the people never ride. There are indeed no roads through the island, unless a few detached beaten tracks deserve that name. Most of the houses are upon the shore; so that all of the people have little boats, and catch fish. There is great plenty of potatoes here. There are black-cock in extraordinary abundance, moor-fowl, plover and wild pigeons, which seemed to me to be the same as we have in pigeon-houses, in their state of nature. Rasay has no pigeon-house. There are no hares nor rabbits in the island, nor was there ever known to be a fox, till last year, when one was landed on it by some malicious person, without whose aid he could not have gone thither, as that animal is known to be a very bad swimmer. He has done much mischief. There is a great deal of fish caught in the sea round Rasay; it is a place where one may live in plenty, and even in luxury. There are no deer; but Rasay told us he would get some.

They reckon it rains nine months in the year in this island, owing to its being directly opposite to the western coast of Sky, where the watery clouds are broken by high mountains. The hills here, and indeed all the healthy grounds in general, abound with the sweet-smelling plant which the highlanders call *gaul*, and (I think) with dwarf juniper in many places. There is enough of turf, which is their fuel, and it is thought there is a mine of coal. Such are the observations which I made upon the island of Rasay, upon comparing it with the description given by Martin, whose book we had with us.

MARGARET
FAY SHAW

❋   ❋   ❋

Folklorist and photographer Margaret Fay Shaw began life in Pennsylvania until, orphaned as a teenager, she was sent to stay with a distant cousin near Glasgow (her great-great-grandfather, John Shaw, had emigrated from Scotland to Philadelphia in 1782). It was here, at a recital in Helensburgh, where she heard Gaelic songs for the first time – from none other than noted collector Marjory Kennedy-Fraser – and became determined to learn more about them. From these humble beginnings Shaw would eventually be recognised as one of the premier folklorists and folksong collectors in Britain. She was married to the late Gaelic scholar John Lorne Campbell. Together they bought and lived on the island of Canna.

'Of all the islands I'd visited, there was something about South Uist that just won me; it was like falling in love; it was the island that I wanted to go back to,' she writes. Shaw lived for six years on South Uist with two sisters in a small cottage.

Shaw is the author of Folksongs and Folklore of South Uist, *which is considered a classic work in its field.*

❋   ❋   ❋

South Uist

from FROM THE ALLEGHENIES
TO THE HEBRIDES:
AN AUTOBIOGRAPHY

I had hoped to be a pianist, but I developed rheumatism, really some kind of an infection which affected my joints, making them terribly sore so that I couldn't play. I had my appendix out and my tonsils and wisdom teeth, and underwent all kinds of treatment to find a cure. Aunt Elsie, who was generous and loving, and lovely to look at, paid all my expenses for all this time; I think I saw twenty-three doctors. The doctor I saw in New York was a specialist, Dr. Russell Cecil. He said to me, when I was getting better, 'Margaret, you have too many relations! What would you like to do?' And I said, 'Well, I've been on a bicycle tour through the Hebrides, and I would like to go back there, to live and to collect songs and learn Gaelic.' And he said, 'Why, that's a wonderful idea! My wife is Australian, but her ancestors came from the Hebrides, and it's a place I've always wanted to visit. That's what you should do.'

So I went back to Glenshaw and announced that I was going to go to South Uist. And they all had a fit! They thought that riding the bicycle – using the handbrakes – was perhaps the cause of the trouble, and getting wet and that I hadn't looked after myself.

When Aunt Mary asked what I planned to do in South Uist, I said I wanted to collect folksongs. In trying to explain, I mentioned that Percy Grainger had done that in Ulster, and she said, 'But *he's* a musician!' And Uncle George said, 'You know, we had a distant cousin called Dude Weighly; her name was Dorothy, but she was called Dude. She eventually lived with the cats and the chickens and became very peculiar. Now you don't want to be another Dude Weighly, surely?' And they thought I was ungrateful, and that I would never amount to anything, and it was a waste of a life, and so on. It was all very sad and difficult. However, something made me go. So I started off to South Uist.

Of all the islands I'd visited, there was something about South Uist that just won me; it was like falling in love; it was the island that I wanted to go back to. Of course, I was not looking for *islands*: I was looking for a way to live my life. I went first to Lochboisdale and stayed in a cottage with a Mrs Campbell for two or three months, but there was too much English, and it wasn't exactly what I wanted. Donald Ferguson, who was a cousin of Mrs Campbell's, asked us to Boisdale House for New Year's dinner. So we went around to South Lochboisdale, where we had a lovely dinner, and afterwards Mrs Campbell said, 'What about Peigi and Mairi giving us a song?' They came in from the kitchen, and Mairi sang a song which was absolutely wonderful to me; I'd never heard anything like it, and I said, 'Would you teach me that song?' And she said, 'Yes! If you'll come and see me, I'll teach you that song.' 'Right, I'll come!'

A week later I was able to get a boat over the loch, to the south side where they lived. I walked up to this little thatched house with a blue door and I thought, 'This is where I ought to stay, this is where I want to be, if she'll take me.' So I said to her, 'Could I come here and stay? Would you take me as a boarder?' And she said, 'Yes, if you'll be comfortable here, of course I'll take you.' And that was the beginning. I said, 'Well, I have to go home to my sister's wedding, but I'll be back in about six weeks.' And so I went home to my sister Biddy's wedding, and I came back and moved in with Mairi MacRae, and I lived there for four winters and six summers.

Donald Ferguson had a large farm in South Lochboisdale and his big house also included the shop and post office. The two sisters, Peigi and Mairi, were his cousins, their mothers being sisters. In Boisdale House they were the servants: Mairi the laundry maid and Peigi was both cook and dairymaid and ruled over all. She had a young lass to help her, for the work was never-ending; they were up at five in the morning and never ceased until midnight. The farm-hands were to be fed as well as their other cousin, Angus MacCuish, who was in charge of the shop.

I would come to the kitchen in the late evenings when they would all be having tea and there would always be songs. Peigi and Angus gave me one in praise of Uist with a fine tune and splendid verses:

> O my country, I think of thee, fragrant fresh Uist.
> Land of bent grass, land of barley,
> Land where everything is plentiful,
> Where young men sing songs and drink ale.

Then follows the verse:

> They come to us, deceitful and cunning,
> In order to entice us from our homes;
> They praise Manitoba to us,

A cold country without coal or peat.
I need not trouble to tell you it;
When one arrives there one can see — a short summer, a
   peaceful autumn.
And long winter of bad weather.

This song reminded me of a woman I met on the roadside who said that since I came from America I might know her son who had gone to Saskatchewan: 'The frost is in their bones and they miss the sea.'

My coming to live with Mairi and her son Donald meant that she no longer needed to work in the laundry. She now had a little money to be independent. It was the same for Peigi when she was old enough to receive the pension and came to live at home with Mairi.

The schoolteacher came to stay with us, Katie Ann Nicolson from Skye. She was a young and jolly girl, just out of teacher's training college. There was to be a *Mod*, a competition on the island, and Katie was persuaded to go, for she had a lovely voice. So we sat on a hill and taught her a song that would be new to the audience. It was really a man's song, but with her full, deep, lovely voice she won the prize. It pleased me to think that I was the one who had given her the song.

Peigi and Mairi's house was a very small cottage. You entered a little passageway, and on your left was what they called 'the room'; and on your right was the kitchen, and then between there was a door to a tiny room which they called 'the closet', *closaid*, where there were two small beds. Mairi's son Donald slept on the bench in the kitchen, and I was given 'the room'. I had my books there, and the spinning-wheel. I had a couch and two upright chairs. When the women came to spin and talk to me, we sat 'up' in my room; when the men came, we sat 'down' in the kitchen.

I had to learn that no one was called by their last name. It was *Peigi Anndra*, meaning Peggy daughter of Andrew, or '*Mairi Mhor an at-Soighdeir*', Big Mary, daughter of the soldier'. If I said that I'd met 'Mary Campbell', Mairi Anndra would say, 'Which one? Do I know her?' I should have said '*Mairi Iain Chlachair*.'

Every night friends would come in to sing and talk. Angus John Campbell was the one who came regularly all the years I was there, and he taught me an enormous amount, in knowledge of songs as well as the Gaelic words for birds and the parts of a boat. These latter were often of Norse derivation from the Viking inheritance. I can see him yet, after a long evening of instruction, taking a live peat from the fire in the tongs and going out in the pitch-black. The wind would make the peat flare up like a torch to light his way home. The path was between deep ditches – peat bogs in which one could drown. A huge Highland bull was found up to his head and there was a struggle to put a rope round his horns, with all the men pulling to save the beast from sure death.

And the storms! The thatch was rounded, and the ends of the houses were rounded, so there was nothing to catch the wind. Everything just blew across it, unless the wind came from the northeast, with rain; then that was hard on the door, and I've seen water hit the door and then just rise up like a little curtain underneath with such force of the wind. The storms used to be so bad in the winter that all the peat, the whole fire, would blow right into the middle of the floor from the chimney. I'd rush, and grab peat and a shovel, and put it back and pound it out.

We always had cats, a dog, and a very good Highland cow for milk, and pet lambs: they made pets of everythig, including the ram. Once when Mairi had a headache and was in the *closaid* lying in bed, I was at the kitchen table, about to clean a little cockerel we were to eat. Mairi called to me to 'take the engine out'. So I started with great difficulty and, as I began to get the inside out, I suddenly looked sideways, and in the door came the ram, a huge thing with great curly horns. He was coming right for me because he wanted to get to a bin of potatoes that was under the chest. I didn't want him to get in, so I picked up a saucepan that was lying on the table, and as I did this, the chicken began to move: the cat was pulling the chicken in my left hand and I had the saucepan with my right, trying to hit the ram. Mairi heard this shouting and swearing and put her head around the door. It cured her headache, she said, to see me. The ram and Fluffy the cat had me at a great disadvantage.

Willy-cat was found as a kitten in the shop on the pier at Lochboisdale. Mr Clark had a shop in which he sold everything from cheese to corsets, and he always had a lot of cats. These kittens were running all over the food and everything, and the boy that worked for him said, 'Mairi, take a kitten, take a kitten!' So she picked up this cute little brown furry kitten and stuck it in her jacket and took it home. That one became Wicked Willy. He was a remarkable cat. When Fluffy had kittens, Willy would bring her mice to her basket. He was the most devoted tom, very sweet, and when I was married, Mairi said, 'You must take Willy with you'. So Willy then went to live on Barra, and then later we brought him to Canna.

They had their own peat-bank just down from the croft, below the house. Everybody had their own peat bog; a certain part belonged to each family. There were about thirteen families in that whole glen, and the men would help each other. The neighbours, with Donald, would cut Mairi's peat one day, and then Donald would go with them to cut Angus Ruadh's peat, and each house that was having peat cut would give them a good meal and would always give them a twist of tobacco and a half-crown if they could afford it. You cut the peat in June, but you wanted good weather for it. You cut it just like chocolate cake, in pieces, and then you took it onto the bank and you put three or four together to dry, and then you added more and more, and then when it was properly dried, you took it home and made the big peat-stack. They had a way of making it so that it shed the water; the ones on top were left wet, but it was always dry underneath. The blacker the peat, the better, for it dries as hard as iron and burns far longer. They would cut enough to last a year. They would never let a peat fire go out but smother it with ash at night and blow it into life in the morning.

In the spring, Mairi and Donald would mark the long strips on their land for what they called 'lazy-bed', and cover each strip with seaweed. Then between each strip they would dig out the sods and lay them on the seaweed. This made a ditch on each side that drained the water. They then made holes in the sods with a dibble called a *pleadhag*, and planted potatoes. These were delicious and the mainstay of our diet.

The seaweed was also spread on the field and the earth was turned over with a foot-plough, called a *cascrom*, meaning 'crooked foot'. The lumps of earth were broken up with a heavy wood rake with five thick teeth, and then a harrow was dragged by hand to smooth the ground and the oats were sown.

The few sheep were carefully tended, the male lambs sold for the money needed to buy tea, sugar and other necessities, the ewe lambs kept to replenish the herd. They would ever eat their own sheep, but the local mutton was the best ever tasted. They were a small breed of 'Blackface' and fed on the salty grass, heather and seaweed so the mutton was never fat and greasy.

They grew potatoes and oats and that's all. They couldn't grow cabbages or anything like that because the sheep could get into everything; fences were expensive, and it was just not done. So we never had any green vegetables, and I was never so well in my life.

I was worried about them when I saw that they didn't have medical attention and proper food. Now, I thought to myself, I can't live without oranges and prunes, and I couldn't afford them, because I'd have had to share them with innumerable children around who'd never seen an orange! But I found that on porridge and herring I could manage very well, and I got my vitamins in marmalade. I never missed the other things. Of course I was fortunate that I could go over to the hotel on Sunday for dinner.

The shop at Lochboisdale was kept by Mr F. T. Gillies. I heard from him valuable accounts from the history of the Hebrides. The sitting room above his shop was where I would spend evenings listening to this learned and kindly man tell of the old days, especially of the evictions when the people were cleared from their land to give it to sheep farmers from the south of Scotland. The people were forced to leave and told that Canada was where they would find a far better life. A ship called at Lochboisdale to take them away. Some men were tied with ropes and put aboard, others hid in the hills.

Mr Gillies' father was a blacksmith in North Uist, known as a man of tremendous strength and independent character, opposing the Church of Scotland which was subsidised by the government and which approved of the evictions. One day the people of his village were all told to come to the church to a meeting. While they were there, the sheriff and his officers began clearing their cottages of contents and burning the thatched roofs. When the smith realised what was happening, he rushed back to find his wife had been carried out with her new-born baby and the furniture was just being

removed by the sheriff's men. He shouted to put it all back or he
would break every bone in their bodies. Their fear of this powerful
man made them do what they were told, and his house was saved.

I used sometimes to cross to Lochboisdale pier in the *St Bride*,
buy my groceries at the shop, and then walk the nine miles home
with them. I used to walk a lot in those days; I loved it. Once I was
carrying home a big, badly tied parcel of groceries. It was a misty
evening; fog was rolling in from the Atlantic. I had on a black oilskin
and a black sou'wester. The road was very lonely; there were no
more than four or five cars on the island at the time. To get home I
had to pass a hill, a low hill covered with rocks and grass, called
Carishaval, which was said to be haunted. There were said to be
ghosts there.

Well, just there the string of my big parcel broke. I got down
on the roadside in the grass to try to tie it up again. A long way off
– Uist is bare, without trees – I could see a cyclist coming along the
road, but he didn't see me. I rose up at the side of the road and said
'*Oidhche mhath*!' 'Good evening!' The bicycle went swerving every
which way down the road; I had given him the most terrible fright.
I'm sure he swears he heard a *bocan* on Carishaval!

Once, on an afternoon in Christmas week, I walked to
Daliburgh at the head of Lochboisdale, to a friend's cottage. I had
with me Mr Gillies' collie, a very young dog. I got there and had tea;
then I thought I'd walk up to the machair and then get back to the
road, making a sort of circle to Lochboisdale. I got out to the
machair, which is a great, broad, sandy, grassy plain just at the edge
of the Atlantic, where the waves were roaring. But a thick fog
suddenly came in, and I couldn't find the road. I couldn't find
anything; all I could do was to keep on walking. And of course in
the winter the daylight only lasts a very short time, and it began to
get dark and the moon came up. The little dog Pat and I had to just
keep walking north, always keeping the roar of this surf steady in
our left ear, because to the East, where we wanted to go, there were
bogs and deep drains where you could drown. I knew I had to keep
on walking towards Askernish, a place about three miles farther to
the north; I thought I might see a light in some house there which
would show me the way to the road.

Now the moon was shining; I could see it above my head,

with this thick fog pouring in, and suddenly, swish, there were wings right in my face: we had walked into a great flock of wild geese. They didn't hear us coming, and there they were suddenly, beating their wings as they roared up. We eventually got to Askernish, a long way up the machair, and I realised from a certain light that I was just past the deep drains, and that I should find a wooden bridge – just planks across. We got through there, and then we had the long walk home. I remember Pat running ahead of me in the moonlight, which was then brighter with the fog not so thick. He would run ahead and then lie down flat, absolutely exhausted on the road until I caught up with him, and then he'd get up and start off again, and so on. Instead of coming home at five or six o'clock, I didn't arrive 'till after midnight, and I found that my feet were getting very, very sore. My woollen socks, which of course had got soaked, had completely disintegrated. I hardly had any socks left when I took my shoes off.

I saw at that time, coming back to Lochboisdale, a very strange phenomenon. The mist was still coming in big fragments, flowing in from the west; the moon was shining, and I saw, on the side of a white house that was well in from the road, my shadow, which was absolutely tremendous. I couldn't believe my eyes when I saw this huge creature going along, and then I realised it was myself with the moon and the reflection.

One time I went up to Grogarry in the north end of South Uist to spend a few days and stayed at the Post Office with a Miss MacRury. There was a theology student from Lewis who was boarding at the farm up the road, and I went to him for lessons in reading Gaelic. I had my grammar, and we always had *Litir a Bearnaraidh*, the late John N. MacLeod's weekly Gaelic column in *The Stornoway Gazette*, 'A Letter from Bernera', an island off the coast of Lewis. This always had a very good Gaelic story. But with the sentences from my book that I had to translate, I was very slow. I remember the embarrassment when I said, 'The cow called. We will have milk on Tuesday.' Well of course to have a cow 'call' means that she calls for the bull. When I said, 'The cow called', my tutor was very much embarrassed, but he didn't explain to me what 'call' meant; only that what I should say was 'The cow calved'.

I remember teasing him, saying that the Hebridean women

worked so hard and they always seemed to be carrying the bundles or the sack on their backs while their husbands walked ahead with a stick, and he said, 'Oh not at all! The Hebridean has the highest respect for his women. What you say isn't true at all.' Well I picked up my book of sentences, which was written by a Lewis man, and read 'John, come in. Mary, get up and give him your chair.' And I said, 'There's my case.'

I made many a mistake with words. One occasion shows how very polite the neighbours were. One who was very poor was suffering toothache and had come up to Mairi Anndra's and was sitting on the bench. I came in and said, 'Would you like to hear my Gaelic? *Cia mar a tha do dheargain?*' Mairi Anndra turned to me and said, '*Deideadh! Deideadh!*' When Peigi Neill had gone, Mairi Anndra looked at me and said, '*Deargain! Agus ise lan dhiu!*' (Fleas! And she full of them!) What I had said was, 'How are your fleas?' With her politeness, she'd never let on that I'd said the wrong word! She knew what I meant to say was 'How is your toothache', and thanked me very much.

They were never curious about my background or where I came from, although they knew I came from America. (I had nothing to connect me with the mainland of Britain.) As far as they were concerned, I was like a strange bird that had flown in from the west; that was the way they took me. They took me for myself. Mairi Anndra would scold me or correct me if necessary, but I had much warmth from everyone. Peigi and Mairi used to call me 'Maighread'. Anyone else always spoke of me as 'Miss Shaw'; I was always known as 'Miss Shaw'. To this very day, after being married many years to John Campbell, when I meet my friends on the road in Uist, they say 'Miss Shaw! And how is your husband?'

It was a life that I loved. I never looked at it from an anthropological point of view or anything else like that at all. It was just for the pure enjoyment. I loved the songs. The tunes were heavenly. They appreciated the fact that I didn't want the songs that were well known: I wanted their own everyday songs, songs that they sang when they rocked the cradle or worked the spinning wheel. These songs had not been much collected before, and had not been really appreciated by the collectors. That gave my friends pleasure, and they were anxious to help.

I had to forget the major and minor scales and listen to modes which I had never notated before. I knew how to do it, but I had to concentrate. I had to learn to listen outside of what I had ever heard before, because, even though I took down the tune as accurately as I possibly could, I couldn't get certain half tones that were in it, and nobody can tell except the singer – and then she couldn't read the music!

I knew that one can't take down a Gaelic song without knowing the words, because the difference between the long and short vowels of the language are so much a part of the rhythm of the tune. So I tried to learn the language, and when I began I knew absolutely nothing. I would get somebody like Angus John Campbell to help me write it down, and, though he didn't know much about writing Gaelic, he knew enough to represent it phonetically. In his writing I could see the stress of syllables, and then in hearing it I could find the syllables that went under the notes of the tune. In Gaelic songs, the tune just carried the words along. If the voice was good, that was very nice, but it wasn't essential. The first thing was to hear the poem.

They were polite when we were gathering in the kitchen; everybody would be asked to sing. There was one neighbour who was a bit feeble-minded, Mary Kate, and she had two songs which she sang to the same tune, but that made no difference. They listened to Angus John singing a very fine song, but she got just the same applause. They made Kate feel just as important as anyone there. And they were very tolerant of me.

ALISON JOHNSON

❀ ❀ ❀

Alison Johnson grew up in Aberdeen, where she earned her first degree, an MA in Medieval and Renaissance English at the university. Later she recieved a second degree from Oxford. After marrying Andrew Johnson, she moved back to Scotland with him. Both found positions as teachers on the Isle of Harris. It was here, on the the west coast of the island, where they converted Scarista House, a derelict Presbyterian minister's house, into one of the most highly acclaimed hotels in Scotland. After more than a dozen years running it, they sold the hotel in 1990. Alison now runs the White Horse Press, publishing books and journals on environmental and social issues.

A House by the Shore is a delightful, often quite funny account, of their years living on Harris and running Scarista House. Anyone who thinks operating a bed and breakfast is a romantic, idyllic way of making a living will think again after reading Johnson's no-holds-barred account.

❀ ❀ ❀

Tarbert

from A HOUSE BY THE SHORE:
TWELVE YEARS IN THE HEBRIDES

Everything continued delightful. As town dwellers, we were in a state of constant wonder at how romantically far north we were. At about 10 o'clock after a long morning twilight, we would see the sun top the rocky edge of Ben Luskentyre to the south. It trundled uncertainly along it for perhaps four hours, casting fantastic shadows on the pale wind-wearied tussocks of grass. By two o'clock it had rolled out of sight, and the west loch was plunged into shadow. As the steep shores darkened, the water paled and gleamed, holding the last reflections of a pearly sky.

The earliest part of the Hebridean year is often our most beautiful time. The weather can be more still and clear than at any other season. By night, the sky is full of stars, stars where one never knew there were any, extra stars in Orion, the Pleiades hopping and jumping to crowd themselves all in. When the full moon shines, she is so bright that the stars recede as if by day. The sea reflects a silver swathe of light. You can distinguish colours clearly, and if you preferred reading by moonlight to looking at the moon, I dare say you could. The Aurora Borealis is visible most nights, once the eye is attuned. Usually it is only a wavering pallor in the Northern sky, but sometimes strong pulses of pink and green shoot rhythmically to the zenith over an arc of 180°. By day, sea and sky are cloudless blue, and every bone and wrinkle of the grey and tawny land is highlighted by the low sun. There is not a scrap of green. Nothing grows yet, in spite of the low incidence of frost: there is not enough sunshine at this latitude. But the days lengthen faster and faster until mid-January, and there is a sense of happy expectancy, like waiting for Christmas. Everyone's small talk is full of it: 'The nights are getting shorter.' 'Aye, we'll know the difference in a week or so.' 'It's lighter in the mornings, too.' Small talk, but no small matter: islanders long for the light nights of summer and dread the onset of winter darkness. At first we thought this quaint, but now in our eleventh winter we are as much in awe of solstice and equinox as everyone else.

For winter in Harris is not all starry nights and clear days. Indeed, I think we have the most vicious winter weather in Europe. Well-informed visitors often tell us how mild our winters are: we have the Gulf stream; we have little frost and snow; how much warmer we are than Kent or Norfolk or Cumbria! But they have forgotten the wind. Winter gales, which usually means the first Force 8 or upwards since perhaps April, can start at the beginning of September and rage for 7 months, in a bad year. The winter incidence of gales in exposed parts of the island is one day in three on average. The violence of these gales is astonishing. The huge seas and white water are no surprise—they happen on any coast in lesser storms. The effects on land are more extraordinary. Motor vehicles are regularly pushed off the roads or flipped over by the wind.

Debris flies through the air as if in some hurricane-hit shanty town: slates, sheets of corrugated iron, bits of caravans and hen-houses. Roofs are ripped off and windows smashed in. We used at first to be horribly fascinated by the behaviour of our kitchen window. The glass would bulge out and in, alternately sucked and blown by the gale, with a dull popping sound, but it never gave way. During one worse than average storm, when I was attempting to teach some rudiments of grammar to a class of unwilling boys, I was disturbed by the shouts of 'Miss, Miss! The roof's blown off!'

'Nonsense! Get on with your work!' I snapped.

'But Miss – '

As I turned to clip the ear of the disruptive element, I saw he was quite right: chunks of the gymnasium roof were sailing past the window.

Such gales blow from any quarter, except due east. Southwesterly is the commonest and fiercest, but land and buildings have evolved to accommodate it. Less of a wind from an unusual quarter may cause more damage, bouncing off high bluffs and catching the corners of buildings, to the detriment of rones and downpipes. It was the northerly wind we feared at Leachkin. The West Loch is a comparatively narrow inlet with high sides, pointing south east to north west. A north west to west wind was straight-forward, screeching gleefully up the loch and over the isthmus to Tarbert, leaving the high wire fences of the school playing-field plastered with flotsam of polythene sacks and broken fish-boxes. A southwesterly reared up over the mass of Ben Luskentyre, hit the centre of the loch in a massive catspaw, or perhaps a smallish tornado, and had spent its rage before lashing our front windows. But the nearly-north wind clawed up the sheer crags on the far side of Gillaval, the mountain which loomed behind our house, often showing a wild spiral of cloud in a blue sky before we felt a breath of its descent. Then it was on us with a shriek and a bang. Its alternate lulling and moaning was restless and sinister. This was the wind that sucked at our kitchen window, flipped our boat over on her mooring, and hurled small birds against our back door. Andrew, in particular, hated it. I disliked it less, as it usually came with drier, brighter weather. During our first few years in Harris, it was the continual dampness I found a misery, as I was used to the hard frosts and dry snow of Aberdeen. The southerly wind was my enemy. It brought evil-smelling mist in summer and a fiendish cocktail of rain, hail and sleet in winter. Occasionally, which was better, it graced us with a snow blizzard. This always resulted in a power cut. The electricity cables run down the road from Stornoway, over a mountain pass, and the iced-up wires soon break in high winds. Indeed, they do not need to be iced up: long power cuts are common and frequent for much of the year.

During out first school term in Harris, we were busy with the new experiences of being employed, and it was not until friends and relatives began to visit us in the spring that we explored the island to any extent. The fortunate visitors were treated, on these trips, to the front seats of our beloved Land-Rover, from one of which we had recently extricated a dead mouse and its nest. The cab still smelt rather of rancid mouse. The Land-Rover was our first ever vehicle and we were very proud of it. Usually it started, and even progressed, with a great deal of noise and smoke, but sometimes there was a difficulty about remaining stationary, as the hand brake was chronically inefficient. Once on, it required a hammer blow to knock it off again, so we tried to avoid applying it. Andrew is fond of driving backwards at top speed, rather than turning round; and as some previous owner had reversed the canvas to separate the cab from the back, thus reducing rear visibility, the procedure was hazardous. Soon we had very few rear lights, and as spares were locally unobtainable, we did without. In the damp climate of Harris, thick green moss grew up inside the base of the windows, which I thought pretty, but I doubt if our visitors liked it. Worst of all, sometimes strange explosions took place under the bonnet. I shall never forget my mother leaping out of the moving vehicle, clutching her handbag, as smoke belched from the dashboard.

On these safaris, I usually sat in the open back, and until overcome by exhaust fumes enjoyed the views immensely. Harris is small, only about 25 miles long, but the scenery is varied. To the north, above the waist of Tarbert (Tairbeart means a place where a boat can be hauled overland) lies a range of grim mountains, a sort of no-man's land between Harris and Lewis. The highest summit, Clisham, is only 2600 feet, but the whole range is spectacularly steep and craggy, conveying a powerful impression of malevolent and watchful old age. The rock is Lewisian gneiss, the oldest metamorphic rock in the world, worn by wind and water to gaunt ribs and ridges. Gillaval and Sgaoth Iosal with their long steep corries crouch like evil old giants over their sour peat bogs. They claim occasional victims, too: sheep, children, shepherds. Beyond them the road climbs over the shoulder of Clisham, whose pointed and tilted summit is always crowned with a streaming scarf of cloud, even on a clear day, for the mountains make their own weather in the moist Atlantic air. North of Clisham, the road zig-zags down to Ardvourlie on Loch Seaforth. On the landward side lies a great natural amphitheatre through which the Scaladale river winds, overhung by misty crags and corries, a fit subject for the most romantic Victorian landscapist. To seaward the prospect is less awesome: a mundane assortment of power-lines, fences, land-drains and 'done up' croft houses, typical of island life.

South of the mountains Harris spreads out lower and rounder. A single track road switchbacks out to the western promontory of Hushinish. Here a sandy beach on the south side looks out over many small rocks and islands. The tiny village huddles on the machair above the bay, and beyond it is the high island of Scarp, quite recently depopulated. The shore to the North rises in steep cliffs towards the mountains. There are more inaccessible sandy beaches, more cliffs, more mountains, till habitation begins again 25 miles round a roadless coast in Lewis.

At Hushinish we would pile the Land-Rover with driftwood for our fires. The visitors turned blue and shivered: having learned from Andrew's optimistic reports that Harris has a mild climate thanks to the Gulf Stream, they never brought enough clothes. They didn't realise he only meant milder than Hudson Bay or Okhotsk which are comparable latitudes. How they must have dreaded the driftwood, too! It spat and cracked and gave no heat. We liked it: it produced lovely green and blue flames, and was free.

Back over the lurching road, past the Edwardian baronial pile of Amhuinnsuidhe, with its salmon falls and neglected gardens, past Bunavoneader with its solitary factory chimney, at the head of a deep bay. A whaling concern operated from here in the first half of this century. Many of the old people can remember it—stinking, bloody work but work nevertheless, in an area of chronic unemployment. In our more whale-sensitive age, the abandoned brick stack has an air of lonely reproach, a cenotaph to many dead. There is another memorial here, too: the Norwegian manager who earned his bread from the death of whales erected a fine tombstone to his beloved dog, Sam. I often think of that contrast; it has followed me through all our years on the island.

To go further south, one has to return to Tarbert, where the island is only about $1/4$-mile wide between the east and west lochs. Eastward the whole length of the island is the Bays, the fantastic rock wilderness which had so astonished us on our preliminary visit. The shoreline is very indented, and in every little cove and creek are houses, stuck precariously on the bare rock. At first we were puzzled as to why so many people lived in the Bays, where only a few narrow strips of hard-won soil are available for cultivation. The answer, as so often in the Highlands, is that the fertile land on the west of Harris was cleared for sheep farming in the mid-19th century, and any of the population who could not be encouraged to emigrate were forced back to the rocky east coast. It is picturesque enough now, in an age of subsidies and unemployment benefit, but it is impossible to forget the abject misery of that overcrowded population, as refugees without homes, possessions or seaman's skills descended on the original fishermen who scratched a living here from the sea.

For the modern householder, though, there are certainly fine views. In clear weather, Skye looks within touching distance, and beyond it, fifty miles away, are the whole line of mountains from Applecross to Scourie. Often their tops are striped white with snow, and sometimes the whole range is entirely covered, floating like icebergs in a blue sea. When we first saw the Alps across the lagoon from Venice, we felt at home: they looked very much like Suilven and Canisp from Scadabay. That is the islander's dream, to find somewhere that looks just like his own island. Gaelic songs are full of nostalgia for home: 'If I had given my heart to it altogether, what made me ever leave the place of my love?' Scalpay men who have sailed the world over will tell you proudly that the seas around Scalpay are the worst in the whole ocean. A class of bored children shown a picture of York Minster shrieked with delight: 'it's just like Rodel Church, Miss!' How passionately people here love their native place! All the more misery for the evicted populations of Luskentyre, Seilebost, Horgabost, Scarista: forced into surroundings only a day's walk away, but as alien as Patagonia.

'The grass on the West Side is most Clover and Dasy, which in the summer yields a most fragrant smell.' So wrote Martin Martin in 1716. This is the distinctive Hebridean machair. In our first summer, we were astounded by the beauty of these coastal pastures. Where the sour peat is sweetened by shell sand blowing from the beaches, there is great fertility. At the end of April, primroses and daisies appear on the seaward slopes. In a week or so the tidal salt-flats at Luskentyre and Northton are entirely pink with thrift, and thereafter comes a succession of bloom—bird's foot trefoil, white and red clover, harebells, knapweed and many more. The sheep are taken up to the hills in late May, and immediately these meadows are sheets of pink and white and yellow, with scarcely a leaf of green showing. The air is laden with honey and lark-song. The flowery pelage extends into the marram of the dunes, and patches of fragrant mauve sea-rocket appear almost at the tide line, mingling with shells and black twirls of dry seaweed. The long clean beaches start white at Luskentyre, and gradually change through cream to pinky gold as one goes south. The colour change is attributable to the different proportions of various shells which compose the sand. At Luskentyre it is mainly cockles. By Scarista, there is a preponderance of bright pink thin tellins. In places delicate swirls of blue-grey resolve into crushed-up mussels. Whatever the colour of the sand, the sea, even on a dullish day, is clear turquoise inshore and deep blue towards the horizon.

No one can fail to be impressed by these beaches. Our visitors shot reels of film, to our gratification. Some even joked about going swimming, and one or two did remove their shoes and paddle.

During our first few months, if we had no friends staying with us we did not move around much. We told everyone that teaching at Tarbert was very easy, and so it was, for classes were small and the pupils docile. All the same, it was quite an adjustment. We had been well on the way to perpetual studenthood, and it was difficult to adjust to punctuality and toeing the line. It was difficult to do as we were told, and difficult to imagine our charges would, or should, do as we told them. Mine never did. I was not surprised. Andrew had slightly more success; as he taught General Science, he could always arrange an explosion if interest was flagging, or wire up the baddest boy for a few electric shocks, to the delight of the rest of the class. But the study of English and History does not lend itself to colourful disciplinary measures. I gave out thousands of lines and they wrote them in science lessons. They did their science homework in English. On the whole, though, they were good-humoured and tried not to spill the beans to the rest of the staff; indeed, they were embarrassingly conspiratorial, once they discovered that we did not have 'the Belt' and anyway didn't know how to use it, which we were forced to confess after crossexamination.

'Miss! You'd better not get one. Mr M—belted Queerie and Queerie took his hand away and Mr M—got it on the thigh.'

My sympathies were not with Queerie, a boy whom I could cheerfully have hanged, but I couldn't trust myself to aim straight, as I can't even hit a ping-pong ball, and so procured no Belt. I pulled out tufts of hair, which can be done from the back when the victim is unsuspecting, and confiscated mountains of sweets and comics. The latter punishment hurt me more than them: if left with sweets and comics, they would at least keep relatively quiet, so that other teachers passing by would think I had a grip on things. On demoralised Friday afternoons, confiscations dwindled. Andrew soon made an interesting and helpful discovery about the effects of fresh air, too. Our first action in the morning was always to turn off the heating and open the windows in our respective classrooms, causing vociferous complaints from our pupils.

'No one else does that! Only you and Mr J. It's freezing!' We assured them it was healthier that way. However, experiment and observation left Andrew to realise that a rise in temperature and lack of oxygen could be made to induce a condition of stupor, most heartily wished for as 4 o'clock drew near: so on went the heating and the windows were shut. I gratefully adopted this procedure, but Andrew was better placed, really, as the soporific fug was increased by leaks from calor gas cylinders and other scientific fumes. Also, he could always escape to his prep room for a few gulps of air. Sometimes, whe he overdid things, the air became so noxious that he had to evacuate the whole class to the playground. As the lab was next to the infant classrooms, this caused great delight among the little children, who hung at the windows waving to their older brothers and sisters. Further alarms were caused by his explosions. On one occasion, after a particularly loud bang followed by screams, the primary school headmistress rushed in to the rescue, expecting wreckage and blood, but it was only some conjuring trick.

The other staff treated us with tact and kindness, which we did not really deserve, for we were undoubtedly both arrogant and ignorant. We started from the unfortunate position of feeling that much of the work we were asked to do was pointless. We knew that many of the children would never get jobs, and that even those who did would not obtain them by growing copper sulphate crystals or perusing *Julius Caesar*. The greatest embellishment of a good pupil would be a crown of 'O' grade passes, perhaps three or four. After that, there was a chance of two years at the Nicolson Institute in Stornoway, Higher grade passes, possibly a college course, possibly university: but very few would get that far, and for those that did, the future was far from assured. They might still be unemployed at the end of it, and at any point along the route, the attempt to cram in more than natural ability would really allow could lead to crest-fallen failures. This is not, of course, particular to pupils in Harris. It pertains across the whole country. Being fresh from lengthy education, and sick of it, we were very conscious of this. As for children who were not set on examination courses, their case was even more discouraging. At 12 and 13 they were still childish, eager for anything new. After that a curtain came down. The girls were dreaming of boys and babies, and the boys of sheep and whisky. They were intensely bored. What could one do to raise a spark of interest? School could never be the adult world after which they hankered, so for them it was meaningless, try as one might. Their boredom cowed me, but I could see no alternative for them. Certainly one cannot encourage 14-year-old girls to breed, and even in Harris there are not enough sheep for all the boys to chase, though there is enough whisky to drown them.

I am sure our lack of conviction showed, and it must have made us a nuisance to everyone, to pupils as well as teachers. After all, there is no point in attacking, even in not defending, established standards unless one has something more relevant to offer.

Educationists are forever propounding some new and 'more relevant' scheme, of course, but in fact each is as worthless as the last – or as worthy: the success or otherwise hangs entirely on the conviction and dedication of the individual teacher. What is taught hardly matters at all; it is the spectacle of an adult devoted whole-heartedly to an ideal that impresses young people.

Well, I was not wholehearted. When a certain youth fell asleep and slid off his seat in a history lesson, I was sorry for him, but not surprised. The pathos of this moustached young giant, trapped in his little school desk, haunted me (and my history lessons) all my teaching days. But really, I was probably wrong. I expect he had been dreaming happily enough of sheep, to which he soon afterwards escaped two months short of his official leaving date. The school attendance officer did not take ship for the offshore island where he lived, so he was safe enough. Good luck to him. But no *real* teacher could have felt any good would come of his truancy, and no real teacher would have bored him into slumber, either.

On the whole, though, I think the children quite enjoyed us. We were an entertaining double act. Andrew is tall and thin and I am short and fat – a good start from a youthful point of view. Our appalling cut-price clothing was another source of glee. I made skirts from hideous-coloured remnants, and Andrew had a very long-legged pair of large-check trousers and a very short-sleeved small-check jacket (in non-matching colours) which he wore for most of his teaching career. I had to listen to so many remarks about these trousers that eventually I put them in the dustbin.

Our other attraction was that we put a lot of time and effort into the school Youth Club. There is very little entertainment for youngsters in Harris. The population is too small and scattered to make the usual clubs and societies possible, as school transport takes the children home at 4 o'clock. Consequently, Youth Club meetings were the longed-for goal of the whole week. We needed no fancy amusements. We encouraged them to sell refreshments, to raise money for equipment, and they were immediately pleased with the things they bought – a dartboard, a home-made snooker table, disco lights, and records. Our club members were very unsophisti-cated compared with city children. When we took them on a summer barbecue to Hushinish, boys and girls tore off their shoes and paddled rapturously, or chased a football on the sand. We had been expecting drinking in the bus and fornication in the sand dunes, but there was no trouble at all.

It was through the Youth Club that our previously much-ridiculed Land-Rover reached the summit of its fame. The children in outlying districts had never been able to attend meetings, but as we could pack a dozen into our bone-shaking vehicle, on different weeks they could be picked up from the Bays, the West Side, Kyles Scalpay or Hushinish. They came with a will, collected money spontaneously to pay for petrol, and were astonishingly grateful. Our battered old wreck now became an object of the greatest affection and esteem.

Unlike teaching, the Youth Club was immensely rewarding, simply because they enjoyed it so much. Out of that enjoyment, we tried to encourage them to do something for other people. We had sponsored litter collections, with the redoubtable Land-Rover pressed into service as a dustcart. The money raised went to charity, Christian Aid one year and Save the Children the next. Participation was gratifyingly enthusiastic, but in spite of their indignation at the new rubbish spread by the next gale, they still dropped sweet-papers in the playground.

We liked to feel we were fostering self-reliance and consider-ation for others, though probably very little of it stuck. But of our three years' teaching experience, I think any good we did was through the Youth Club, simply because we felt ourselves it was worthwhile. We regarded it as ours, and so did the children. By the time we left the school, they had forgotten there had been a Club before 'The J's', and were unfairly oblivious of the part played by other teachers in supervising it. Our pleas to Mr Beattie not to ban meetings after misdemeanours, and to allow the divine Scalpay maidens to attend, were transformed into epic battles in school folklore. Our personal involvement with the club was what what counted—the wholeheartedness that we did not give to teaching. We have found exactly the same process in our hotel business. It is the level of emotional involvement in one's own efforts that trans-forms them into a worthwhile communication with others; trouble taken for the love of it blots out failures and excuses short-comings, it seems. We scarcely recognised our shabby furnishings and

ALISON JOHNSON / 237

amateurish cooking in the glowing praise of our first guests: now our standards are much higher, but we are less single-minded, and our clients, I suspect, less pleased.

But to return to Sir E. Scott School in 1974. Two salient features emerged on our first day there. One was that almost the whole class register began with 'M' – MacDonald, Macleod, Morrison. The other was that every naughty boy would have half a dozen brothers to plague you coming up the school. Both point to a dominant factor in Hebridean life: families are typically large and extended, and the ties of kinship are vital and intricate. 'My cousin in Canada' may well be a third cousin twice removed, whose forebears left Harris over a hundred years ago, and who has never been seen on the island. A cousin he is, nevertheless. Islanders still have an exceptional memory for oral knowledge, and most people carry many-branching family trees in their heads, covering not only their own relationships but their neighbours' as well. It is almost as necessary to know other people's cousins as your own: otherwise you could inadvertently give offence, and in a small community it is important not to fall out with neighbours. This accounts in part for the delightful courtesy and discretion shown in conversation with newcomers to the island. The following conversation between an old gentleman of Harris and two foreign tourists is accredited and relevant:

'It is a lovely day today. Are you enchoying your holidays?'

'Yes, we like Harris very much.'

'Well, well, it is not much of a place. But I am glad you are enchoying it. And where would you be from yourselves?'

'We are German.'

A stunned silence from the old war veteran. And then:

'Well, they say Hitler was a very clever man.' After all, they might have been Adolf's fourth cousins.

The need to establish strangers in the context of their relations is deep-seated. Islanders are at first rather wary of newcomers who settle here. For them, the sole and sad reason for leaving home and relatives is to find employment. Why on earth should anyone from the rich mainland leave parents and cousins and come to Harris, where jobs and housing are scarce? Surely such a person must be a black sheep at home, to have abrogated the duties of care for aged relatives and mutual assistance to younger ones, and fled to Harris. When we lived first at Leachkin, we were amused to notice that the decorous Sunday afternoon walk permitted to Church of Scotland families (but not to the stricter Free Churches) switched from eastwards up the Caw to out the West Side, so that we could be kept an eye on. We rudely put it down to sheer nosiness, but I think now it was an attempt to discern our roots. Once our families had been seen to visit us, so that people had a clearer picture of our background, these perambulations ceased. Nowadays, of course, more and more mainland families are settling in the islands. The standard explanation for these removals is now acceptable, and quite rightly occasions local pride: that the islands are a refuge from the violence, overcrowding and status-seeking of the cities.

One would think that the steady trickle of mainland refugees might cause conflict in a rigidly traditional society. In fact, I think we are remarkably well tolerated. Every incomer is a stranger and also someone's neighbour, and benefits from the ancient customs of hospitality and neighbourliness, long atrophied in industrial society. The crofter next door may well despise and dislike the newcomers, with their loud English talk and irreverent Sunday habits, but he will still help them find their feet. They will be brought buckets of potatoes, legs of mutton, chunks of salmon. If these attentions cease after a while, the incomer should review his own behaviour: he, too, is someone's neighbour, and should have cemented the ties by giving unobtrusive gifts and doing small services, and by trying not to tread on local corns. For the heavy-footed mainlander, this is very difficult. For a start, with the best will in the world, he is bound to desecrate the Sabbath. Island Presbyterianism is ferociously Calvinistic and relies on very literal reading of the Bible. The mainland Christian as much as the mainland atheist will find himself in confusion, for parts of Deuteronomy that never see daylight over the Minch are here brought into play. Conversely, the great festivals of Easter and Christmas are totally ignored here by the religious: the Bible has not given us firm dates for them, so why follow Popish tradition? Popery, one feels, is the unforgiveable sin encompassing all others, and as one grim old patient told a young Anglican doctor here, 'The Church of England is chust next door to the Church of

Rome.' The most remarkable feature of island life is the strict obser-
vance of the Sabbath. Not only may no work be done, but no leisure
activities are permissible except for reading the Bible and the
Christian Herald. However, as it is a day of rest, it is respectable to
spend the entire day, between the two long church services, in bed
with drawn curtains. (The temptations of such recreation must, I am
sure, occasionally further procreation, but no one has yet
researched this.)

Even the islanders do not all live up to the rigours to which
they are enjoined. They are also quite tolerant of incomers' aberra-
tions. As long as one's breaches are not defiant, one will be treated
with restraint. The pulpits and letter pages of the *Stornoway Gazette*
thunder every week against the abominable practices and vile
blasphemies of people like me, but in practice no one expects any
more than we be discreet in our abominations. The first time one
hangs out washing on a Sunday, a mild rebuke will reach one at
third or fourth hand: 'they were saying that some of the old people
do not like it.' The second time, no one will say anything, but it will
go down as a deadly insult. I think it is sometimes so intended: it
always puzzles me that people who love the place enough to want to
live here cannot conform on such a trivial issue. But human
relationships are full of absurd stances: wars are indeed fought over
which end an egg should be eaten from.

Very similar attitudes prevail in the matter of the Gaelic
language. This is still the language of home for many people,
perhaps most families, but contact with the mainland and television
are steadily eroding it. Not surprisingly, the islanders are sad,
though resigned. Occasionally, in print, they will rage against the
arrogant incomers who are hastening its demise. But in fact, no one
will force you to learn it or even listen to it. We have always found
that if we go into a room or a shop where Gaelic is being spoken,
people will immediately change to English, even amongst
themselves, for fear that we should find them rude. I am sorry to
admit our attempts to learn the language have been abortive: I feel
we owe a debt to island courtesy in not having taken the trouble.
There is great pathos in the delight our Gaelic-speaking friends
have shown because our young daughter is fluent in their language.
Yet no one considers it remarkable that her Gaelic-speaking

contemporaries have to pick up English in infancy. Really, the islanders do not expect much of incomers, and their tolerance is commendable.

We would have found Harris life much more puzzling at first if we had not had kind local friends. The first person we met on our arrival was Mrs Peggy Macaskill, who held the keys of our rented house for the absent owner. She was full of kindness and useful advice. Often she would call us in as we passed her house for a cup of tea and her own delicious baking, and send us home laden with gifts — pancakes, scones and 'maragan', the home-made black and white puddings that are an island speciality. Having arrived in Harris with no money, in fact in debt to the tune of one old Land-Rover, we were especially grateful for these tactful gifts. John Macaskill sub-let the croft on which our house stood, and soon became a familiar figure. He was a big, burly old man, who had to come through our narrow back door sideways, to his own great amusement. He was forever with his sheep, dosing, dipping, shearing, lambing, or just leaning on his crook watching them benignly. Though in his seventies, he would heave a pair of sparring rams apart, one in each fist, or toss a strayed ewe on his shoulder with a flick of his wrist. Often he stood deep in thought, with a lamb tucked under one arm, or inhaling blissfully the sweet scent of newly-cut hay packed into his little byre against the winter. He drove an old black van, in which his friends and family feared greatly for his safety, for if he saw a particularly interesting or a troubled sheep, he would stop dead or veer right or left the better to look at it, oblivious of traffic. The same disconcerting halts occurred if he spotted a likely-looking stone for the fine wall he was making at his house, for he was a talented mason, and in fact he and his sons were builders. But how could he distinguish good stones from bad at a glance, among all the rocks in Harris? We were very fond of John, and also in awe of him. His mixture of childlike enthusiasm and thoughtful observation made his conversation a delight. He died some years ago, but when we pass Leachkin I still expect to see him in his fore-and-aft cap, leaning on his crook. I never hear sung 'He shall feed his flock like a shepherd' without thinking of John Macaskill, whose care for his flock was more illuminating than any number of theological commentaries.

When we first arrived in Harris, we ate what we could scrape up, on account of the unpaid-for Land-Rover. As spring and the first visiting relatives drew near, however, young married pride demanded some more respectable provisioning. We bought a small second-hand freezer, and looked around for things to put in it. Where was the butcher in Harris?

'Go and see the Macaulay Boys at 1, Ardhasaig,' we were told, 'the house with the trees at Caolas na Sgeir.' Ardhasaig is next to Leachkin. 1, Ardhasaig is not the first in a street, but the first croft in the Ardhasaig township: the system of numbering sounds oddly urban to an outsider. As we neared the gate, a figure that might be a Macaulay Boy appeared shyly between the trees. I was not surprised that the Boy seemed to be older than us, as we had already discovered that island boys remain boys well into their forties, and into their nineties if they never marry. We were welcomed politely and asked how we liked Leachkin and the school and the weather. Being in a hurry to get back to filling my tiresome new freezer, I rudely (in retrospect) cut the pleasantries short by asking,

'Are you the butcher?'

'No. I am the butcher's brother. Calum is out with the van just now. Will you come in and wait for him? I'll make you a wee cup of tea.'

I hastily demurred, and handed over an order for the actual butcher to deliver to us. On the way home, Andrew was plaintive. He would have liked to have tea with the butcher's brother, he said. We never went anywhere or made any friends. Why on earth hurry home? And anyway, I had been horribly rude.

So I had. I became very cross.

A few days later, the Land-Rover being off the road with seized brakes, we were walking back from work when an oncoming van stopped and out jumped both Macaulay boys, Calum and John Angus. They shook hands cordially and enquired after the Land-Rover. On hearing of its troubles, they promised help: they would see we got the spare parts: we would have them next day. And when would we come down for a ceilidh? We promised to call the following Saturday.

Next day, to our amazement, the Land-Rover parts duly

arrived. Peter Mackinnon, the postman, a cousin by marriage of the Macaulays, had been called in to help, and had stripped the required pieces from an old vehicle of his own. Twelve years on, it is still the same story: if there's something you need, ask the Macaulay boys. If they don't have it, they won't rest till they find someone else who has. There have never been such neighbours, not only to us but to everyone they encounter.

That Saturday we went for our ceilidh, the first of many. A ceilidh does not mean the studio performance folk-concert suggested by television representations: it is simply a leisurely social call, with plenty of yarn-swapping and (of course) refreshments. John Angus's 'wee cup of tea' is legendary, and puts many five-course dinners in the shade. In the coming months we learned his technique of hospitality. We would start making 'must go' noises at about 10 o'clock.

'No, no, you'll just stay for a wee cup of tea! I'm just going to put the kettle on.'

John Angus's kettle is trained to boil only when his guests make their next attempt to leave – about 10.30, perhaps. Then he disappears into the kitchen, to return with plates laden with goodies—bread and cheese, cakes, chocolate biscuits, or in extreme cases platters of salmon and salad. The consumption of this repast takes a good half hour. Sometime before midnight we try to leave again—and John Angus and Calum go hither and thither, fetching us things to take home, fruit, sweets, household goods, books and magazines. Their hospitality and generosity are astounding. Parting, we are always reproached with, 'you didn't stay long enough!'

Nothing we can ever do could repay the Macaulays for their kindnesses. In those early days, it left us constantly perplexed, taxing our ingenuity to do little things in return that would please them. Their mother, a gentle, uncomplaining lady bent double with arthritis, liked scones rather than bread, but could no longer bake her own easily. I used to make some for her, and horrible they were – hard as rocks and half burnt: I can't bake like the Harris women. But they were as politely grateful as if they had been manna – and promptly set about showering us with yet more gifts, and time, and trouble.

DEREK COOPER

❋   ❋   ❋

Radio and television broadcaster, Derek Cooper is considered one of Britain's finest journalists and broadcasters. In 1984 he won the Glenfiddich Award as Broadcaster of the Year for BBC television's Food programme, and in 1973 and again in 1980 won the Glenfiddich Trophy for excellence in food and wine writing. He is the author of numerous books, including Skye; Guide to the Whiskies of Scotland; The Whisky Roads of Scotland *(with Fay Godwin);* Hebridean Connection: A View of the Highlands and Islands, *and* Road to the Isles, *which received a Scottish Arts Council award.*

In The Road to Mingulay, *he takes a journey from Lewis to Barra en route to his final destination, barren Mingulay where his grandmother Seonaid was born. Along the way he talks to ministers and priests, crofters and fishermen, teachers and doctors. Unlike many journalists, who are in awe of the genius that falls from their pens, Cooper allows the people he meets on his journey to tell their own stories. In his travel books, the voices of the people are truly heard. In this selection he visits the island of Berneray.*

❋   ❋   ❋

My Gaelic Went Into the Sea

from THE ROAD TO MINGULAY:
A VIEW OF THE WESTERN ISLES

Mrs Macleod is married to Dr Roddie Macleod, the Church of Scotland minister. She used to teach in the school. Tea is ready. Homemade tomato soup and to follow a taste of cockles, the first time, I tell Mrs Macleod, anyone in the Western Isles has ever offered me this free, delicious and nourishing bit of shellfish. Unfortunately the cockle has always been associated with famine in

243

the Hebrides; a necessity you ate along with whelks when all else failed but better used to bait hooks for something really worth catching.

There is roast beef, mashed neeps and boiled potatoes and a lemon pie to follow, with grapes. In the visitors' book everyone seems to have fallen on their feet with Mrs Macleod. 'Heaven after camping for two weeks,' wrote the Sharp family of Carlisle. Jenny and Bob Ward of Cambridge noted their 'delicious drop scones which finished a good day on the island' and there were thank yous in German and French.

After supper I walked up the road to the manse and Dr Roddie came out to meet me. He'd been tapping out a sermon on a small and ancient typewriter. A Gaelic activist, Roddie had been a member of Comhairle nan Eilean and is at the eye of every political storm which blows over the island. Like many parts of the Outer Hebrides, Berneray is still privately owned. When Lord Leverhulme died in 1925 his lands were divided into small parcels and disposed of at knockdown prices – Galson estate seven miles south of the Butt of Lewis went for $2^1/_2$d an acre. In the currency of those days that was the equivalent of 57 acres for a bottle of 'Johnnie Walker'! Berneray was virtually given away as well.

'There was a man named Hitchcock at the sale,' Roddie tells me. 'He was owner or manager of the Lochmaddy hotel at the time. They asked me for bids and there weren't any. So the auctioneer said in desperation will *anyone* make me an offer. A voice from the back, Hitchcock, said £500 and it was sold for £500 which I don't think he had at the time. He managed to borrow it from someone and the first time he collected the rents he paid it back.'

The rents have remained charitably low ever since; until recently they were the same as they had been in the 1930s. I asked Roddie if he had ever met the owner?

'No, he's dead now. Maybe his widow is still alive, but it's probably the son who owns the estate. He's a seed saleman in Essex or somewhere. We would prefer to have the island in community ownership operated by a committee elected by the community. People would feel they had more of a say in what was happening.'

Berneray is not much of an investment. There is, as in many other townships, an insoluble problem of unemployment. 'The boys can turn to fishing or crofting but there's nothing except marriage to keep the girls here. They tend to go into nursing or teaching so we have very few girls between the age of 15 and 30 on the island.'

But the emergence of Comhairle nan Eilean in 1975 put a spring in everyone's step. Even the replacement of a light bulb suddenly became simple and more logical. The bureaucracy of Inverness was replaced by common sense in Stornoway.

'We've got navigation lights', says Roddie, 'on the jetty. Now under Inverness, if the navigation lights went out I used to telephone to say they were out and they sent a man with a van from Inverness with a bulb! What happens now is that the Council leaves a supply of bulbs for a local man here to replace.'

Roddie talks about the mainland mentality and its obtuseness. 'When the new council houses were being built in Vatersay we discovered they were all-electric.' In a community where peat is free and hospitality around the fire is traditional it was like building a hospital without beds.

'It wasn't only that they ignored the need for fireplaces to burn peat in but the supply of electricity was a very fragile one anyway – it came by cable from Barra and Barra got its power from South Uist, so you had two chances of being cut off from your only source of heat! We tried to have fireplaces put in but they were at such an advanced stage of building it wasn't possible. That's the kind of thing that used to happen when your architects are sitting in Inverness; it was such a huge county they couldn't visualise what the needs of a remote island like Vatersay were.'

Central control weakened the enterprise of many a community and paralysed initiative. Now it's much easier to get things done.

'We have a community council here that meets once a month on a Saturday. On Monday all the things we've agreed on Saturday can be done. We operate a minibus that takes people to the post office and the shop and at that monthly meeting we decide who's going to arrange all the drivers for the next four weeks.'

For Roddie small is beautiful and above all practical. 'On North Uist they have a community council but there are sixteen people on it and they only meet every second month and then they disperse and may not see each other for eight weeks. Here where you're meeting each other every day you're much more likely to get things done.'

It's not only a new spirit that's abroad in Berneray but more money too. 'There was talk of a causeway at one time but it was going to be too expensive so we got the car ferry instead – that cost the best part of a million and we wouldn't have got that if we'd still been under Inverness. We've had six new council houses, they cost £200,000 and four more have just been completed along here at a cost of £170,000.'

Three township roads have been built too; that cost £300,000. Just past the passenger jetty a new harbour is to be built with the help of the E.E.C. which will cost a million or so. It seems a lot of money to spend on 130 people – £3 million in the last ten years. But the minister does not believe that you can balance human lives against pounds and pence.

'The contribution of this island to Britain can't be measured like that. We've provided ministers and missionaries, scores of school teachers and doctors.' There's the record in two wars as well: the islands suffered losses in both wars more than twice as heavy, in proportion to their populations, as the rest of Britain. In the Great War out of total population of 29,603, in Lewis alone 6,172 men were on active service; hundreds of women were away nursing and on war work, and of the men more than 1,100 lost their lives. The other aspect is that although money can help a community like the one on Berneray to survive no amount of money could rebuild that society elsewhere.

'There's something about a group of people like this and there aren't many of them left in Britain; it's like a big family. You might have an old person living alone; in other places they would cart him off to hospital. Here you might have two or three people working shifts to be with them all through the night rather than have them forced to leave the island. We had a funeral here not so long ago; a Berneray man who lived in Kyleakin on Skye. He was drowned when his dinghy capsized going out to his boat. A lot of people came from Skye for that funeral – there was a lady next door who with a friend provided lunch for 38 people! You can't buy that kind of generosity.'

So where does it spring from?

'It's got a lot to do with religion I think. This island is almost entirely Church of Scotland with just a few members of the Free Church – just the opposite of Scalpay which is mainly Free Church as you saw for yourself. Religion is part of the family atmosphere, it's one of the things that binds people together. Some of the strongest features of Highland society, like hospitality and kindliness and helping each other, are really Christian principles as well. In the old days when a bard praised a chief it was always his hospitality and kindness that were singled out.'

People on Berneray, then, were still ceilidhing with each other?

'No, they're not. TV has certainly spoiled all that. It tends to keep people in their homes a lot more.'

And the programmes they are exposed to all too often celebrate the urban values of a consumer society. Even more disturbing is the almost complete absence of enticing Gaelic programmes for young children. When Roddie came to Berneray eighteen years ago all the children were Gaelic-speaking and in the playground nothing but Gaelic was spoken. Now of the fifteen children in the school only about five have parents who are both Gaelic speakers.

'There was a little girl here who just started school, she was about four. Her parents speak nothing but Gaelic at home. After a while she stopped speaking Gaelic; she spoke only English. I would speak to her in Gaelic and she would answer in English. And I would say to her in Gaelic 'Do you have any Gaelic?' and she would say 'No!' One day I said, 'What happened to your Gaelic?' and she said, 'It went into the sea.'

❊   ❊   ❊

Back at Mrs Macleod's we have tea and biscuits and I look at her Gaelic library in the sitting room. They are closed books to me, incomprehensible. I feel a great sense of loss, a longing for something I never had – the language of my grandparents which would add so much to this journey.

'You have no Gaelic?' said somebody in Lewis.

'No,' I said.

'Well then you might just as well be wandering around the Western Isles like a blind man.'

I'm beginning to think he's right. Mind you, being blind wonderfully concentrates your sense of hearing.

BETTINA SELBY

✳   ✳   ✳

In The Fragile Islands *veteran travel writer Bettina Selby fondly recalls a long summer spent in the Outer Hebrides, which she refers to as 'a marvellous but fragile world on the edge of a wild ocean.' Equipped only with an 'all-terrain' bicycle and a small tent, she ventures to places most people have never even heard of and meets people not encountered on the typical tourist routes.*

Selby is also the author of Riding the Mountains Down; Riding to Jerusalem; Riding the Desert Trail; Riding North One Summer; Frail Dream of Timbuktoo; Pilgrim's Road *and* Beyond Ararat. *She is a thoughtful and highly sensitive writer. In* The Fragile Islands *she offers a fair and balanced portrait of a surprisingly complex part of the world.*

✳   ✳   ✳

from THE FRAGILE ISLANDS:
A JOURNEY THROUGH THE OUTER HEBRIDES

I had planned that my last few days on the islands should be spent around what is certainly my favourite bit of Lewis, if not indeed of the whole of the Outer Hebrides. It is a smaller bay to the south of Loch Roag and Gallan Head called Uig and close up against the hills of Harris. No-one who has been there when the weather is good can ever think of a more beautiful place. Although this particular August was more like April with cold gusty showers sweeping across the sea out of the south-west I was still determined to spend my last available week there.

It takes most of the day to cycle around the coast from Callanish and all along the wastes of the moorland roads there were showers followed by rainbows, like arches spanning the twisting way. After many hours in the saddle I was still only just opposite

Great Bernera, on the west side and only three miles from it as the crow flies. Then the rain stopped and the evening turned fair and golden and I cycled on around the west side of Loch Roag and through the Valtos glen, which is a strange narrow depression between Gallan Head and the slopes of Suainaval, out of which one bursts suddenly upon the enormous expanse of Uig Sands. Two spurs of land slope down to enclose this perfect stretch of beach, one on each side like arms reaching out to shield it from the battering of the sea. Just a narrow entrance remains which gives on to a bay sheltered from all winds except strong north-westerlies. These are the ultimate sands of childhood, a place of endless discovery and limitless horizons.

Beyond the great spaces of Uig Sands the road meanders on for another seven miles, up and down, around headlands, past the turnings to isolated hamlets and tracks to the shore, getting narrower and less purposeful, until just beyond a slanting faded sign which reads *Tigh an Cailleach Dubh* it comes to an end altogether. The sign marks a few rickles of stones that was once a Benedictine Nunnery 'The House of the Old Black Women'. It is a strange deserted spot besides a beach called Mealista, a place of such haunting beauty and atmosphere that it is where I would build a small house if I could, and stay there. It is a place at once peaceful and yet somehow challenging, a combination that occurs not infrequently in the Outer Hebrides and is not I think purely caused by geographical features for always such sites appear to be associated with religious centres of one sort or another.

Once this coast between Mealista and Uig was thick with settlements and the hills behind sheltered countless summer shielings. The whole coast, all along the cliff tops still wears the raised weals of old lazybeds in an endless, convoluted pattern like Celtic carving, bearing witness to an extensive population. Now just a few fields are worked in the townships of Mangersta and Brenish and the last inhabited house on the road belongs to English white settlers who make a living from weaving and pottery for tourists. Not that many tourists come this far or stay the night if they do venture. Local people who had up B&B signs claimed that the tourist office in Stornoway advised visitors that there was nowhere to stay on the west coast – 'In the pay of the Stornoway

Hotels they are,' claimed a local woman darkly.

Circumstances dictated my last camp ground by the heavens opening just as I was level with the cliffs above the spectacular Mangersta Sands. There was a circular enclosure on the cliff top, about fifteen feet across that looked as though it had once been an ancient dun. Only a few courses of stone were left and even these had mostly mouldered away and were grassed over, except in one section where the wall had been roughly raised to about four or five feet to afford shelter from the prevailing south-westerly wind, which was presently driving the rain hard before it. This spot had sheltered a small tent before mine as the pale scar on the grass showed. Some old folk in Mangersta who asked me in for tea later on told me that it was in Red Murdo's garden that I had camped and that there was often a small tent there as the spot seemed to attract campers, though who Red Murdo was or when he had gardened there they had no idea, it was well before their time they said and they were both over seventy. It made a good camp site and I stayed there for several days exploring the coast when there was some respite from the rain and otherwise eating and reading and finding pleasure in coping efficiently in my small space. I had never spent so many nights in a tent in any one year and now that I was acclimatised to the hard ground and to cooking and eating in a prone position I was finding that I quite enjoyed it. The rare nights when I slept for seven hours or so without once waking seemed a triumph. I made a candle holder out of any empty bean can and this gave me a quite disproportionate sense of achievement – I was digging in, home-making.

My surroundings were spectacular in the extreme. Below me and inland, huge waves rolled in to thunder and break upon Mangersta Beach with an uninterrupted force and grandeur I had not seen elsewhere up here; normally such fury expended itself against the cliffs or on the boulder-strewn storm beaches and the sandy bays were more sheltered spaces. Directly before the tent's opening and at no great distance from it, the land fell away to the edge of the sheer headland, in front of which were slender stacks like huge needles in a giant's pincushion. There was a way to scramble down to the sea and wander about in the sheltered shingle coves at the feet of these stacks. It was from there that the older inhabitants of Mangersta could remember launching their twenty foot, open fishing boats and sailing out over the Atlantic on still summer nights, beyond the sight of land.

There was no still weather at all while I was there. I'd wriggle out of the tent in a brief dry spell and my wet clothes, soaked by the last shower would be wind dried in minutes, as I made my way across the tops of the cliffs, concentrating on keeping my balance and not being blown over the edge. The ground I walked on was covered with a close-growing vivid green weed that looked from a distance like the finest bowling green turf. Another bullying herring gull, suspecting that I had designs upon his territory added to the excitement by stalking me and suddenly flying close, his harsh cries echoing around the rocks.

One day when I was walking on Uig Sands I met a group of youths who were camping there and canoeing. They were bright boys mostly in their last year at the prestigious Stornoway secondary school and one was in his final year at University. They asked me in for a cup of coffee and having run out of meths, in the true island style of making do, they managed to prime their stove with bits of fluff pulled from a towel. We talked while a minor gale raged outside their roomy but leaky kitchen tent and I asked them what they thought their futures were likely to be. Of the ten there only two thought they would stay on Lewis, the rest were quite resigned to leaving the islands. One of the two was the under-graduate and he said that after two years away he knew that he had to live on Lewis no matter what work he did as it was the only place he wanted to live.

When I asked them what was the worst element of life on Lewis as far as they were concerned, I was surprised that they unanimously plumped for religion. I was even more surprised that it was not the restrictions of religious observation that they found so galling but the hypocrisy of it all. Sundays they painted as a day of constant fret and niggling, with parental injunctions to turn radios down and come away from windows to avoid neighbours seeing or hearing them do what they ought not to be doing, and that comprised anything at all other than reading the Bible. They were quite insistent about it – it was not the deed itself but other people seeing it that made it heinous – pure hypocrisy they said with all the absolute conviction of youth. Pressed further they admitted that it must be a genuine belief for some people but they still insisted that for the majority religion was simply social pressure, fear of what your neighbours thought in a place where neighbours were so important to life. You had to conform they said otherwise life was made unbearable for you. The youth who was planning to stay said that he too would be forced to go through the motions of conforming and he would do so even though the thought made him angry, because you cannot live on an island if your neighbours ostracise you.

There was currently a religious revival they told me and people were becoming 'converted' even at school but it seemed to them that this was largely play-acting or at best, hysteria. Life in Lewis was dominated by the Free Church they said and its people were in all the positions of power; particularly in the schools, where they claimed indoctrination was in operation from the first class onwards. If they felt so bitterly about it all, why didn't they openly rebel? I wondered and their response to that was that they couldn't possibly because it would rebound upon their parents. I think that reply showed me more about the social cohesion of the islands, its strengths and its weaknesses than anything else I saw or heard there.

Towards the end of that last week there came a day when quite suddenly I craved comfort and had had enough of wet clothes, cramped quarters and hard ground. I had anticipated this and had my plans ready to move into a guest house I had heard of which overlooked Uig Sands and sounded like the exact antithesis to the rough self-sufficiency of the previous months. *Baile na Cille* it was called and was yet another ex-manse, one with a sad history for the last incumbent had hanged himself there. He'd been cooking the books for ages, claiming that he had a healthy, flourishing congregation at a time when every Parish Church on the Protestant islands was virtually empty, the folk having deserted *en masse* to the Free Church, and every Parish Church minister was sick with anxiety because they were paid by results. In reality his only member was his housekeeper who couldn't desert for obvious reasons and when the Establishment in Edinburgh, eager to learn how he had succeeded where every one else had failed informed him of their impending visit,he couldn't face the shame of exposure.

I had been told about the guesthouse by the Vaughans at Ness and in fact their lovely busy-painting of the cricket match had been commissioned by the owners, Richard and Joanna Gollin. I found it a place where the term 'no expense spared' meant a quiet solid comfort, rather than brash ostentation. The Gollins are young and have succeeded in what they set out to do in a relatively short time. Both come from the home counties and both visited the Outer Hebrides when they were still at school and decided then that it was where they wanted to live. A judicious claiming of available grants and a great deal of hard work have provided them with a splendid home and business. The 18th century manse has been improved and refurbished to a standard of affluent comfort – good taste without too much individualism. At £24 a night for dinner bed and breakfast it offered tremendous value, for the food was excellent and plentiful, the rooms were attractive and the site, overlooking the full sweep of the sands was superb. I was lucky to get in because with so few places to stay on this lovely coast it was quite full, but the Gollins kindly allowed me to take over their small daughter's room at a reduced rate and in return I showed them how to rig the sailing dinghy they had just purchased. The Gollins have two young children and Richard also has a teaching job in Stornoway. They work tremendously hard for very long hours during their short season and then take their own holidays in winter when there are no guests.

While I was there a young German whom the Gollins had met on the Continent the previous year, arrived with his tent. He had been intrigued by what they had told him about their island life and had decided to come and camp in their grounds and see it for himself. He was a highly intelligent, rather waspish youth with his attitudes to life neatly worked out – 'Typical English food is fish and chips, marmalade and baked beans.' As a result his instant surrender to the spell of the Outer Hebrides was all the more surprising. The first night we all went for a moonlight walk in a rare spell of milder weather and before we had gone a mile along the marvellous empty sands, beside a sea that was full of soft murmurings and silver shadows, he was declaring that he had found Paradise and would travel no further, for what was the point when perfection was there within his grasp?

I'm glad his visit had coincided with mine, for his unequivocal response reminded me of what I had felt when I had first come out here. It seems to me that he was clearly stating what this string of 'precious fragments' was really all about. It is 'Paradise' to individuals who want what it has to offer and don't mind doing without many of the modern trappings which modern Western man thinks are essential to life. It is one of the few places left in Britain where an individual can choose to live differently in a habitat where nature is still the most dominant presence. I'd come expecting to find something else – an older culture, a communal way of life with a social structure strong enough to withstand alien pressures, something precious preserved over the centuries. I didn't find that, which is not to say that it doesn't exist in a few small pockets. For me the old life style seemed on its last legs with people paying lip service to past values and ideas, while taking on all the expectations of the modern cosumer society and it seemed to be the alien values that had won. I heard lots of talk about a valuable cultural heritage, but I saw glimpses of it only amongst the few and those mostly the oldest of the population. Television soap operas were as much the daily cultural fare as anywhere else in the country and the Gaelic language seemed to be disappearing fast. Nor had subsidies prevented much of the land falling into disuse, lending such an air of desolation and neglect to the landscape.

I was often told of what 'the government' ought to be doing for the islands – creating work so as to halt the population erosion. While I sympathise with anyone out of work, particularly the young, I don't think it's the 'government's' job to keep people anywhere, nor can they do so except in prisons and if it is the 'government's' job to create work then there is the rest of Britain to consider too and the numbers in all the Outer Hebrides are just a drop in the ocean of unemployment.

Terrible injustices have been perpetrated on the people of the Outer Hebrides; the last two hundred years of their unenviable history is as black a period as any. It is small wonder that so many of them have looked elsewhere for a more satisfactory life or that children raised on stories of such inequalities should seek their future away from the islands. Something very precious has indeed been destroyed. But it is not only the people who have suffered, the islands themselves have been exhausted under a regime that put profit first and destroyed much of the fertility of the soil. It didn't seem to me that subsidies were doing much to reverse these centuries of misuse. I read in one modern sociological treatise that the people don't really feel the land belongs to them yet and this was why they were not prepared to effect real, long-term improvements. If they really feel that way will they, I wonder, be able to resist pressures to turn the place into a nuclear dumping ground or an advanced missile base or a testing ground for chemical warfare?

What gave me most hope for the future of the Outer Hebrides were the individuals who had chosen to live there. Whether 'white settlers' or returned natives, they were the ones who had made a rational choice between different value systems and decided that they would be richer in their own terms, living there than anywhere else. Where people make that sort of commitment, a level of caring ensues which is seldom matched by people who simply find themselves in situations. Such people have a clear idea of what the islands give them – which is of course the sum of what they themselves give to the islands.

I was thinking of the people I'd met out there as I steamed back across the Minch, past the Summer Isles to Ullapool. Many of them would I suppose be considered 'dropouts' in some societies, because they are so unambitious in worldly terms. I thought of Jack and Polly in the manse garden on Barra; Chris Spears in the house he'd made out of a byre on the edge of Berneray; the Vaughans; Margaret Ponting with her passion for prehistory; the Miles, the Gollins, and the man whose name I've forgotten, who'd come back to his small village near the island of Scarp. I see these people as the new inheritors, upon whom the rest of us have to depend to preserve this fragile chain of precious islands.

W. R. MITCHELL

❖　　　❖　　　❖

Born in Skipton, in Yorkshire, W. R. (Bill) Mitchell lived and worked in the Dales all his life. In 1943 he joined the Craven Herald *as a cub reporter, where he met Harry J. Scott, founder of* The Dalesman; *in 1948 he went to work for Scott at the magazine, where he has been on the staff for almost 40 years. He has also edited its sister magazine* Cumbria *and has written more than 60 books, including* The Changing Dales *and* Changing Lakeland *and* A Dalesman's Diary.

Every spring Mitchell and his friends crossed the Border to explore a different part of Scotland – their ultimate goal always being Muckle Flugga, the lonely lighthouse in the Shetlands, where Great Britain truly ended.

In this selection, Mitchell reaches another personal milestone by setting foot on St. Kilda, the remote and enigmatic Atlantic island that was evacuated at the request of its inhabitants in 1930.

❖　　　❖　　　❖

At the Edge of the World
St. Kilda

from IT'S A LONG WAY TO MUCKLE FLUGGA:
JOURNEYS IN NORTHERN SCOTLAND

St. Kilditis, an incurable disease, is neither painful nor debilitating. It is characterised by a deep longing for St Kilda, that scattering of volcanic islands and stacks some 50 miles off the Western Isles. St. Kilditis is alleviated by reading about them or by making the long, sometimes stormy crossing to 'the islands at the edge of the world'.

I was afflicted some 40 years ago, when I read *With Nature and a Camera*, a book written and illustrated by Richard and Cherry

Kearton, grown-up men who reverted to a mental age of 11 when let loose on some remote island. They were boys at heart. Having visited St Kilda in 1896, they left a graphic account of their adventures. It began with the sea crossing:

> When we got clear of the Hebrides, and were fairly launched upon the bosom of the mighty Atlantic, the waves began to make themselves felt, and to render the after-deck uninhabitable except for such as could don oilskins ... Towards noon, the weather thickened considerably, and a drizzling rain commenced to fall. The steamer was now rolling and pitching ...
>
> As we passed Rock Lavenish, the ship got the full benefit of wind and tide on her port, and, in consequence, rolled fearfully. Her decks were often at such an acute angle that the sailors themselves were obliged to hold on to whatsoever stable article lay within reach.

Happily, in Village Bay, on the main island of Hirta, the water was calm, although they did hear the tide growling in the caves of Dun, which forms a natural breakwater.

On the voyage to St Kilda, the weather can be so calm that seabirds admire their reflections in the Atlantic, or so bad that even the seasickness pills turn green. I wrote to the National Trust for Scotland requesting a place on one of its summer work-parties. They put my name on the list of those going in June. All that remained was to hope for a calm sea and a pleasant voyage.

So that year, while Fred, Ron and George – together with the 'lasses' – went to the glens of Perthshire, I voyaged 100 miles west of mainland Scotland. The Weather Clerk was in a benign mood. The only white water I saw was the sea-foam at the bows of MV *Monaco*, a converted trawler now concerned with cruising alog the Scottish seaboard. The National Trust for Scotland were using *Monaco* to transport its work-parties. Cubby MacKinnon, the skipper, delights in the tumult of water at the bows of a sea-going ship. He derives as much pleasure from it as someone else might get from looking at the varied forms and shapes in a good coal fire. He and his wife Kate work together on *Monaco*.

My adventure began on a bonnie morning at Oban. A dozen of us, all cheerful volunteers, with Ron Hardie as the party leader, stood on a quay looking down, down, to where *Monaco* waited at low tide.

There was work to be done – a fortnight's food supply, plus our luggage, to stow away below decks. The stock of food formed an impressive heap, for St Kilda is more than a day's sailing from the nearest supermarket. With the boat's deck far below the quay, we lowered the substantial items of food and kit by rope. Vegetables were dropped and 'fielded' by someone on deck. Holidaymakers on the quay stared open-mouthed at the spectacle of free-flying bananas and cabbages.

The eggs, in their papier-mâché boxes, were passed from hand to hand. It was ironic that we should be taking eggs to St Kilda, where several million seabirds lay eggs. Years ago, the St Kildans consumed seabirds and eggs, storing any surplus for use in the winter.

At noon, the propeller of MV *Monaco* stirred some life into the calm water of Oban Bay. The boat left a herringbone pattern on the Sound of Mull – a pattern that became complex when our wake was crossed by a MacBrayne car ferry and then by a tall-masted ship from Ireland.

Rounding Ardnamurchan, I looked eagerly for the familiar shapes of the Small Isles. I bowed gravely towards the Cuillins of Skye and winked at MacLeod's Maidens (a group of stacks). A friend of Cubby pointed to one of the last two of the diesel-powered puffers, the 'workhorses' of the Western Isles, which had just delivered a load of coal to Dunvegan and was returning to Ayr. 'Coal's cheapish just now ... '

For years, my dreams had been coloured by accounts I had read of remote, little-visited St Kilda, which came into being with the flaring of a large ring volcano some 60 million years ago. The islands and stacks are what remain and they are being ceaselessly eroded by the mighty Atlantic which, in a few more million years, will have gobbled up the lot.

For centuries, the self-reliant folk of St Kilda were in part a 'bird people', relying on the nesting seafowl for food, for lamp-oil and for feathers to be bartered with the Factor for necessities brought from the mainland. The traditional way of life ended when the population declined to 36 and, in August 1930, was evacuated.

St Kilda was visited by yachtsmen, by naturalists or trawlerman until, in the 1950s, a small military base was established on Hirta for monitoring the launching of rockets from Benbecula. Today the islands are owned by the National Trust for Scotland, who have leased them to the Nature Conservancy Council. They were declared a National Nature Reserve in 1957 and appear on the World Heritage List. The Ministry of Defence sub-leases a small area.

Humans are vastly outnumbered by the seals and the seabirds. Hereabouts is the world's largest gannetry and the oldest and largest colony of fulmars in Britain. Here the puffins fly like bumble bees pouring from a hive and eiders sit tightly on their nests like streaky brown puff-balls.

On that first day of voyaging from Oban to St Kilda, the sun set redly, among a mass of blue-black cloud. I had the impression that the western sky was bleeding. We reached Lochmaddy on North Uist under the binoculared gaze of an officer on the bridge of the MacBrayne car ferry – a huge vessel ablaze with electric light. Cubby made a neat job of securing *Monaco*.

For several hours we slept; the boat's engine was still. Then Cubby and Kate were up and about, the boat came back to life and I reached the deck in time to observe that magical moment at dawn when all is still. The sea was as calm as the proverbial millpond: if a jellyfish had surfaced, I would have noticed the faint ripple.

TheSound of Harris was our route to the Atlantic. We did not know what conditions to expect beyond the natural breakwater of the Western Isles, so Kate dampened the cloths on the tables of the saloon to provide extra adhesion for anything placed upon them. In the galley, the knives began to rattle, but the crossing was 'nae so bad'.

We left a clear sky and slipped under a canopy of cloud. It was not actually raining but sometimes the air had such liquid consistency it might almost be called drizzle. When St Kilda came into view, afar off, the islands wore poultices of cloud.

I had a peculiar pleasure in seeing St Kilda as a smudge on the horizon when, for so many years, it had been familiar only through photography. The archipelago consists of four islands – Hirta, Dun,

Soay and Boreray – each appearing to leap directly from the sea, such is the spectacular nature of cliffs rising to over 1,000 feet. Some of the attendant stacks were tall enough to tickle the passing clouds.

Cubby ignored our final destination, Hirta, and made directly for Boreray, four miles away, intent on showing us some big colonies of seabirds. We had the company of birds that had been feeding. They had yet to run the gauntlet of the great skuas.

Gannet, puffin, guillemot and razorbill flew purposefully, overtaking the *Monaco* with ease. Gannets rose the air currents with stiffened wings, the auks working their wings so briskly I half-expected some of them to break off. All were heading for Boreray and its stacks.

We approached a grey wall, topped by summer-green pasturage for the many sheep that were left here at the time of the evacuation and which now are the unofficial green-keepers of this uninhabited island, keeping it neat and tidy.

The *Monaco* came close to cliffs that held rows of growling gannets, some of which flew to join the traffic in a bird-busy sky. The presence of the boat did not alarm them. Years ago, a tourist spectacle was provided by the skipper of a steamer when he sounded the whistle and thousands of gannets rose simultaneously into the air.

We rounded the island and saw Stac an Armin, Britain's highest sea stack, whitened by nesting birds. We passed Stac Lee. These geological remnants rose like the fangs of some monster. Gannets, silhouetted against the sun's glare, wheeled above the rock.

The *Monaco* was now directed to Hirta; we reached Village Bay. The Keartons wrote of the 'sombre grandeur of the place'. That was before an Army camp was constructed, and before Gemini inflatable craft with outboard motors scurried across the bay like brightly-coloured water beetles.

An Army landing craft slipped by on the high tide and allowed itself to be stranded on a crescent of fine sand until the next tide. The beach is present only in summer, for winter storms disperse the sand in deeper water. When the LCL (Landing Craft Logistics) are unable to land, the St Kilda detachment is supplied by helicopter or by Cessna aircraft.

The Cessna specialises in dropping containers with stores and mail on to a tract of flat ground on a hill overlooking Village Bay. One day a luckless soldier on the ground was injured when a bag burst and he was struck by a flying chicken. That chicken was like a missile, having been plucked and frozen!

I eagerly looked beyond the Army complex to locate the famous Street, between the old meadowland and the hill. Archaeologists have detected several phases of habitation. What remains of the small Victorian houses are the most prominent features in the Street. They were small, 'two ee's and a moo', yet, with their chimneys intact they have a dignity even in decay.

Most of the Street itself is grassed over. It was here that the St Kildan males met each workaday morning as the Parliament, discussing the tasks to be carried out that day. The Street, with its sixteen houses, once held a large population. Now the area where the St Kildans lived, loved, raised children and died is patrolled by fulmars which stare at intruders unblinkingly. St Kilda wrens try to infuse a sense of life into an ancient settlement by singing at full volume.

The Street is mown daily by the Soay sheep, one of the most primitive types in Europe, which on St Kilda are virtually untouched by human hands, being allowed to live their lives without interference. The sheep also litter the Street with moulted wool, chestnut or black. The wool has moulted naturally; once it was a valuable crop, being plucked, not shorn.

I watched a researcher training a group and collecting fresh droppings in small glass jars for study. She had also developed the art of catching sheep at dead of night by sneaking up on the cleits, the old storage places of the St Kildans, which the animals use as dormitories.

The Soay sheep are on St Kilda by the right of 1,000 generations. No one is sure how they got here, but they might have been brought by the Vikings. Unlike mainland sheep, which can be enticed by food, these Artful Dodgers would not tolerate close scrunity. They were flighty creatures. If I stopped, they soon bounded away. The population builds up and then crashes, which is a natural way. It had recently lost about 50 per cent of its strength, but the survivors would soon restore the old numbers.

Soay sheep are spirited animals from birth. I watched two small lambs head-butting. The small black lamb gave way, turned and began to graze. The chestnutty lamb ungallantly butted the other from behind. I mentioned this to a retired vet who was in our party: he smiled and forecast a bright future for the chestnutty lamb!

All the masonry in the Street had been made secure by work-parties of the National Trust for Scotland; they had also roofed and refurbished five of the houses. In the first, our meals were prepared and served. We surreptitiously sprinkled a few crumbs on the floor for the St Kilda mice, which turned up at about 10 p.m.

The island sub-species of long-tailed field mouse is quite a character; it scutters about the Street in the gloaming, and by invading houses it occupies a niche once held by the St Kilda house mouse, now extinct.

It was never really dark. The Hebridean summer night is brief enough; on Hirta, the orange glare from sodium chloride at the Army base tinted the clouds, and the throbbing from the generator house provided a rhythmical background to the strident voices of the oystercatchers and mingled with the voices of storm petrels coming in from the ocean to their nests in the big wall between the old Factor's House and the Feather Store.

Anyone who yearned for the noisy pleasures of civilisation might go to the Puff Inn, at the Army base, an establishment described on a leaflet available locally as being famous (or infamous) for its low prices and flexible opening hours. One might drink to the accompaniment of a juke box. Everyone was friendly.

In the bar, one evening, I was shown a Union Jack shredded by a winter gale. The flag had been raised on the mast just before the gale arrived, and the force of the wind was such that no one could recover the flag for days on end. One blast of wind topped 195 miles an hour.

The commanding officer told me that Spring arrived on the first of April. That was the day when the first puffin was reported, when the first Soay lamb was seen and when it was possible to walk out and about without going ankle-deep in mud.

Many of us kept unsociable hours. A Midlander went fishing from the rocks and returned, sometimes in the wee small hours, with a score of fish. A braw Scot took his sleeping bag up the hill and slept under the stars, blithely ignoring warnings about sheep tick and 'keds'. My chief nocturnal pleasure apart from sleeping was visiting the wall where the storm petrels nested, listening to the guttural voices of the birds and occasionally seeing bat-like forms in the sky as the time for a change-over in nesting duties arrived.

The Hebridean night was vibrant with the 'bleating' of snipe which went into shallow glides, extending the outer feathers of their tails so that the wind passed through the stiffened barbs, with a wavering sound. Snipe were common nesters around the village.

Walking could be combined with bonxie-dodging. Wherever I went – through the Gap to the cliffscape between Conachair and Oiseval, or along the western rim to the Cambir, or even to the western limit of Village Bay, at Ruaival – great skuas made the air crackle with their guttural voices. They were nesting on the drier parts of the hills. Off-duty birds perched on knolls and tussocks. The voice of the skua – 'keg, keg' – punctuated my excursions as birds wheeled, taking the upthrust of the breeze on wings with an impressive span, some four-and-a-half feet. The skua weighs over three pounds and is therefore among the avian heavyweights.

No self-respecting bonxie fears a human intruder into its territory. If I had not taken note of the calls, then I could not ignore the dive, with the hefty bird passing my head at a range of a few inches. The first bird to dive on me used guile as well as physical strength, tending to fly towards me from the rear. A sudden 'whoosh' of displaced air was followed by another round of cackling.

Skuas usually nest in treeless northern places where there is no possibility of securing a stick to hold above the head as a deterrent. I was on Hirta at the time when eggs were hatching. Now and again I came across a downy youngster, waddling on webbed feet that seemed a few sizes too large for the bird!

Great skuas were the guardians of the Tunnel, a natural rock arch on the northern shore. As I slithered down the hills towards it, the large brown birds lumbered into flight and then let the rising air carry them aloft. I was also entertained to the air display of the fulmar petrels; the birds disappeared and reappeared at the edge of a cliff, and made dramatic movements of wings and tail feathers to maintain their equilibrium in a fierce updraught.

The Army provided a Gemini inflatable to convey us across the Bay for a landing on Dun, the jagged outline of which had become a familiar feature during our stay in the village. An eider duck cruised by with a duckling on its back. Rafts of puffin in the Bay testified to the high population on Dun. We landed to the croaking of fulmars, which had settled on every suitable cliffscape, high or low.

Dun is dominated by birds and the sea. Every niche on the long narrow ridge was being used for nesting. The sharp crest of the island gave it a special character, dividing the southern side – where the cliffs were up to 500 feet high – from the northern, where steeply shelving slopes were riddled with puffin burrows.

Kittiwakes had plastered their nests against the merest knobs of rock in a shallow cave. Razorbills, immaculate, clad in black and white, like birds in a dress suit, did not sem to mind being peered at from close range. Puffins alighted with glistening sand-eels in their beaks, testifying to the presence of young in the peaty burrows.

We had work to do, of course. One group completed the re-roofing of the first house in the Street; another had some joinery projects; a third was concerned with the renovation of cleits. Each cleit was numbered. I became a member of the 123 Club when I visited Cleit 122 and crawled along a tunnel into the beehive-shaped Cleit 123. Our veterinary friend, emerging slowly from the tunnel which he virtually filled, used his vet's knowledge to extricate himself. 'The first principle of calving,' he announced, 'is to get one shoulder through first.'

Then we thought of home. One of our party made a 'St Kilda mail-boat' – a small, boat-shaped piece of wood, hollowed to accommodate mail and capable of being sealed to make it watertight, attached to a buoyant object. Years ago, an animal bladder was used; we found a plastic container.

When the boat had received its items of mail and had been sealed, it was taken to the Point, to be placed on the ebb tide and, hopefully, to make good progress across to the Western Isles, where it would be picked up and the contents posted to our homes.

The boat was released on the evening of June 16. The postcard I had placed in it was delivered to my home in Giggleswick, Yorkshire, on June 27.

On my return home I gazed at the picture on the card. It had been taken from Hirta, looking across four miles of sea to Boreray and the stacks. The main island was poulticed by cloud. It did not need much effort to imagine the gannets plunge-diving into the sea and to hear the croaking of many fulmars.

I was beginning to get more pangs of St Kilditis. I must return before long to 'the islands at the edge of the world'.

THE
NORTHERN
ISLES

EMILY HIESTAND

❊ ❊ ❊

Winner of a 1990 Whiting Writers' Award and author of a book of poems, Green the Witch Hazel Wood, *poet, writer, artist, and naturalist Emily Hiestand creates word paintings. Whether her preferred method of expression be prose, poetry or a canvas, the result is always the same – a marvellous collage of emotion, sensuality, and gentleness. The poetry editor of* Orion *magazine, Hiestand lives in Cambridge, Massachusetts.*

In 'South of Ultima Thule', she travels with her Presbyterian mother to Orkney. Indeed, it is her mother, an avid birdwatcher, who suggests that they visit these northern islands, as much to escape to the strangeness of a strange land as to return to the part of the world where her forebears originated. It is an emotional journey for both mother and daughter, full of unexpected linkages. Hiestand recalls how the fiddle music of Orkney reminds her of Tennessee bluegrass and of how the music of Scotland in general, and the Highlands in particular, are connected – as if 'the Appalachians and the Highlands are really one mountain chain connected under the Atlantic Ocean.'

As a traveller, Hiestand is unfailingly gracious towards her subject; as an observer, remarkably non-judgmental – a true innocent abroad in the best sense of the word.

❊ ❊ ❊

South of the Ultima Thule

from THE VERY RICH HOURS

There are some sixty islands in the Orkney archipelago, although many of these are best described as *skerries*, large rocks that are overwashed at high tide. In 1933, twenty-eight islands were inhabited, but the more marginal human habitations have gradually faded and the primary island communities now number sixteen: Mainland, Rousay, Egilsay, Wyre, Gairsay, Shapinsay, Westray, Papa Westray, Sanday, North Ronaldsay, Stronsay, and Eday are the North Isles; Hoy, Burray, South Ronaldsay, Flotta, and a scatter of tiny others are the South Isles. Mainland is so much larger than the others that it makes up nearly one third of the total land area of the chain. The startling first impression of the big island is of a treeless, unsheltered landscape that stretches away to the sea in wide plains and gentle hills. In the Scandinavian way, farmhouses are widely dispersed across the land, creating a sparse terrain. With no imposing hills and no forests, and few villages to act as a break, a strong southwesterly wind is always blowing, singing, howling, or whistling over the island, carrying in its teeth a saline tincture that saturates even the most inland areas. Gale winds blow for twenty-four days a year on the average, and the combination of caustic salt and wind is so potent that it has long been considered an eccentricity to attempt to grow a tree on Orkney. Planted in the lee of a house or barn, a sapling will begin to grow, but no sooner has it outgrown its protector than the trunk begins to bend in the wind, eventually keeling over nearly ninety degrees toward Norway. The southeastern prong of Mainland is articulated by a thin neck of land, an isthmus shaped as though an oceanic thumb and finger had slightly squeezed a warm hunk of dough, leaving two fat bays on either side of a narrow land bridge. This strand corresponds with the crossing point of two huge geological rifts: the North Scapa and Brims-Risa faults. Kirkwall town is nestled on the isthmus along the northern bay, perhaps a half mile from the intersection of the faults. Rising up from a plateau in town, halfway up a slight slope from the sea, is St. Magnus Cathedral. 'Kip carrrrryin' doone, Leddies, kip carrrrryin' doone,' are the melodic, accurate directions we receive from two little lads playing on the hill above the kirk.

In a world of grey flagstones, grey seals; fences, buildings, and streets made of grey stone; and a rhapsody of grey skies dripping over a grey sea, the peoples of Orkney have responded not by a stubborn resistance, not with intrusions of gaudy paint and bright cloth, but by melding themselves and their artifacts into the landscape. The palette of earth, sky, and sea has sufficed and has schooled the local eye in subtlety and proportion. Out in the countryside, over the course of a day one might see three splashes of vivid human colour: a purple door in a grey farmhouse facade, a hunter-green painted gate in a grey stone wall, one outlandish pink house by the bay in St. Margaret's Hope, leaping from the grey continuum of the village. Departures from the grey-scale are prominent events and they pose a question: what danger would be courted by a more lavish deviancy, by a rash of magentas and pinks, yellows, cerulean blues, carmine reds? Would some fibre be weakened, leaving the community more vulnerable to the careless accident that comes of a momentary distraction, the frayed rope that leads to the splintered wreck on the shoals? The embrace of grey must arise from an old calculation in which morals and aesthetics have merged to mirror the palette of the surround. The colors that do appear – the green gate, the purple door, even the vibrant pink house – all arise from the colors of heather, grass, and petals. Even the ratio of painted door to grey stone facade follows that of tussocky heather to vast black moor, primrose petal to salt-lashed cliff. Very like the strategy of those animals who assume the protective coloration of their habitat, this human aesthetic has grown from and is semaphore to the surround.

Tuesday comes up wet, cold, raining, and grey. Drizzles probe into showers then recede to drizzles throughout the day. We make a trip to the post office in Kirkwall town. By chance, we are here during the culmination of celebrations for the birthday of Her Majesty the Queen Mother. As one might expect, a celebration of things English and royal does not especially stir the Scottish spirit, but this Elizabeth is from the Highlands, so shops offer a great line of souvenirs with her portrait applied woozily, slightly out-of-register to plates and ashtrays banded with gold. Best of all, the Philatelic Office has issued a stamp series in her honor: four stamps showing four stages of life. The first is a sepia-tone picture of a young wild-haired girl that at first glance seems an ethnographer's photograph of a half-feral child. Then comes a pale blue stamp: Elizabeth as Duchess of York, in her twenties, in ropes of pearls, a regal set of head already established, just beginning to contend with Wallis Simpson. The third is a stamp of a woman encrusted in a crown and massive necklace, her mild face firmset with concern. The last stamp is a release into vivid turquoise and fuchsia pastels:

a blousey, calm old woman, wafting in her signature costume, a floral suit and a sort of floating, gossamer garland of flowers emanating from her broad-brimmed hat.

In the post office, as in banks and city halls, there are prominent spindle racks holding brochures about family programs, health care services, and how to get your old-age pension. Just as the Glasgow vibration hinted, in Scottish island society there is everywhere the surprising message that life will be a possible proceeding. In the America I know, the sensibilities of even optimistic souls are tinged with a competitive, anxious edge that hovers like a cautionary tale: very little about our society suggests that the average person can raise a family or grow old gracefully. Even the rich live with a grave wound: the knowledge that the economy that yields their material affluence dooms many others to misery. This short spell in Orkney invites a vicarious entrance into a slightly more secure world. The society cannot be all satisfactory, for I see in the paper that the youth are bored with farming jobs and are beginning to drink alcohol in public. It is a greyer society; it does not lightly tolerate the outlandish and speculative; yet there are many signs that islanders have a kind of inherent well-being lost even to the materially affluent in my country.

After the post office, we wander up to the main market street to buy scones, fruit, and local Orkney cheese for the next day's field trip. The streets are narrow, made of blue-grey flagstone slabs, crowded with shoppers and tiny cars that weave slowly through the pedestrians. Women push their round-headed babies in prams that are uniformly fitted over with clear plastic rain jackets that can be opened or zipped up in a trice. When the rains begin, as they do at some point nearly every day, mothers and fathers all up and down the street are suddenly bending, zipping up the hoods of prams. The babies process placidly throught the wet streets with splots of rain bouncing and beading on their plastic ceilings. When the sun comes out again and the hoods are unzipped, the babies must experience a miniature version of what is happening over the whole landscape: the abrupt parting of a blanket of clouds that renders the island a sudden bright, wet jewel, all the more astonishing for its rarity. On a sunny day along these streets, one commonly sees a practice that in most other cities could only be found today in a book of old statistics: in front of meat shops and tea rooms and bakeries, there are parked pramfuls of babies, wee ones left outside near the warm stone walls, safe and unattended save by the passing people of Kirkwall. From one blanketfold comes a peedie, tiny hand, stretching out to the sparkles in the grey stone wall. Well underway are the countless perceptions and sensory minutiae that will cause this baby to relish greys. Orcadians are said to be wary towards outsiders, and one can easily imagine that the climate engenders a stoic and braced psyche. Yet a community that can leave its tenderest members unattended for a spell, on its busiest street, during market hours, has preserved a kind of trust that is elsewhere only a memory. Perhaps it is not too much to say that such a trust and the National Trust that tends the landscape of Scotland are two faces of one virtue.

LAWRENCE MILLMAN

❊ ❊ ❊

The author of five books of fiction and non-fiction, including Our Like Will Not Be There Again, *an account of his travels in Ireland and* An Evening Among Headhunters, *as well as hundreds of essays, short stories, and poems, Lawrence Millman is one of those writers whose non-fiction work reads like a novel.*

Millman's first book of poetry, Northern Latitudes: Prose Poems *(New Rivers Press), celebrates the landscapes of the far north, including arctic Canada, Greenland, Labrador, Iceland, and the northern fringes of the British Isles. In 2000 a revised edition of* Last Places *with a new introduction by Paul Theroux was published by Mariner Books.*

Millman is the quintessential loner. He plays the role of restless wanderer to the hilt – the stranger in town who heeds the call of faraway places and whose adventures, often surreal encounters that sometimes flirt with violence, make for wonderfully vicarious thrills. In Last Places *he loosely follows the Viking trail from Norway to Newfoundland by way of the Shetland Islands, the Faeroes, Iceland, Greenland, and Labrador. Here he makes a stop-over in Foula, reportedly the last place in the British Isles where the old Norse tongue, Norn, was spoken. Fans of the cinema will also remember that Michael Powell's classic 1938 film* The Edge of the World, *ostensibly inspired by the evacuation of St. Kilda, was actually shot on this lonely, forgotten island.*

❊ ❊ ❊

Birds of a Different Feather

from LAST PLACES:
A JOURNEY IN THE NORTH

Ten hours out of Bergen the *Norrona* came in sight of the Shetland Islands.

The Shetland mainland is a long attenuated backbone of peat and stone shaped like a dagger and pointed toward the British mainland. The offshore islands lie helter-skelter in the sea like a bunch of mercenaries undecided whether to stab the British lion or float off to join some other hireling cause. One of these islands, Foula, sits by itself, impervious to such nonsense, a chunky meditative bulk brooding only on its own diehard rhythms. Indeed, Foula sits so far off on the horizon that it was once thought to be the legendary Thule. It wasn't, and isn't. The only authentic Thule is the giant American air base at Cape York, Greenland, whose radar commonly transposes flocks of migrating geese into a Soviet nuclear attack.

Foula has always been a little too far away. It was overlooked in 1469 when Norway pawned Shetland and Orkney to Scotland as part of a royal dowry, a slip that allowed Foula to continue on, with its own Norse king and queen, until the middle of the seventeeth century. It became British largely by geographical default, since Norway hardly knew it still possessed a colony in the British Isles. Being British (or Scottish) did not mean a thing to this pawky little piece of Old Red Sandstone so hermetically sealed off from the rest of the world that it was omitted from a good many maps. Foula was not on the road to anywhere. Even now Foula remains the odd island out in a group of odd islands out, the Shetlands, which belong to Scotland, itself on the fringe of the United Kingdom. North Sea oil has brought Shetland more or less to the public's attention. Not Foula: it is still left off the map occasionally.

I decided to inaugurate my Viking trip on Foula because it was the last place in the British Isles where Norn, the old language of the Vikings, was spoken. In 1759 an Englishman named Low visited the island and took from the lips of one William Henry of Guttorm a thirty-five stanza Norn ballad about the daughter of a medieval king of Norway. The nineteenth century saw the demise of Norn as a living tongue, yet I'd heard rumors on an earlier trip to Shetland that odd snatches of the language were still being spoken in thick-walled houses by the squally sea, among a company of secretive old men. If true, this would be a remarkable thing in the Britain of Liverpool Eight, Paki bashing, and punkhood, rather like finding a passenger pigeon in a contemporary zoo.

'Foula?' said the skipper of the Norrona over a glass of schnapps. 'Haven't the lights gone out on Foula?'

'Not quite,' I said.

Here was a man who'd sailed as far south as the Roaring Forties and as far north as Sisimiut in West Greenland. That he knew so little about this particular outcropping in the sea gave me, I must admit, a certain pleasure and confirmed (if I needed confirmation) my decision to visit the island. Later we checked his charts on the bridge and there was Foula – graphically not forgotten by at least one cartographer. All around the island WKS (wrecks), RKS (rocks), LDGS (ledges), and OBS (obstructions) warned the prospective mariner to stay away. Foula's waters were a dazzling minefield, which made the island inhospitable to yachtsmen, day-trippers, and even Her Majesty's public works brigade, though not – I learned in a few days – Jehovah's Witnesses.

At two am I got off in Lerwick, Shetland's tiny capital, an enclave of gray granite rowhouses and staunch churches peering from their hillside roost down on the prickly antennae of the fishing fleet. Like all good towns at this hour, Lerwick was fast asleep, but like all sailor's towns, it was also wide awake. Little roving bands of Russians and Norwegians had received shore leave from their factory ships and were looking for a good time. One of the Russians stopped me and asked somewhat forlornly where all the girls were. 'At home in bed,' I replied. He looked even more forlorn. Clearly he felt a sailor's town ought to have at least one or two waterfront whores to lend it some respectability.

The Norwegians, on the other hand, had been coming here for too long to expect more than booze from a Shetland waterfront. A thousand years ago the islands offered them refuge from King Harald; more recently, in the 1940s, the so-called Shetland Bus ferried them across the North Sea after the Nazi invasion of

Norway. Now their visits were less politically charged, unless you consider the depletion of fish from Shetland waters a political issue. Lerwick must have made them feel right at home, with its Norwegian lifeboat, Norwegian welfare center, and fishmeal factory run on Norwegian capital. Local shopkeepers cheerfully accept this capital – much more cheerfully than they accept Mrs. Thatcher's debased pounds.

Since there wasn't any action on the waterfront, apart from a few teenagers trying to neck and eat greasy chips at the same time, I took to the road. In lieu of the morning bus, I decided I'd walk the fourteen miles to Walls, port of call for the Foula mailboat. For I wanted to renew my acquaintance with the bald glaciated Shetland earth, remind it of my presence, let it sniff the leather of my boots and feel their stomp, so that when it came time for me to visit Foula's steepdown cliffs, this earth would recognize me and not be inclined to fling me overboard twelve hundred feet into the sea. A bootless prisoner of a motor vehicle might not be so lucky; he might be perceived as an undesirable alien and, once he left his cage of metal, be catapulted to his doom.

Shouldering my rucksack, I climbed up cobbled lanes so steep they required handrails and threaded a maze of dark wynds and rowhouses. Near the Iron Age broch of Clickhimin, which stood across the road from a modern housing estate, I paused to chat with a man walking his dog. He was a baker, he said, and no more terrible ('*Turr-r-rible*, laddie!') profession existed in Shetland. It was well-nigh impossible for him to get apprentices anymore. All the young lads were heading up to the Sullom Voe oil terminal, where they earned three times as much as they could earn in his shop. But wasn't a good loaf of bread, he asked me, more valuable than a big blob of North Sea oil? He opened his shop and gave me a loaf of soda bread with the specific gravity of lead. Then we went our separate ways, I overland to Walls, he – it would appear – to an early retirement.

I'd met quite a few other Shetlanders who admitted to a powerful dislike of the side effects of oil. They muttered in their pints about the widening of roads, dead seabirds, crowded pubs, crowded shops, ugly housing estates, overpriced wares, and the accents of imported British and American oil workers. *Accents!*

When local folk fuss about someone's accent, you know there's more to it than meets the ear. You know they're not just fussing because the Scots part of them likes to fuss. Rather, they're worried about an assault no less deadly than an assault by a lockstep army: an assault to the gut of their own pridefully rundown and outmoded way of life. Perhaps they're also trying to drum up a little support for a species – themselves – threatened by extinction. What oil supplies to the community chest, it takes from the marrow.

Yet the farther you travel from Lerwick, the less evidence there is of this upstart oil. The only accents tend to be Shetland accents, triumphantly impenetrable. And except for the main north-south road to Sullom Voe, the roads are all narrow twisting lanes on whose asphalt a thunderous oil lorry would be an impertinence. Also, it wouldn't fit.

After I left this main road, I climbed up and down a series of heather-and-sedge hills bulldozed clean by Shetland's own miniature ice cap during the last Ice Age. I cut across a switchback and scared off a few sheep who were busily cropping the grass down to its roots, a reminder of why there are no trees, scarcely even bushes or shrubs, in Shetland. Soon the wind (another reminder why there are no trees) picked up and my cap was whisked into a small loch. Five minutes later it was blown off again, now into a peat cutting. Fifteen minutes later it was impossible to light my pipe even with my supposedly windproof matches. In half an hour my ears felt like they'd been tacked to the amplifier at a rock music concert. Yet this wind was a gentle breeze compared to the cyclonic blasts that sweep eastward from Iceland and strafe Shetland with their artillery. In 1963, 177 knots were registered at Saxavord on the isle of Unst before the wind seized the anemometer and carried it off to parts unknown. I had heard accounts of brawny men thrown off their feet and babies wrenched from their mother's arms. And on my earlier visit to Shetland, when I'd gone to the island of Fetlar to observe snowy owls, I had heard this story:

In the early 1970s the roof of a house belonging to an elderly Fetlar woman was blown away. As if that wasn't bad enough, the wind whirled down and picked up some of her possessions, including a cache of letters, and distributed them about the island. The woman had been known as a person of lifelong ascetic, if not resolutely virginal, habits. The letters, written years before, proved otherwise. These ardent declarations of love to a certain sea captain contained detailed notes showing that their union was not strictly platonic. Everyone on the island possessed elaborate testimony to this fact. They mentioned it, not disapprovingly, to the old woman, who by slow turns died of shame (her lover had died many years earlier, in the Great War).

After Tingwall, the site of the old Viking parliament, the road wound round arthritic inlets and perched atop gray sandstone cliffs, angling through one dark bog after another. Bog cotton, like spent spume, fluttered along the pavement. I saw a few of the celebrated Shetland ponies, their foals flung on the ground like rag puppets. They had the same off-white, skewbald, fawn, and brown colors as the sheep, and they were losing their coats in the same early summer fashion as those sheep, too. Shreds of hair stretched from their hocks or floated behind them in the wind.

Dawn was approaching with typical high-latitude light, a kind of perpetual muffled gray with a few brighter spots thrown in for variety's sake. At seven am, the first car I'd seen in hours drove up and stopped. A reddish head with charcoal eyes peered out at me. Obviously a head built for bulk so that the infamous Shetland winds would not dislodge it from its body and send it rolling over hill and moor.

'Hop in, laddie.'

I was too close to my destination to hop in. Would Mallory, Irvine, or even Hillary have hopped in at this point? But the man would not be put off so easily. His massive head hung there with a coaxing grin on its face. I wondered if Shetland hospitality, a bequest from Viking times, *required* that he give me a lift, else the god Thor would exact a cruel and unusual punishment from him for forsaking a lone traveler on the road. But then I heard him snoring lustily and noticed that his breath was 86 proof – another Viking bequest.

At Bridge of Walls I passed a number of derelict, roofless crofts which, if this were the tropics, would have been buried in the all-encompassing underbrush or at least strangled by a few creepers. Here they were *memento mori* that gave the lie to their own transience, not decaying naturally with the years but just *staying* decayed while less stolid organic matter was sucked back into the earth. Then I arrived in Walls itself, a tiny village that had been languishing ever since the salt-fish trade died. Walls was 1912 preserved in amber. Its streets had a quality of eternal peace denied to places carrying on through gainful endeavor. I saw only one very old woman; she was herding a very old cow. When I asked her where everyone was, she replied, 'Everyone's drowned at sea or repairing helicopters at Sullom Voe ... '

At the pier I sat down to wait for the *Westering Homewards*, the Foula mailboat. It came right on time, two and a half hours late.

Foula is twenty miles from Walls, but the sea makes it seem at least twice that far. A strong tide runs between the island and the mainland and has the odd habit, not of flowing in one direction and ebbing in the opposite, but of flowing from every point on the compass in turn. Thus the trip had the tumult of a tea leaf in a boiling pot. It was made even worse by the boat itself, a thirty-five-foot former Royal Navy lifeboat that appeared to have seen action during the Battle of Trafalgar. One of the two-member crew had to nurse its single-cycle Perkins diesel engine the whole way to prevent it from dying. The other member of the crew was steering by compass and solemnly informed me that radar was a 'superstition'. My only fellow passenger was an islander named Tom whose abscessed tooth had been fixed in Lerwick (nothing so extravagant as a dentist lives on Foula). We screamed at each other to be heard above the engine, which kept exploding into noisy life and sending up smoke rings in magical profusion.

Tom called himself an 'Antipodean dropout', since he had come originally from Wellington, New Zealand. As a boy, he'd read *Treasure Island* sixteen times; this seemed to have had a formative effect on his later years. Good books, he said, were even more insidious than bad parents. He was trained as an epidemiologist – his people had been in the medical profession all the way back to the Maori Wars – and did his internship among the Fore tribe in the highlands of New Guinea. The Fore were then being decimated by a rare, extraordinary disease called kuru, transmitted through ritual cannibalism; pregnant women and children would eat the brains of their dearly departed to acquire their virtues, along with the lethal kuru virus. When the Fore were told to stop eating brains, the disease was cured. Tom's interest in a medical career was cured, too. ('In one year, 1971, Albert Schweitzer changed into Long John Silver.') In Port Moresby he married an Australian nurse and convinced her to homestead with him on the most isolated island he could find in his vest-pocket atlas. This turned out to be Pitcairn Island, home of the *Bounty* mutineers. They settled there but could never seem to get along with the Pitcairners, all Seventh Day Adventists who eschewed the dark satanic brews of tea and coffee for a more godly drink made from bran husks. Tom and his wife left Pitcairn, travelled for a while in her ancestral Scotland, and – lo! – ended up on Foula.

JOHN McKINNEY

❈   ❈   ❈

In the mid-1980s freelance writer John McKinney journeyed to Shetland to observe life in these remote isles to the north of the Scottish mainland. More specifically he came to see what North Sea oil had wrought. 'Would the islands be essentially unchanged, or yet another victim of industrial rape?'

What he found was a land of paradoxes, populated by a people more Scandinavian than Scottish, and who love their native soil with a fierce sense of pride.

This selection originally appeared in a 1985 issue of ISLANDS magazine.

❈   ❈   ❈

Beautiful Between Weathers:
The Shetland Islands

A North Sea gale rattles the storm shutters of the Saint Magnus Bay Hotel, but it's business as usual at the hotel bar. Two oilman, a farmer, a fisherman and a marine biologist whom everyone calls 'the professor', sip McEwan's Export and grouse about the dockers' strike, the coal miners' strike, the prime minister and this godforsaken weather.

We retreated here when the soft and misty afternoon rain began falling in blinding sheets with the approach of darkness. Our walk in the rain along the great bay of Saint Magnus from Esha Ness in the north to Sandness in the south was vintage Shetland. Over the treeless, peat-patterned headland we tramped, our boots making squishing noises on the wide grassy platforms shorn by a multitude of sheep. Offshore was the most Gothic of spectacles –

arches, pinnacles and grotesquely sculptured pikes of ancient red sandstone called The Drongs.

With its art nouveau furnishings unchanged since World War I and its dour help, the Saint Magnus Hotel is the ultimate Edwardian hotel, an ideal setting for an Agatha Christie murder mystery. Provided no mad knife-wielding duchess lurks in the solarium or stalks the dark hallways, it should be a quiet, though somewhat morose, evening around the bar. Part-time bartender/part-time philosopher Ian dispenses the draft and the Shetland weather report: 'Some people say we have two seasons here – nine months of winter and three months of bad weather.'

'Which season is this' I ask.

'It isn't always raining,' he continues, ignoring my sarcasm. 'Shetland is beautiful between weathers.'

Ah, but will I ever see the islands between storms?

The fisherman is telling the professor about his grandfather. Grandad, it seems, was provided with a boat and tackle by his landlord in exchange for all of his catch. 'How could man make a living like that?' the fisherman asks. 'It's the same today; there's plenty of work but no money.'

Paradox: the isles are full of it. The Shetlanders around the bar boast of the native talent in Lerwick and Hillswick and Scalloway, then complain that everyone with half a brain has fled south to Scotland. They denounce the U.K. welfare state for its misappropriated largess, then advise each other on how to obtain the latest national health insurance benefit. They deplore the islands' poverty, while in the same breath brag about the boom times brought by North Sea oil. They grumble about the invasion of foreigners, then confess how much they enjoy extending their hospitality to Germans, Swedes, Dutch, Russians and Americans.

Bar talk. Rainy night talk. Mick Jagger sings 'Sympathy for the Devil' to a congress of wet wool. The clock strikes 10 and the boys around the bar switch from beer to whiskey, Scotch of course. Shetlanders are a melancholy lot. The black clouds forever overhead define both meteorology and the islanders' collective psychology. The long bitter years when families struggled in near-serfdom for despotic landlords are not forgotten. The islanders of old never knew when they might be evicted to make room for the more profitable sheep, and the Shetlanders of today seem to have a similar insecurity, unconvinced that the prosperity brought by the oil boom is here to stay.

Into the barroom gloom march a dozen short, squat senior citizens of unknown nationality. Ian lines up beer glasses atop the bar as if expecting an invasion. 'The Faroe Island pensioners,' he whispers conspiratorially.

'We will do our national dance now,' says Olga, the feisty leader of the Faroese. Ian dutifully moves the Stones from the cassette player and puts on what sounds like the Faroese Stomp, a loud heavy-footed melody. In a minute we're all shuffling around the pool table, I and the whiskey-sodden Shetlanders, trying to keep up with the lively pensioners. Soon the melancholy of the evening dissolves. 'We make the rain go away,' shouts Olga, dragging me around the room.

No reflection on the Faroese holiday-makers, but their folk dancing does not make the rain go away. Geography is responsbile for the rains; the Shetland Islands are caught between the stormy tantrums of the North Atlantic and the North Sea. Westward lies the Faroes and Iceland. Eastward stretches the Norwegian coast, whose Vikings ruled the Shetland archipelago until the 15th century. North of the islands lie only Spitsbergen and the North Pole. The islands float above the 60th parallel; that's the same latitude as southern Greenland.

I came to see what changes the discovery of North Sea oil has brought to the long-isolated islands. Would the islands be essentially unchanged, or yet another victim of industrial rape? Would I find another dreary story of a native culture pulled kicking and screaming into the 20th century, or canny islanders like the Bahrainis or Taiwanese who outfoxed the capitalists?

At the far northern end of mainland Shetland is Sullom Voe, site of Europe's largest oil and liquefied gas terminal. The facility handles production from a dozen oil fields located in the East Shetland Basin midway between Shetland and Norway. The North Sea treasure pours through pipes from the offshore fields to the terminal for storage and loading onto tankers. On a gray day, Sullom Voe's smokestacks and massive tanks project what corporate architects call 'industrial drama'; other observers suggest it would serve as the perfect locale for some German expressionist filmmaker to remake *Metropolis.*

Whatever its aesthetics, Sullom Voe clusters its buildings in one isolated harbor; this location was determined by the adroit local politicians who controlled the project's development. Shetlanders, figuring that they were the ones being inconvenieced by oil they didn't need, demanded and won over a per-barrel percentage of oil profits. Shetland's share of the oil revenues, which funds social programs and promotes Shetland's traditional industries, is aptly called 'disturbance money'.

'We've been disturbed for 500 years,' declares Andrew Williamson, curator for the Shetland County Museum in Lerwick. Williamson works to preserve the islands' artifacts – the Stone Age statuary, the Viking weapons and the curiosities washed up from the many shipwrecks off Shetland's shores. The curator also has a passion for preserving living culture, such as Shetland's unique music, dance and language.

'Shetlandic should have been dead 300 years ago, but it's persisted,' Williamson lectures. 'English professors say it's only a dialect of lowland Scot mixed with Swedish and Norwegian; I say it's a wholly separate language. But it's been removed from the public schools, it's assassinated by the telly and all we get from the BBC is a gabble of bloomin' English. Only a few cranks like me want to preserve Shetland's tongue."

As Williamson paces about his office in the museum's storage room, he grows increasingly agitated and I fear he will grab a Pictish hammer from storage and wreak mayhem on the nearest cultural imperialist. The Shetland Islands were influenced not by the Scots but by the Norse, Williamson emphasizes. 'There's a big difference between a Shetlander and a Scot as between the Irish and the English. You won't find kilts or bagpipes here or anyone named MacThis or MacThat. My old grandmother – if you called her a Scot, she'd thrash you.'

Williamson points out another difference between Scots and Shetlanders: 'On most Scottish islands, the islanders have been farmers, who happened to have been born near the sea, while Shetlanders have always been fishermen and traders, who used their islands as safe harbors or for a wee bit of crofting.'

For Shetlanders, the sea is the ultimate paradox, both creator and destroyer, giving rise to a love-hate relationship that controls their pattern of living. The sea is at its most dramatic at the end of the south mainland, where a raging tideway of white water known as The Roost crashes against the brooding promontory of Fitful Head. One resident of the Head was Sir Walter Scott's bizarre witch Norna, 'Mother Doubtful, Mother Dread, Dweller on Fitful Head.'

It was Sir Walter who named nearby Jarlshof, considered by experts to be Britain's most important archaeological site. Jarlshof appeared in his novel *The Pirate*, but has since acquired greater renown as a site that chronicles separate periods of human habitation over a span of nearly twenty-five hundred years. Dating from the Bronze Age are stone huts and cattle stalls; from the Iron Age are a broch – fortress – and some structures known as wheel-houses, which consist of partitioned recesses with 10-foot-high walls spoked around a central hearth. After the wheelhouse-building settlers came the Norse, who occupied the islands from A. D. 900 to 1400 and left an architectural legacy of longhouses. The foundations of a medieval homestead and the crumbling walls of a 16th-century manor testify to the presence of still-later arrivals.

The nearby heath, populated only by the ubiquitous sheep, appears drained of all goodness. I wonder how these ancient people lived, how they farmed. And I wonder how farmers of the last century or of this one eked out a living on this poor land.

The croft, or family farm, is now worked only on a part-time basis. Few islanders make a living from the land, but enough is produced to have fresh eggs and milk, some vegetables in season and plenty of mutton. Crofting, even in the old days, was never intended to provide a complete livelihood, but was a way to grow basic crops and raise a few animals while the men earned a small income from fishing.

In Boddam, a croft house has been reconstructed and furnished as if the date were 1850. Straw thatch has been placed over cut turf and the whole works is supported by driftwood beams. The chairs have wooden backs to keep out the drafts. The expertise of crofter/curator William Manson is required to make any sense of the old crofting tools in this mechanized age. The *tushkar*, the traditional peat-cutting tool, is still used, but the odd-looking ploughs and threshing machines belong to another age.

The land around the crofts seems fit only for sheep. Near the shoreline, where the lime from seashells neutralizes the acidity of the peat, are rich meadows, ideal for grazing. Sheep have been kept on the island since the Stone Age, and although there has been some interbreeding with British varieties, Shetland sheep have retained two distinct characteristics – their small size and an intelligence that enables them to avoid patches of bog and to defy most fences.

Most of the breed is white-faced and white-wooled, but a small number produce other shades of wool such as fawn, gray and brown. The colored sheep are kept in separate flocks by the more careful crofters. The sheep's soft and and hardy fleece is transformed into sweaters by island knitters, who rework traditional patterns using the natural colors. One problem with Shetland wool is its inclination to shrink; every household possesses that relic from the crofting days, the jumperboard, upon which sweaters are stretched while drying. Another problem with Shetland wool has developed more recently – crofters now lime their fields, producing lusher pasture, which in turn results in healthier sheep. These hardy sheep grow thicker coats, which is worse for knitters, who prefer to work with thinner wool.

Crofts, more than any other part of the traditional Shetland landscape, have changed the most since the oil boom. The sheep and the vegetable garden are of secondary interest to a man or woman working full-time for wages. The crofter, neither farmer nor fisherman, is likely to be driving a lorry, repairing helicopters or supplying vessels for the oil rigs. Even the land itself has changed. Where whaling and fishing stations once flourished, aluminum warehouses and oil storage tanks now stand. Bulldozers have scarred the green, readying the land for a deposit of prefabricated housing.

Lerwick, the capital city, is where a third of all Shetlanders now live, about seven thousand of them. Ships from all over Europe call at its port and many languages are heard in the pubs, giving Lerwick a cosmopolitan air. Sailors aboard their anchored ships enjoy the best view of Lerwick, of old triangular-shaped stone houses clinging, rears to the sea, to steep hillsides. Behind the waterfront winds narrow flagstoned Commercial Street, lined with knitwear shops and numerous fish and chip establishments. Grizzled Norwegian sailors exchange amused glances with Lerwick's punk teens, who sport the latest in orange and purple hairstyles. Pedestrians on Commercial Street are close watchers and will not be dissuaded from their sport of people-watching even in the midst of a downpour.

When darkness and downpour fall upon us, we retreat to Hamnavoe on the island of West Burra, to a guest house operated by Joan and James Wood. As we arrive, our hosts are retreating too. James carries an ice chest full of fish with one arm and his golf bag with the other. 'Could've broken a hundred today, if the wind would've stopped blowing my balls into the loch,' he declares. Joan also has her arms full; she is returning from a flower and produce show and carries a gale-battered flower arrangement and a basket of vegetables. She chairs the Shetland chapter of the Scottish Women's Rural Institute, and today the members held an exhibit of their gardening skills. 'I took first prize for "Best Begonias" and "Best Vegetable Arrangement." ' she modestly informs us after some coaxing from her husband.

As James prepares the fish and Joan her prize-winning vegetables, they ask, almost in unison: 'How do you like the food on the islands?'

I think of gluey porridge, the mouth full of bones that is smoked kipper and mutton, mutton, mutton. 'Lots of fish and chips,' I venture.

'Ah, you haven't had real Shetland cooking then,' Joan declares. My image of endless fish and chips is not flattering to Shetland cooks, she counsels. 'Crofting women are especially good bakers and even if our cooking is simple, it's very wholesome.'

'Have you tried haggis?' asks James with a twinkle in his eye.

'No,' I cautiously reply.

He explains that the haggis comes out only at night and is hard to catch. The haggis, as his story goes, is a one-legged, tartan-crested bird that flies over from Scotland and lives in seclusion around Shetland lochs.

I suspect that James is pulling my leg.

'Actually there really is a haggis,' Joan interjects, 'but I better not tell you about it; some folks lose their appetite.' She hesitates a moment, then decides that I have a strong stomach. 'Haggis ... you take a sheep paunch, stuff it with heart, liver, oatmeal and onions, then boil it for three hours. It's served with mashed potatoes and turnips.'

Yum.

James is a better fisherman than golfer; his whitefish is splendid and so are Joan's prize-winning vegetables, homemade gingerbread and first-rate pear pudding topped with fresh cream. Shetland cooking has been redeemed.

Thus sated, we gather round the telly to watch 'The Scottish Gardeners Show', an advice program for people with problem plants. Four distinguished gardeners tour Scotland, each week videotaping their show in a different locale. Last week the show was taped in Lerwick, and the Wards eagerly watch for the appearance of their neighbors. With the misery only fanatic gardeners can display, the Shetlanders present their jaundiced plants to the illustrious panel, whose members try to determine what rust or rot plagues the poor specimens. A lady from Scalloway hands her troublesome tomato plant to one gardener, who bursts out laughing. 'Nothing would grow in this Shetland soil. Nothing!' The panel agrees unanimously.

Though the soil is poor, the islands have a picturesqueness all their own. Muckle Roe, Norse for 'Big Red Island', is the core of a 350-million-year-old volcano. Unst, the most northerly of British isles, is the remote and beautiful home of the trolls of Shetland literature and a delight for the hiker. Papa Stour was formerly the site of a leper colony. Noss is a nature reserve full of Arctic terns, puffins, razorbills and kittiwakes.

I see these islands – their tattered coastline, brave little Shetland ponies, neatly patterned fields – in a dark mist. Lost in my anorak, I wander the soaked hillsides down to beaches of gray boulders and watch the Atlantic swells pound the skerries. Mesmerized by the windshield wipers, I drive from village to village. From Sumburgh to Muckle Flugga, wherever I go, the rain follows. Heavy. Hypnotic. Relentless.

And then one day it finally comes – a clear day. From Sandwick I catch a ride on a fishing boat out to the small grassy isle of Mousa. The isle is uninhabited except by grazing sheep, a colony of seals that sunbathe on the deserted beaches and the fulmars planing to and fro in the air currents.

The screaming terns overhead call attention to the island's claim to fame, an amazingly intact Iron Age tower. Constructed of red sandstone, it rises to a height of 43 feet, swelling outward at the bottom to withstand an enemy's battering rams. Nowhere else in Europe was such a great height achieved. Archaeologists disagree about the origins of the people who built the broch or even why it was built. In the Norse sagas, the Broch of Mousa is a popular rendezvous for eloping couples. In 1153, Erland, son of Harold the Fair-Spoken, kidnapped and brought to the Shetlands Margaret, the beautiful but less-than-virtuous mother of Earl Harold Maddadson. Earl Harold beseiged Mousa, but found it 'an unhardy place to get at'. Needing his army elsewhere to defend his kingdom, he had to retreat and consent to the lovers' marriage.

The Shetland Islands are once again being invaded, this time by 20th-century industrialists, as competitive and disruptive to the culture as their Viking predecesors of A.D. 900. Progress has caught up with Shetland, once the terra incognita of the North Sea, and I wonder if there are enough native Shetlanders sufficiently committed to a Shetland way of life to preserve what is left.

The gathering around the peat fire and the fiddle playing have largely been replaced by oil-burning central heating and the telly, yet some customs die hard. Perhaps few Shetlanders make their living as fishermen, but many a fellow fishes after work and on weekends, often in a boat built with his own hands. And if few crofters work full-time on their land, most keep a vegetable garden or potato patch.

For now, Shetland remains a great paradox: a poor land surrounded by a bountiful sea, a culture so permanent yet so fragile, islands subjected to the ugliest of tempests, yet beautiful between weathers.

FURTHER READING

※   ※   ※

Bray, Elizabeth. *The Discovery of the Hebrides: Voyages to the
    Western Isles 1745-1883.* Edinburgh: Birlinn, 1996.
Chapman, Malcolm. *The Gaelic Vision in Scottish Culture.*
    London: Croom Helm, 1978.
Cheape, Hugh. *Tartan: The Highland Habit.* Edinburgh:
    National Museums of Scotland, 1991.
Defoe, Daniel. *A Tour Through the Whole Island of Great Britain.*
    Edited by P. N. Furbank, W. R. Owens, and A. J. Coulson.
    New Haven, Conn.: Yale University Press, 1991.
Delaney, Frank. *A Walk to the Western Isles: After Boswell and Johnson.*
    London: Harper Collins, 1993.
Devine, T. M. *The Scottish Nation: A History 1700-2000.*
    New York: Viking, 1999.
Finlayson, Iain. *The Scots.* Oxford: Oxford University Press, 1988.
Glendening, John. *The High Road: Romantic Tourism, Scotland,
    and Literature, 1720-1820.* New York: St. Martin's Press, 1997.
Hunter, James. *On the Other Side of Sorrow: Nature and People in the
    Scottish Highlands.* Edinburgh: Mainstream Publishing, 1995.
    Scottish Highlanders: A People and Their Place. Edinburgh:
    Mainstream Publishing, 1992.
Kay, Billy. *Scots: The Mither Tongue.* Edinburgh: Mainstream
    Publishing, 1986.
Lyle, Emily, ed. *Scottish Ballads.* Edinburgh: Canongate, 1994.
Lynch, Michael. *Scotland: A New History.* London: Century, 1991.
MacDougall, Carl. *Early Days of a Better Nation: A Search for
    Scottish Identity.* London: Aurum Press, 2000.
MacLean, Fitzroy. *A Concise History of Scotland.* London: Thames
    and Hudson, 1988.
    Highlanders: A History of the Scottish Clans. New York:
    Viking Studio Books, 1995.
MacLean, Malcolm, and Christopher Carrell, eds. *As an Fhearann:*

From the Land. Edinburgh, Stornoway, and Glasgow: Mainstream Publishing, an Lanntair, and Third Eye Centre, 1986.

McCrone, David, Angela Morris, and Richard Kiely. *Scotland the Brand: The Making of Scottish Heritage*. Edinburgh: Edinburgh University Press, 1995.

McLaren, Morey. *The Highland Jaunt*, 1954.

Maclean, Charles. *Island on the Edge of the World: The Story of St. Kilda*. New York: Taplinger Publishing Company, 1972.

Macleod, John. *Highlanders: A History of the Gael*. London: Sceptre, 1996.

No Great Mischief If They Fall: The Highland Experience. Edinburgh: Mainstream Publishing, 1993.

Powell, Michael. *Edge of the World: The Making of a Film*. London: Faber and Faber, 1938. Reprint, 1990.

Prebble, John. *The Highland Clearances*. London: Penguin, 1963.

Rogers, Pat, ed. *Johnson & Boswell in Scotland: A Journey to the Hebrides*. New Haven, Conn.: Yale University Press, 1993.

Shenker, Israel. *In the Footsteps of Johnson and Boswell*, 1982.

Sinclair, Marion, ed. *Hebridean Odyssey: Songs, Poems, Prose and Images*. Edinburgh: Polygon, 1996.

Thomson, Derick S., ed. *The Companion to Gaelic Scotland*. Oxford: Blackwell, 1983.

Withey, Lynne. *Grand Tours and Cook's Tours: A History of Leisure Travel, 1750 to 1915*. New York: William Morrow and Company, 1997.

Wordsworth, Dorothy. Introduction, Notes, and Photographs by Carol Kyros Walker. *Recollections of a Tour Made in Scotland*. New Haven, Conn.: Yale University Press, 1997.